Yoga inVision 3

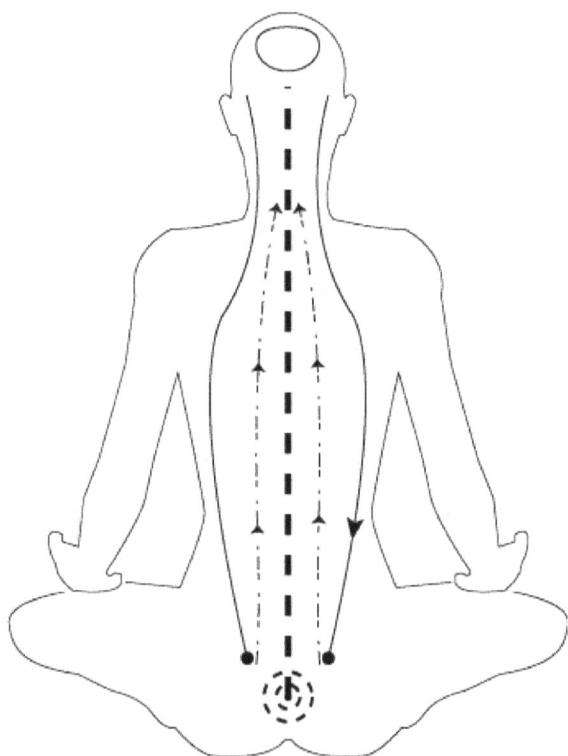

Michael Beloved

Shiva Art:	Sir Paul Castagna
Illustrations:	Author

Correspondence:
Michael Beloved
19311 SW 30th Street
Miramar FL 33029
USA

Email: axisnexus@gmail.com
                michaelbelovedbooks@gmail.com

Paperback ISBN: 9781942887126
LCCN: 2017913013

Table of Contents

INTRODUCTION

This is the third in the series of Yoga inVision reports.

Considering these details of yoga practice, and the persistence required to get even these small results, one may ask why anyone would endeavor for this. It is no wonder that many persons, in fact most of those who pursue spiritual life, avoid yoga austerities and take to a simpler and less involved strenuous process for freedom from material existence.

If yoga was like eating, sleeping, mating and defending in terms of maintaining a material body, something which even animals are expert at, then I would not practice. If I could attained these realizations by a simpler method, I would not practice. You too may avoid yoga if you can get desired results by another process, especially by a simple method.

How much interest do you have in spiritual discovery?

What investment of time and energy are you willing to invest in austerities? Are you satisfied with what you get from the preferred religious process? The answer to these questions would determine your willingness or unwillingness to do yoga. By reading the Yoga inVision series, you may access the benefits of yoga. You may decide if it worth the effort.

Part 1

Yogeshwarananda

He said, "Bring down the hearing sense separately.

"First, bring it down from the strongest side, then from the weaker, less-used, side, then from the balancing point of both. Carry that about in the psyche as you did with the visual sense. See how that is retracted into the intellect.

"When doing yoga, it is important to focus in the sushumna nadi, the central subtle channel. The various nadis below the head run into the central subtle channel. Focus on that central place. Keep that passage cleared."

Remark:

These are instructions about sensual energy withdrawal and focusing of that withdrawn energy into the central channel when doing breath-infusion for clarifying kundalini chakra.

Yogeshwarananda

He said, "Each sense should be retrogressed separately. When the visual sense is retracted, the others may effectively stay in their out-orbits, focused outside the intellect or resting in a condition of alert for external focus. Thus each should be deliberately retrogressed."

Remark:

This pertains to sensual energy withdrawal. It requires a sincere lack of interest in the gross and subtle material existence. First one conquers desires for the gross existence. Gradually over a long time of practice, one conquers one subtle level after another, from the heavier subtle dimensions to the very light and flimsy ones. The more light and flimsy a dimension is, the harder it is to retract one interest in it and to regulate one's mandatory involvement with it.

March 10, 2001

Yogeshwarananda

He said, "Bring this subtle sense. Systematically connect the others in ascending order."

Remark:

On the previous day, Yogesh taught an ear pull-down pratyahar sense withdrawal. This is a technique for retracting the sense of hearing into the intellect and into the causal body. First I did the right side, then the left, then the balancing center point. This practice is not difficult but since it entails a very subtle action, one requires acute mystic perception to execute it.

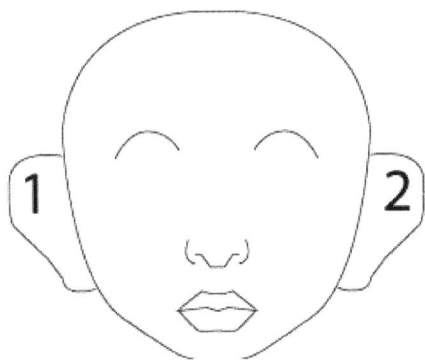

ear 1

then ear 2

then center of head

between eyevbrows

Yogesh had me do this to one of the working senses, the sense of evacuation. At first one has to pull the urine/bladder operational sense. This is a subtle power. One trains that sense to criticize and rectify its own operations rather than to criticize bad functions in the body of others. One pulls it up into the kundalini chakra and then into the intellect and then into the causal form. These are subtle actions.

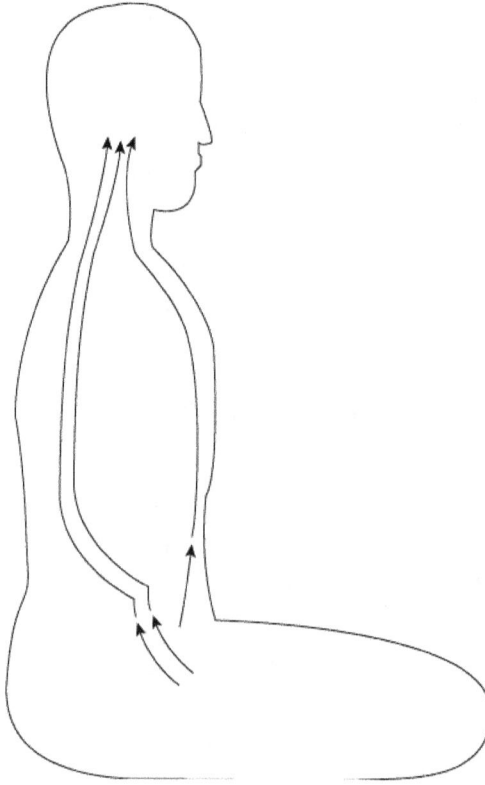

March 11, 2001

Shiva

He brought to my attention that the early meditation before rising from bed, before doing the early morning session of exercises, reveals the silent condition of the intellect. The flickering light called the lalata chakra, is actually the intellect's energization for sensual pursuits. Usually this light flickers without being noticed. The average human being experiences this light as an awakened condition of mind. He or she does not see a light. A yogi may not see it every morning but only periodically. The early meditation can show a yogi how to calm the intellect and bring it to a habit of remaining calm, rather than being habituated to excitement which leads away from meditative states.

Remark:

Shivananda brought this to my attention years ago. Due to a habituation to excitement, I could not put what he said into full practice. Shiva gave a revision lesson on this.

March 12, 2001

Yogeshwarananda

He gave a celibacy technique which works on the area where the thigh connects with the buttocks. This is for getting control of sex drive in the subtle body, by working on the gross and subtle simultaneously. This is done with breath-infusion with full attention on the stretch, with the eyes closed and the mind being attentive to the movement of subtle energy.

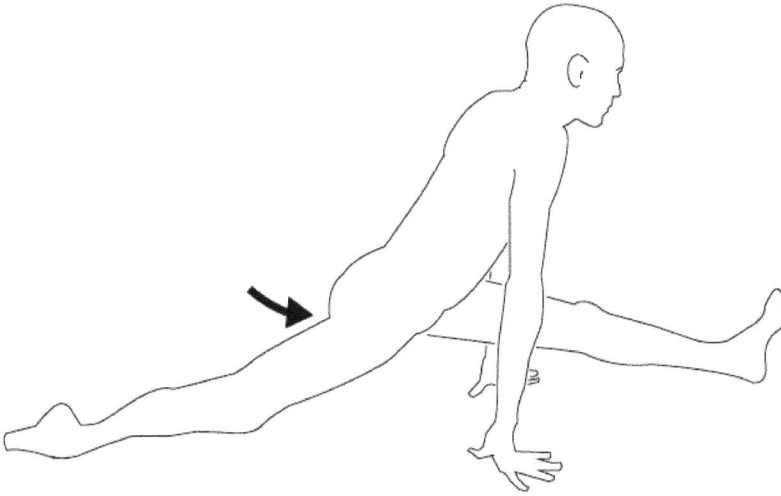

March 13, 2001

Yogeshwarananda

He gave a strong-side / weak-side practice.

Remark:

In each body, there may be a dominant side to each sense. For instance the right eye may be more used and more assertive, than the left one. Subsequently the right one may absorb more energy from the subtle reserve of power.

Thus the balance between each side may not be in the center. One has to find the balancing point even if that central place is not exactly in the center.

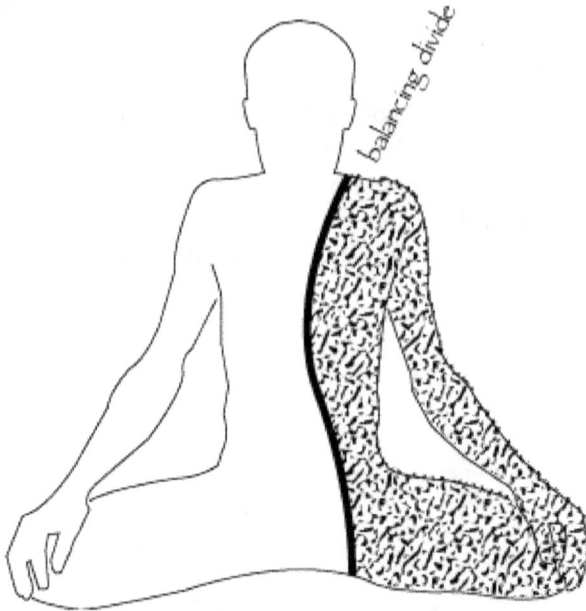

balancing divide

March 14, 2001

Yogeshwarananda

A sound-vision down-in-under the thighs method.

This concerns withdrawal of the tendency to look down into the thigh area for sexual energies. As dictated by social existence, one does this within one's body and to the body of others. This concerns sexual attraction. Some of the visionary power is lost in the sexual energy and needs to be withdrawn for complete celibacy. One should be aggressive in his pursuit of celibacy.

The gross body is not the problem with sexual indulgence. It is a very small and insignificant part of that. Unless one curbs the subtle form, the celibate effort is a sham.

In the process for retracting the sound-vision energy which is invested in the sexual area, one should retract the energy from the areas of the subtle body as shown in the diagram. This is a mystic practice, which is facilitated by postures, muscular locks and breath-infusion.

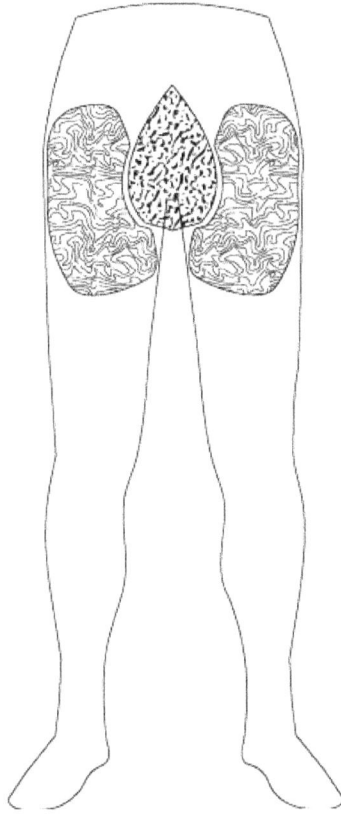

March 23, 2001

Yogeshwarananda

On this day he showed how to use the intellect in the brahmrandra zone. This proves conclusively that certain mystic practice cannot be learned unless one is shown by someone else. Some mystic techniques, cannot be learned from our position in the gross existence. One must take some lessons directly in the subtle world. Thus it is necessary that one develops the mystic skill (siddhi) to see into and communicate accurately in the subtle world.

Some teachers condemn the desire for mystic ability, for siddhi. However they are wrong if they think that one can avoid developing this on the spiritual path. It must be developed sooner or later. Furthermore it is a natural development on the spiritual plane, since the siddhi capabilities are not astounding powers but natural abilities of the various levels of manifestation of the subtle body and of the causal system. Just as the physical body of a human being has certain natural capabilities, the subtle body has certain functions. As soon as one is stationed on the subtle side, he naturally experiences these skills.

Yogesh showed that if one rises early around 2 am, by going to bed very early in the late afternoon just after sunset, one may experience the intellect in its restive state, when it shines easily with a shimmering flow in the middle of the subtle head. By persistent practice, one learns to move the intellect from the center to the top of the head, the crown area, the brahmrandra zone.

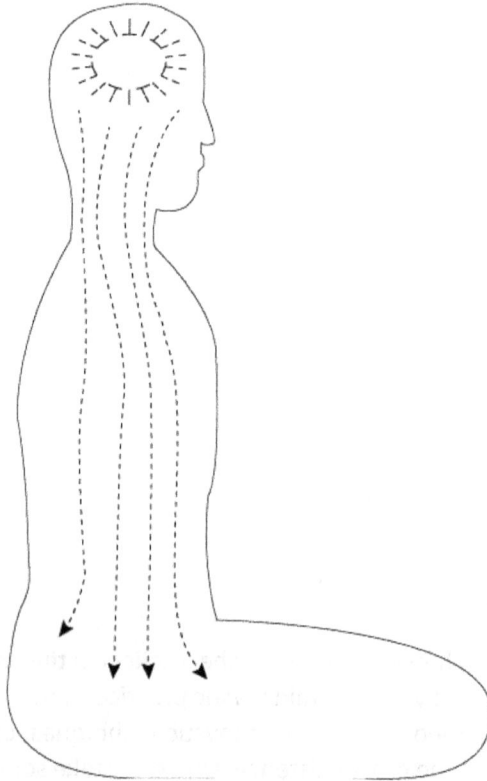

He taught a focus/unfocus concentration. This is taught to understand the method of nature, whereby the intellect and the mind focuses and unfocuses continually. These organs and the breath, go through a process of focusing and unfocusing. When one takes seriously to meditation, he begins to realize that this is the nature of the subtle system; to focus and unfocus in rhythm. In the practice I moved back and forth, from the base chakra composite energy to the intellect position in the brain.

March 28, 2001

Yogeshwarananda

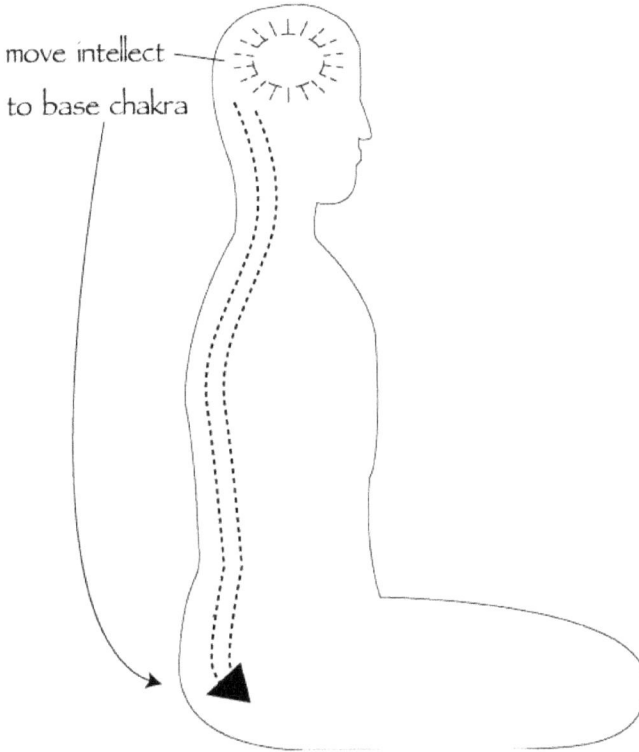

move intellect ―

to base chakra

The base chakra composite energy consists of the base energy, the sexual energy and the navel energy combined. This is experienced differently according to one's level of advancement.

March 30, 2001

Yogeshwarananda

He taught an in-and-out procedure using the subtle penis apparatus and the subtle sex nerve. One pulls these aspects to the intellect. In this mystic action, the intellect stays in one location in the brain. One identifies the light orb of energy which operates the sexual functions. The location of these energies are diagrammed below. It concerns celibacy.

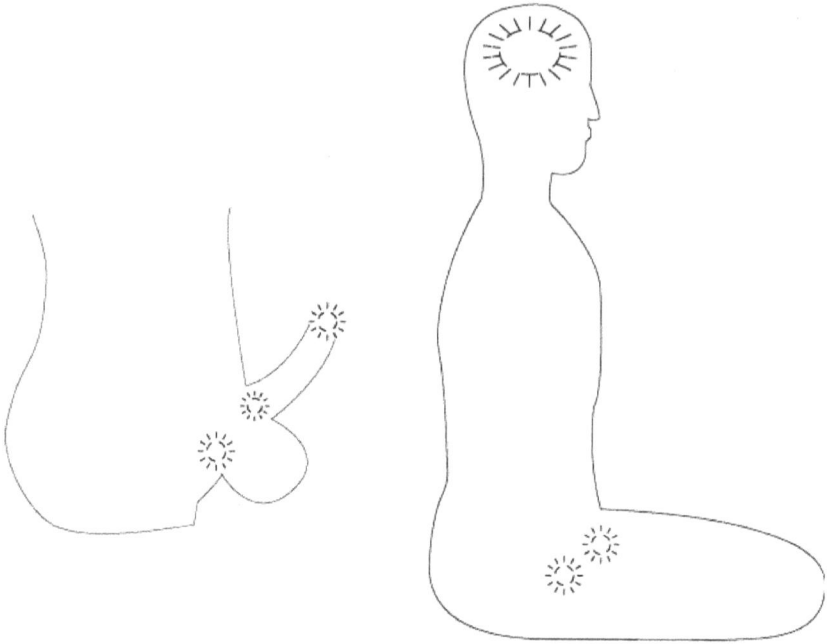

March 31, 2001

Yogeshwarananda

He said, "Study the mind's tendency. Work with the mind for the best results. Your mind was forced enough. Study the effects of the subtle energy. Study its moods. Do thorough asana postures with rapid breath-infusion."

Remark:

This was an instruction to study the effect of subtle energy on the mind. The state of the psychic energy has much to do with mental attitude. Even though the mind can be forced, and even though it can be pressured, still in the long range, one should displace used/polluted subtle energy with fresh energy which is ingested into the psyche by breath-infusion. This fresh force will cause the mind to desire spirituality and thus decrease the need for forcing it along the spiritual path.

April 1, 2001

Yogeshwarananda

He gave a method for communication of energy between the causal cove and the intellect.

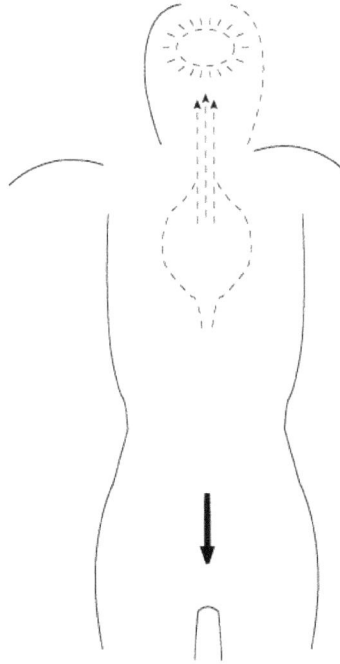

April 4, 2001

Yogeshwarananda

He said, "Release that energy. Let it go to the person freely. The sense-of-identity, ahankara, desires it but it converts into suffering and responsibility. As soon as you perceive that they invoked it, release those wayward but otherwise sticky and undesirable subtle energies."

Remark:

This pertains to non-sexual energies which are aroused in the psyche by proximity to others. Like sexual energies, these forces are aroused on the basis of past activities either in this or previous lives. There were so many millions of previous lives with trillions of such connections, that wherever a person may venture in the subtle or gross material existence, one would encounter connections from the past.

However if one learns how to release these pent-up energies, one would end many of the entanglements. One must learn how to keep the sense-of-identity detached. It has much to do with the entangling tendency of the intellect. Usually in males, the organ has the tendency for complex analytical operations. This discourages spiritual advancement.

Yogeshwarananda

He gave some small energy-absorption practices:
- energizing subtle energy to intellect blast
- intellect out-focus after breath-infusion
- intellect in-focus after breath-infusion
- intellect still-stun after breath-infusion
- any combination of the above

He gave a causal cove absorption practice.

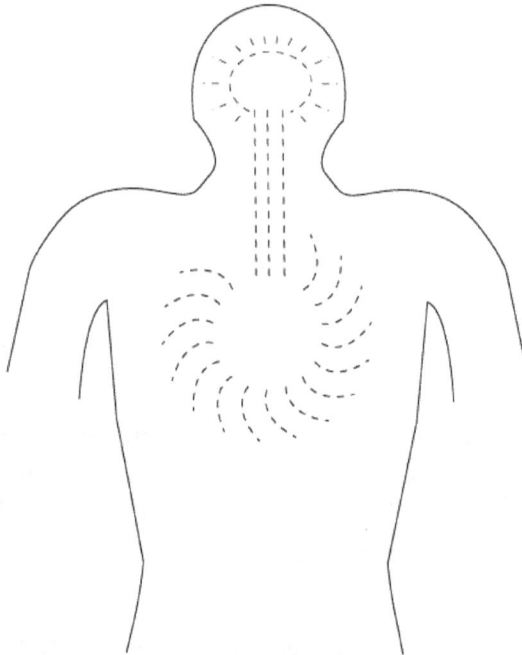

The small absorptions are practiced when the energies are stirred by an intense session of rapid breath-infusion, when the energies are organized by the application of the locks and concentration. The **energizing subtle energy to intellect blast** occurs when one can reach the level of nourishing energized subtle energy either in the head or in the chest of the subtle form. One then directs that energy to enter into the intellect for its refreshment.

The **intellect out-focus** occurs after an intense session when one does no concentration but instead observes the energy of the intellect pouring outward. If the energy is pouring outwards in all directions spherically, one restrains it inward. If it pours outward through a small opening like a hole in a container, one observes that and applies a mystic force to cause the out-pouring to either re-enter the intellect or to do down into the causal cove. If this re-entry into the intellect or downward flow into the causal cove is maintained for some time, it converts into a connection with the cosmic intellect. This cosmic intellect is a vast pool of subtle bliss energy which is an aggregate of many new intellects which are combined with the intellect of the primal creator. This pool of power is enriching to the individual intellects which are involved in transmigrations. The problem is that usually, the individual intellects which transmigrate never reach a pacified state. They do not make the connection with the cosmic intellect. Subsequently they are never recharged enough to make higher decisions.

In the yoga system, there is a practice called tratak. Initially I rarely practiced this. It consists of staring off into nowhere in a blank way. If one does this, the eyes may water or burn. If they do, one should shut them for a time and then open and stare again. After staring for a time, one may see flashes of light or see the aura of subtle energy around objects.

This vision of auras is preliminary. Yogeshwarananda explained that when a person does tratak without doing postures, locks and breath-infusion, he does not get the intended result which is to enter absorption. Yogesh said that many people, without perfecting preliminary yoga, try tratak and then acquire the wrong conclusion.

He showed that tratak is useful in diverting the flow of **outward-bound intellect energy** so that the energy re–enters the intellect or goes into the causal cove. It causes the individual intellect to connect with the cosmic intellect. Eventually the yogi's causal body connects with the cosmic causal form.

The **intellect in-focus** consist of noticing when the intellect loses interest in outward focus and instead remains intently interested in itself. This is a form of absorption. In that experience, one can move the intellect from one place to another in the subtle world either in the psyche or out of it. This state leads to various types of savikalpa and nirvikalpa absorptions. A savikalpa samadhi means one with an objective research intent. A nirvikalpa is one with a subjective research intent, where the self is given over completely to the experience and does no analyzing during the phase.

A yogin may experience nirvikalpa as a loss of the individual self but when one loses track of that, he interprets it as a mergence. Subsequently many persons condemned the absorption practice stating that they do not want to lose their individuality since they desire that it remain in objective existence to serve a divinity. However they too misunderstand what nirvikalpa is. That absorption is simply an observation of certain higher levels of consciousness from a subjective stance. It does not erase, permanently absorb nor destroy anyone's individuality, nor can it cause the permanent dissolution of anyone into anything else.

The **intellect still-stun** is a condition of the intellect being held in suspension because of its moving into an environment in the subtle world, where it simply stops its functions. Since the intellect moves at a high speed, at the flash of thought, its stabilization is sensed by the spirit as a stunned condition. This is not a void but it may be interpreted as such from certain perspectives. Even this state is not eternal, since the intellect will again shift and resume rapid movement.

One need not fear any of these states. None of them is eternal. Some mahayogins are able to remain in touch with the cosmic intellect or the cosmic causal body for some time, even for a period of millions of years, but even that is not eternal. Yogesh is one person who used to be in the cosmic intellect and cosmic causal form but now for the time being he is out of it. He told me that there is no guarantee for a limited being, a finite spirit, to remain in any condition. He said that the limited beings are not in control of their destinies. His view is that in so far as we have little control, we may make efforts and achieve for a time but not for all history.

April 3, 2001

Shiva

He instructed that I do ashwini mudra, just as I do abdomen pumps in various directions as follows:
- up down
- up forward, down forward, clockwise circle
- up backwards, down backward, anticlockwise circle
- down to the right side, clockwise then anticlockwise
- down to the left side, clockwise then anticlockwise
- down gradually, slowly, bearing pressure down
- up gradually, slowly, bearing suction up

Usually ashwini mudra is done pushing out and pulling in the anus, just as a horse does after evacuating. The Sanskrit word ashvin means horse.

April 3, 2001

Yogeshwarananda

He gave mystic guidelines for absorption practice.
Yogesh gave three types on this day:

- sensation
- relocation
- in-location

Sensation Absorption

This occurs when the intellect stays in one location, usually in the brain area of the subtle body. From there it emits a light into an object, penetrating and surrounding the object in part or whole. The light then transmits information to the intellect for the intellect's interpretation. The derived meaning may be accurate or inaccurate according to the sensitivity and clarity of the energy thrown out. The observing self then rates the information. It assesses impressions which are instantly relayed from the intellect. Here, as in all cases with the intellect, it is not so much the accuracy or inaccuracy, but rather the type of energy which it uses at the time of the absorption. Yogesh clarified that if the intellect uses dulling energies, its conclusion will not be insightful. If it takes to passionate energy, the conclusion will be from that perspective. If it takes clarifying energy, it will be insightful and truly informative.

Relocation Absorption

This is when the intellect goes near the object being surveyed. In that case, the intellect moves out of the subtle head and travels to wherever the object is located. In proximity of the object, the intellect throws out rays and surrounds the object in part, while penetrating it with other rays. These are light rays and subtle energy radiation. By its proximity, the intellect makes an impression about the object surveyed.

As I typed this, Yogesh from within my brahmrandra, instructed a correction. He said that only those yogis who use physical and astral bodies, have their intellect centered in the physical and subtle brain. Those who are use only subtle bodies, may have only a subtle brain to house the intellect. Those like himself who have eliminated kundalini lifeforce, use the intellect as the subtle form.

Such yogins move with their intellects directly and do not have to use a physical or astral body for reference. For them, the intellect is the subtle body. They do not use a kundalini survival lifeforce.

When doing the relocation absorption, one is subjected to accuracy and inaccuracy according to the type of energy ingested by the intellect. Yogesh said that if the yogi takes in clarity energy (sattvic prana) his intellect becomes reality-perceptive and is called insightful (ritambhara) intellect.

In-location absorption.

This is the highest absorption. Some believe that it means a permanent mergence. Some condemned it as a loss of individuality. However one cannot lose individuality. It experiences objective suspension but it is a permanent feature of reality. When a child's embryo develops in the body of a mother, the spirit involved may be said to have merged into the mother. Actually it is a superficial union. The embryo's individuality will be displayed later when the embryo matures and is expelled on delivery. In the in-location absorption, the intellect penetrates and surveys from within the object.

April 3, 2001

Yogeshwarananda

He showed an anal funnel touch-point in a curve just below the esophagus in the throat. This is an absorption practice for cleansing the base chakra and gradually eliminating it, making it possible to transit to higher places where kundalini is not used. The anal chakra is usually hidden in dense subtle energy, such that the intellect regards it as non-existent. However if one practices postures, locks and breath-infusion, the heaviness evaporates. A colored energy becomes manifested, first with a brownish glow, then with a reddish hue, then with an orange glow and then with a crystal clear light.

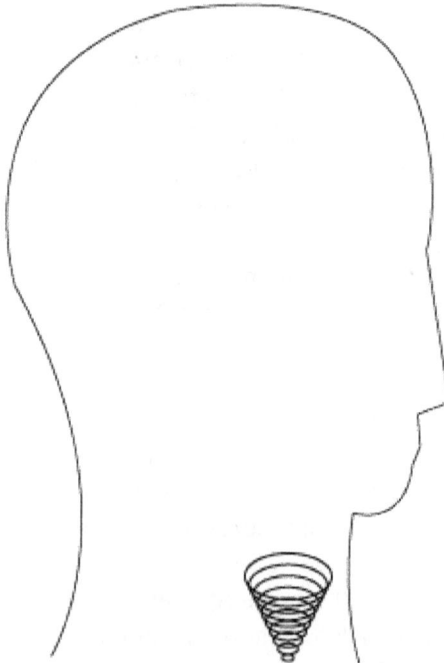

April 4, 2001

Yogeshwarananda

A Ganesh chakra pump.

This Ganesh chakra is the anal pouch. In this practice the anus is contracted and relaxed, in and out, with the lung being full of air at the time.

The abdomen is flexed afterwards with the lung devoid of air. Flexing the abdomen in this way affects the lower intestines which are connected to the anal pouch.

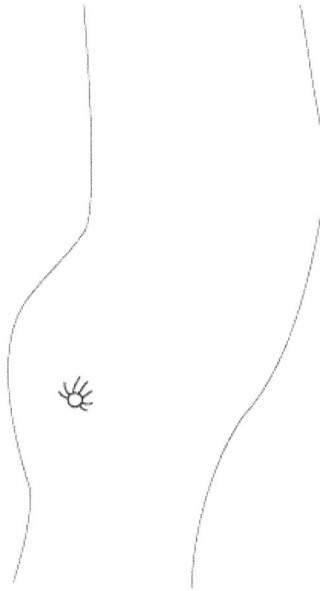

A fan-shaped tube in the astral buttocks.

This fan-shaped tube is located in the subtle buttocks. Yogis who advanced beyond the need for a kundalini chakra and who no longer maintain one, do not have such a subtle body which resembles a human form. Others however should remove polluted and used energy from the subtle body, so that its energies are no longer of a dark or opaque hue but are of a crystal translucent clear type

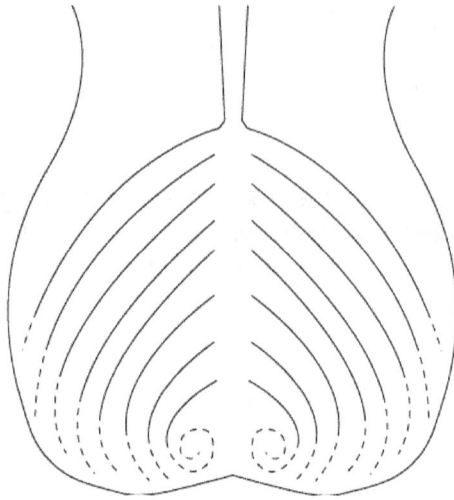

To develop and eventually see this fan-shaped tube, one should do breath-infusion rapid breathing, pumping the air between the heels, with the fingers pushed down. This posture is shown below. When the polluted opaque subtle energy is cleared from the trunk one may peer into the lumbar area.

Yogeshwarananda

He said that one system is to start from the lung and move down the front of the body going around the pubic area. When the sex drive is curbed, move to anus flexing and clearing.

He insisted that at the last evacuation of the day, one should be sure that no stools linger in the anal pouch or lower intestines. There is a way to force lingering stools out of the anal pouch. One squats to evacuate. Then one uses the fingers of the right hand to push in the abdomen from the outside. When the fingers are pushed in, one applies a downward pressure and this may cause any remaining stools to be expelled. One may do the left middle finger anal pouch check. One can clear waste matter by inserting that finger directly into the anus while squatting.

To do this properly, one has to control daytime eating. One should not eat during the late afternoon or at night. Food should be taken in the early morning, even before sunrise or soon after. One should always have enough liquid with the meal so that the stools are not compact or hard during evacuation. In addition one should not use hot peppers, even though these could render a watery stool. One should do the in-location intellect absorption regularly, making the endeavor to move the intellect down into the lower trunk of the body

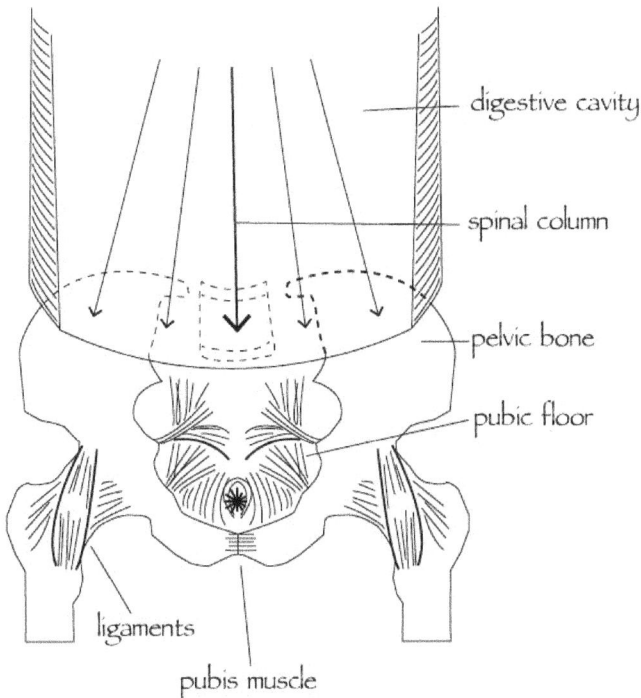

digestive cavity

spinal column

pelvic bone

pubic floor

ligaments

pubis muscle

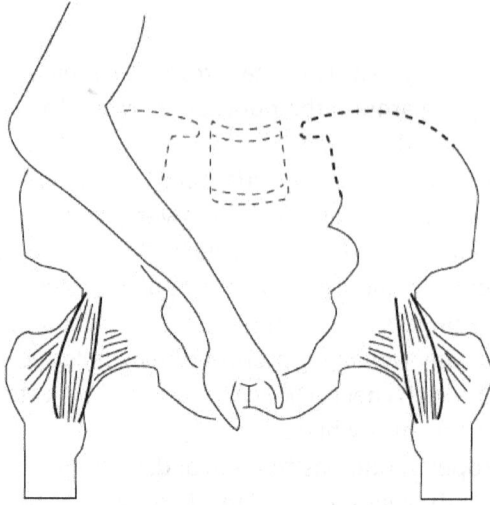

April 7, 2001

Yogeshwarananda

He said, "Do the preliminary wake-up meditation noting the mind's ability not to keep focused."

Remark:

Shivananda introduced this. It concerns waking up earlier than usual at the first call, sitting up in bed, and meditating to observe the mind's ability to focus. Generally when resting, there is a first call about 4 or 5 hours after the body takes to sleeping. Usually human beings ignore this first call. However a yogi should heed it. He should awaken, sit up in bed and meditate, carefully observing the movements of the mind, the life force, as well as noting the subtle memories of whatever occurred on the astral level during resting. Unless we study the movements and developments of consciousness, we cannot attain absorption and cannot understand the psyche in fact.

April 7, 2001

Shiva

He said, "Immediately after the exercises, do down-draw in tight lotus. There should be no gap. Do down-draw, hold breath. Then do down-draw again and hold breath repeatedly. Get up periodically and do down-draw in lotus.

Remark:

Such instructions may be given to be applied once or as a daily application.

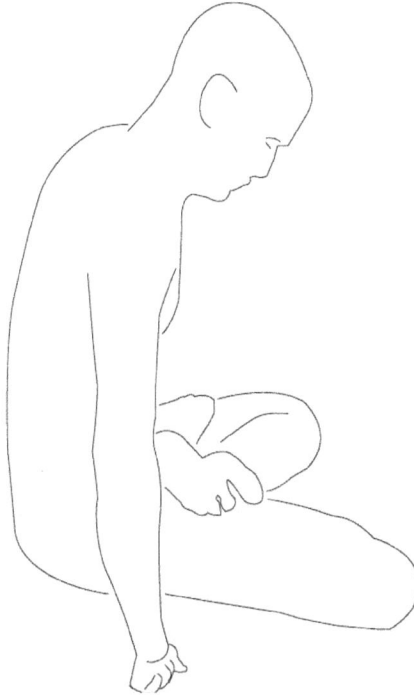

Down-draw breath, may be one breath drawn-in-and-down into the base chakra of the spine or drawn down into the testes or pubic area. It may be one, two, or three breaths in succession. If it is two or three, the first pull-in of breath, is the largest draw of air, while the others are shortened in turn but are drawn in immediately after. Down-draw works after an intense session of breath-infusion when sufficient air was pumped into the psyche. Down-draw·is effective in clearing the sushumna passage. First one must do rapid breathing in various postures to stimulate and move polluted energy out of the body. When this is done sufficiently, one can do down-draw.

April 7, 2001

Shiva

He said, "Recline after the abdomen foot-kicks on the back. Do down-draw when you fully inhale. Do so slowly to the maximum capacity of the lungs. Push out the abdomen slowly. Do not over-force the abdomen. Stop pushing when the abdomen is full. Do not strain. Do this several times. For the last time when the abdomen is pushed out finally move the hands away from the body.

April 9, 2001

Ramana Maharshi

He said: "This was where I stopped in hatha yoga, where I was discovered and started taking disciples. At this point, higher celibacy begins. I did not go further in hatha yoga, but I progressed in meditation through mauna, which is a method of stopping the emergence and compilation of thought images. Mauna, the silent mind technique, is effective when one must deal with disciples and superficial visitors."

Remark:

When he said this, I did these postures.

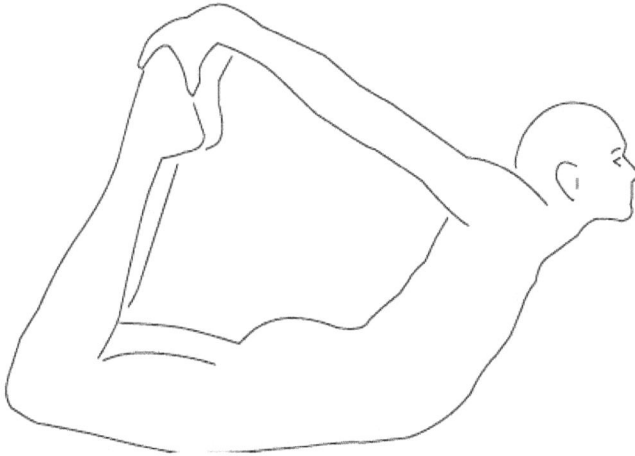

Those postures concern celibacy. At a more advanced stage these postures liberate the sexual functions and allows the yogi to move on to higher practice. He may either stop with hatha yoga here or go further. Personalities like Gorakshnath and Gambhiranath went further. Great Tibetans yogis like Milarepa and Marpa went further. It depends on one's destiny. Sometimes by the influence of disciples, a great yogi is diverted from further practice. Avoiding the stalling force of disciples is a special technique that a yogi may develop. Without that it is hardly likely that he would complete the full course of hatha yoga. Just recently I had a few visitors; two persons who were interested in kundalini yoga and celibacy. During their visit my practice came to a halt. While training them, my progress ceased.

The morning after the last visitor left, Yogesh peeked out from a cloud in my brahmrandra. He said, "Are they gone? What nuisance, these disciples are to a serious yogin. Do not take disciples."

Later that same morning a sculptured form of Babaji called me. When I got close, he said, "Do not take disciples. It will destroy the practice. Helping someone every once in a while is acceptable but do not form the habit."

In the two postures shown which Ramana Maharshi commented on, most of the body stretches. Subsequently a little hormonal essence is taken from each cell and is contributed by subtle energy command. This hormonal essence is the same stuff that flows out on the physical and psychic planes during a sexual orgasm, when it feels as if the whole body becomes involved in sexual ecstasy. Instead of waiting for a sexual release, the yogi releases this energy daily during the exercises, thus freeing his physical body and psyche from the need for sexual indulgence. This is how the yogi foregoes the need for sexual pleasure.

Hatha yoga with breath-infusion is the prime means of replacing sexual intercourse. It is the substitute for sexual pleasure. During a sexual orgasm, all hormonal secretions which are stored in each cell of the physical and subtle bodies is contributed for the formation of a new body, a baby form. In these postures, that same energy is released. One should note that the testes and ovaries hold hormones and collect energy from all other cells as well. From the testes in the subtle body, such hormone is stored in a bulb called a kanda. However, in the advanced states that storage is eliminated entirely.

April 11, 2001

Yogeshwarananda

He said, "Do down-draw to the elephant trunk chakra. Put the thumbs on the small of the back. Let the other fingers pass down around the buttocks.

Remark:

This is a hatha yoga procedure for purification of the anal region. The elephant trunk chakra is the subtle anal pouch apparatus which is shaped somewhat like an elephant's trunk. Ultimately this technique leads the yogi to the subtle body and the base chakra energies. It causes the purification of the nadis in the subtle body in the region of the anus. When these are cleared sufficiently, the subtle body changes from an opaque energy form into one of transparent crystalline light. That is one type of yoga siddha body.

On May 6 of the year 2001, Yogesh told me that a yoga siddha body can be assumed if one completely purifies the lower portion of the subtle body, otherwise it would not be possible. He made this remark as I observed the transparent sun-light producing subtle body of Babaji. Yogesh said that Babaji could very well relinquish that siddha form and just live in the intellect mechanism without a kundalini. He explained that only when there is subtle kundalini, there is a subtle body which resembles the human form, but which is made of transparent or multicolored lights.

It appears that by the instructions of Shiva, Babaji maintains a yoga siddha form, even though he can very well move to the causal plane. Yogesh said that one does not need a kundalini attached to the intellect. He said that a yogi can still give instructions to students even if he does not have a kundalini.

April 4, 2001

Shiva

He said, "Observe how psychic perception is ruined by the reactive process of the mind. When impulses come into the mind, it reacts by recalling previously related or near-related incidences and references. Stop that mental action. If you unwillingly accept a signal, do not react to it. Stop participating in the mind's reactions.

April 12, 2001

Yogeshwarananda

He said, "Keep this cleared and brightened."

Remark:

Cleared refers to physical body pollution clearance by asana postures, breath-infusion and proper diet. Brightened refers to the subtle form by clearing polluted subtle energies, displacing these with higher energy which produces a clarified crystal-clear bliss-yielding subtle form.

In this respect, Yogesh pointed to the anus region.

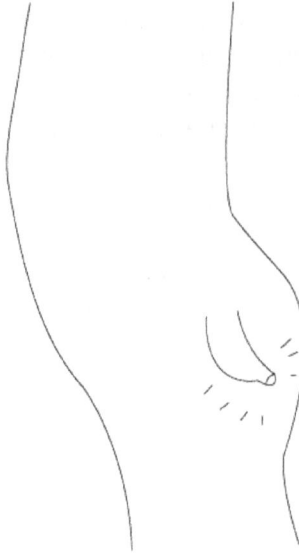

April 13, 2001

Yogeshwarananda

He said, "Bottom, then top, then areas in the abdomen and organs, one by one. Study charts."

Remark:

This refers to purification of particular areas in the order given, beginning with the bottom of the body. When doing this, one should repeat the procedure over and over until attaining a yoga-siddha body or until one eliminates the kundalini chakra.

The attainment of a yoga siddha body, hinges on the grace of Mahadeva, Shiva, but if one is specially gifted one may eliminate kundalini chakra and terminate, for the time being, social involvements on the lower planes. Babaji uses a yoga siddha form. Seeing him is just like looking at a person whose body is made out of clear sunlight. Such a person can hardly be seen. Yogesh eliminated his kundalini chakra. According to him, this is done by being completely unresponsive to whatever there is on the gross and the corresponding subtle planes.

One should do kundalini yoga to clear pollutions at the bottom of the body, to get rid of the anus impurities, the sex organ indulgence tendencies and the lower abdomen command over the psyche. These are technical practices. By doing breath-infusion for about three years, steadily twice per day, one can get a foot-hold on this. If one does asana postures alone, it will take much longer. If one does other gentler breath-infusion it will also take much longer. For general information, I state that the gentler breath-infusion will not work on a person whose body has much impurities. Such breath-infusion is effective if one's body has only a few impurities, in as much as a clogged tube cannot be cleared by gentle methods. This is why breath-infusion was given by kundalini masters like Harbhajan Singh. I learned that from him during the years of 1971 and 1972. I am grateful. With the polluted psyche I developed in this birth, it was impossible to clear it by any other method. Breath-infusion is a standard process. It includes the preliminary breath-infusion known as kapalabhati, but some teachers say that breath-infusion is dangerous.

Kapalabhati is rapid breathing with forcefulness on the exhale. In bhastrika the inhale and exhale are done forcefully. In addition there is the down-draw breath, which is done during pauses of breath-infusion. These can be learned from a teacher. They may occur spontaneously if one is regular in the practice.

At first in trying to do kundalini yoga, one tries to raise kundalini, but many people are at a loss to define and perceive kundalini. Years ago, a Western mystic researcher by the name of Sir John Woodruff (Arthur Avalon) wrote about kundalini. He described its power in glorious terms. Subsequently many conceived of it as the mysterious force. Actually, kundalini is common and is known in the Western world as sexual power. In the Western countries many people adore the sexual power for deriving the ecstasy of sexual pleasure. This is the same kundalini chakra in its downward expression.

Due to an attachment to sensation and its resulting excitements, a beginner desires to raise kundalini to experience sensations in the body. This is not the purpose of kundalini yoga but it serves as a beginner's motive. If the novice sticks to that reason for practice, he will progress further.

When the sexual force is turned upward, and comes up the back, front or middle of the body, instead of exuding through the sexual organ, it is understood that kundalini, was aroused in that person's psyche. Otherwise a human being experiences the aroused kundalini in sexual orgasms.

When kundalini goes downwards in a rush of ecstatic power, it is called a sexual orgasm. This is experienced even by animals. A bull experiences this when the semen is expelled during an arousal and so does a human being. In fact the quality and intensity of the· sexual electric rush of pleasure is the same in each case. Due to the sensitive nerves at the pubio-coccus muscle and in the head of the penis of the male human being and bull, the electric sensations pass through these parts of the body with lightning speed. It acts as a short circuit with an uncontrollable current of power. In the female bodies with the corresponding pubic-coccus muscle and clitoris sexual part, the same occurrence takes place.

Just as there is a set purpose for the flow of kundalini energy in the sexual organ, so there is a set purpose for its flow through the spine and brain and through the nerves of the solar plexus and chest area. If any of us are to be liberated, that person will be required to rid himself of the kundalini power. But that is easier said than done, and the implications of that accomplishment are the end of that person's cultural interest in this world.

Teachers who say that raising kundalini is dangerous may not perceive that the same power which is used in sexual indulgence and which culminates there in sexual orgasm, the most pursued pleasure in the material world, is the same power which when turned upwards may bursts into ecstasy in a thrilling excitation in the nerves, brain, mind and intellect of the psyche. How dangerous can such a power be, a power which is the same as the power experienced in sexual orgasms?

After one worked and worked according to how much endeavor is required for one's individual practice, one can focus on the top. In other words, first one has to purify a greater portion of the body, and then one may try to purify its head. This second phase of the top-of-the-body or head purification, involves developing the brow chakra, as well as the central force in the head.

When one worked somewhat on this head, one should use the acquired skill to tackle the middle portion; the navel and chest regions. These abilities are acquired in due course. Some students experience an acceleration in one phase or another, depending on individual good luck.

After mastery of the kundalini chakra, one becomes inspired to control the intellect in the head of the subtle body. This organ acts independently in a person who has not controlled the psyche. That control is reliant on purification of the psyche and detachment from sensations and excitements. According to Patanjali, yoga means the suspension of the excitements which stimulate the mind. These excitements are called mento-emotional constructions.

The intellect is not easy to control because the entire material world, including the subtle material formations, are enacted on the basis of it. It is very sensitive and reacts to the slightest stimulation when comes in through any orifice of the mind. If the mind is carefully guarded, it becomes possible to limit the intake of excitements and clear the psyche of the old impressions which promote social involvements and discourage yoga practice.

Generally people experience the intellect as their understanding, their ability to perceive and analyze but it is actually an organ of perception. To realize this in fact, means to reach a very subtle stage where one can see the organ and use it as a searchlight.

The intellect is called the light of knowledge, jnana chakshu, in the Bhagavad Gita. This organ is fueled or powered by the slightest or most incidental interest of the observing self. But this empowerment is so natural that the self's deliberate consent is not required. In advanced yoga, the yogi tries to reduce the reflection of his core power to the intellect just for the sake of slowing down the intellect and controlling its interactions. This takes a tremendous amount of time and energy. It involves the practice of asana postures, breath-infusion, pratyahar sensual energy withdrawal, dharana deliberate transcendental focus, dhyana spontaneous transcendental focus and samadhi prolonged transcendental focus, which are the six advanced stages of yoga practice. With these one must incorporate the two preliminary stages which are yama restrains and niyama permitted behaviors.

Those who are satisfied with the material world and who are addicted to various belief systems of religion, find no necessity to master these six stages of yoga. They deride the process as being difficult and time-consuming. However, leaving aside their view, one can honestly practice and form an assessment.

The intellect and the kundalini force usually remains apart, just as two ends of a log remain separate through connected at all times, or as in a building the top story is ever separated from the ground floor. However we should bring these two forces together so that in our interest, one can assist the other.

The independent and whimsical operation of the two forces cannot suffice for spiritual freedom. They must be curbed. Their independence needs be taken away. It is yoga practice that gives one the ability to better regulate them.

Yogesh said, "Bottom, then top, then areas in the abdomen and the organs, one by one. Then to study the charts."

When one attends to the bottom, he deals with kundalini chakra. Then he tends to the intellect in the brain and then by pranavision he looks down into the abdomen regions. This concerns the kundalini. For a tighter control of the back spinal kundalini power, one has to purify the front part of the body from the navel region to the groin. When all this is said and done, one may again try to purify kundalini chakra more and then control the intellect more and repeat the procedures to be sure that nothing is overlooked.

The charts are the various diagrams given in Yogesh's books and in writings of other yogis of repute, as well as diagrams they revealed in the astral world. Ultimately these diagrams must be realized by being shown the various parts of the subtle body. This occurs in the astral world when yogis of repute enter one's subtle form and show from the inside what is here and what is there. One also sees some things by visual-vision and by pranavision when doing asana postures and breath-infusion.

Shankara

His realization about the motivative nature of the mind-intellect-lifeforce complex.

Remark:

Shankara, while debating with a Pundit, explained that the analogy of the two birds relates to the atma as the superior one and the psyche of the atma as the inferior one. In part, this is incorrect. In part this is correct. The misrepresentation has to do with the fact that in some renditions of that analogy it is explained that the superior bird is the Supreme Person (paramatma), and the inferior one is the limited entity (atma). One cannot change that meaning. However in so far as he wanted to explain another important aspect, we should not neglect the idea.

In fact, in the very advanced stage of technique yoga, one realizes what Shankara explained. In the Upanishads it is established that in the atma cannot be fruitive. When it is in submissive proximity to the psyche, it appears to be of the nature of the psyche, even though it is in fact different. It is like the supposition that the person-self is temporary because the body it uses is not eternal. For a want of a firm understanding of its own nature, the self adopts the nature of whatever it identifies with.

The psyche consists of life force, mind space, intellect organ with sensual extensions, sense of identity and resting space. These comprise the psyche or the cultural personality. According to Shankara, this psyche is motivational or fruitive but the spirit is unmotivated and distinct as a detached witness. In the higher stages of technique yoga, one experiences the parts of the psyche as just that, as parts only. One sees where the sense of attachment originates and where the fruitive mentality is rooted. Such a mentality is certainly embedded in the psyche but it is not in the core-self which is in proximity, and which powers the psyche in part.

When a yogi can identify the psychological parts of his being, he can understand how the mind feels disappointed when an idea is not fulfilled, just like a hungry man who is instructed to stand near the entrance of a kitchen but who is destined to be served as the very last customer, and who will be served the smallest most insufficient meal.

That man may hope for the meals which passed him by on trays but which were served to others. It traumatized him. He grieved. When he was finally served a meager amount he felt insulted and deprived.

Part 2

Yogeshwarananda

He said, "Begin to apply a reverse force in that direction, otherwise no matter the aspiration, superficial endeavor or faith, you will go there. The system is meant to keep you tied there."

He pointed to the womb apparatus.

Remark:

Yogesh spoke of the circular spell-binding process through which one takes a body, works with it, becomes frustrated in its old age, and then is pushed out of it by force of time. Then again one takes another body helplessly. Many spiritual masters, even some who hail from reputed lineages, fall under this spell-binding force. However they shrewdly convince the followers that they are exempt from it. Since the followers cannot track transmigrations, they cannot check to see if the teachers are in the circular process. Thus life after life, one falls under such spiritual teachers who repeatedly return with the same slogans, selling faith to followers. It may seem that this is a cheating process but the gurus themselves do not understand how they transmigrate. They are part of the energy of superficial fulfillment, whereby human beings get satisfaction from considering relief of a chronic problem. The problem remains but the human beings feel an ease, thinking that they have solutions.

Many spiritual parties offer a salvation that their followers never realize but it serves the purpose of easing their troubled minds. Only a person who has mystic perception can see where his teacher is located on the spiritual path. Only he can know if the guru is freed from material existence. Others are easily caught in the trap of self-conviction by belief.

It is only by deep meditative absorption that one can interrupt the path of birth and death, otherwise no matter the religion, one will have to return in ignorance and again take another or the same religious process, following another or the same teacher or teachers, and again go through the same belief and dogma.

For myself, despite endeavors which are to an extent unusual for a human being, still if I am not careful I will return. It is easy for me to again be born after a few years from another woman's womb. Even though some people regard me as the teacher, I do not keep disciples. I am not representing a specific sampradaya or disciplic succession. I took initiation in more than one of the Indian lineages. I can say now in all honesty that I cannot tell anyone for sure that I will not take another body. I do not desire one. If anything I can take one willingly if I am instructed to do so by Shiva for one purpose or another. Otherwise I do not feel to take one, but that does not mean that I may not gravitate towards another womb situation accidentally or due to inattentiveness or by sympathy or attraction to such a place.

I endeavor now to be sure that this will not happen but I have more discipline to perform. At the present time my aim is to acquire a yoga siddha body to the extent that I can stay with some mahayogins like Yogesh when I am vacated from this body. As such I am not interested in disciples or in people who say that I am the teacher. I endeavor to get myself in order and to achieve my own priorities for spiritual freedom. Having disciples is a distraction. There are a few people like Sir Paul Castagna who would be with me regardless of what I do or where I go but besides these few I have no deep concern for others. In fact, even for Sir Paul, I do not have to care since he is existentially connected to me in such a way, that wherever I go he would follow. It is like that. It is not that I am looking to carry him here or there. Thus a few people will follow causelessly.

Yogesh stayed with me now for some time. Subsequently I make some firm progress under his supervision by the mercy of Shiva and Krishna/Balarama. Babaji watches over me to be sure that I get out one way or the other, but otherwise there is no guarantee even for me. Yogesh explained that in this existence it took billions of years for us to get into the fix we are in. He said that it may take billions again for us to get out. Those who follow instant salvation gurus, can go on believing and accepting the processes that satisfies them.

The moon or moons of a planet stay in that planet's orbit and are helplessly dragged here and there by that planet, and so certain wombs may drag us against our will. To gain freedom, requires a tremendous amount of power. This is a conjoint power of ourselves doing the yoga austerities and our freed teachers influencing our lifestyles. We alone cannot do it. They alone cannot achieve it either. Both powers must work in unison.

April 17, 2001

Shiva with sages at his feet

He explained, "In the subtle energy concentrate (chitta), there are no tools of excitement like the mind's sensing energy and the telescoping intellect. Thus when under that influence, there is rest or dreamless sleep. There are no mental impressions, just peace and compacted subtle energy. "

He gave this technique.

On the way out of the material world, one has to enter the chitta subtle energy concentrate. One by one, one enters various levels of reality. Generally people mistake the subtle heavenly worlds for the kingdom of God. They usually leave their material bodies and try to transit to one of the subtle paradises but these places cannot be the kingdom of God unless we define such a kingdom as merely a subtle mundane situation. Beyond that subtle mundane situation, there is the level of chitta subtle energy concentrate that is called the causal plane. In that place there are no subtle or gross objects. It is an objectless environment. It is itself the source of the subtle objects just as soil serves as the foundation for vegetation. Even though, as Shiva described, the chitta subtle energy concentrate is free from excitement, it is still the actual cause of our excitement. This stimulation came from the subtle energy concentrate, but in the concentrate the excitement remains dormant as compacted non-expressed energy. This same energy when divested in the atmosphere which we perceive takes the form of various sensual stimuli, which stimulates desire energy in our psyches.

April 19, 2001

Shiva

He said, "The regulation of breath comes naturally from sincere practice. Begin by inhaling uniformly using the whole diaphragm. Hold the breath, then exhaling uniformly. Concentrate on the left and then right in a balanced way or the left or right singly or alternately. Then gradually you will develop a method."

Remark:

On this day, the left channel opened completely. The full moon was visible, showing its influence on the psyche. As I looked down into the lung, I saw a silverish clear space.

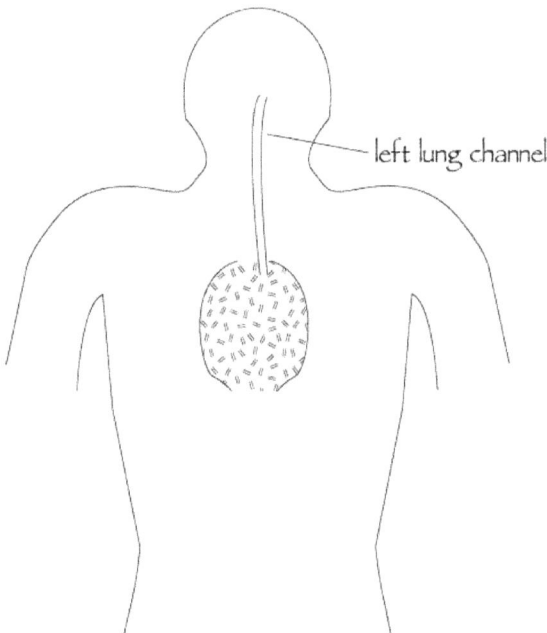

left lung channel

April 21, 2001

B.K.S. Iyengar

On this day, he showed proper alignment of some yoga postures. There are some experts in asana postures. Some others are expert in breath-infusion. A meditation master may not be so expert. Meditation experts may focused on-self-purification and not on postures and breath-infusion. In any case, a certain amount of alignment is necessary for full benefit of postures. Some hard-to-reach areas of the gross and subtle bodies, are only reached by proper posture alignment. Sometimes I take help or I get help from such masters as B.K.S. Iyengar and Swami Sachidananda. These are ancient mahayogins who took new material bodies for the sake of teaching us the science of how to use material forms to upgrade our existence.

If one takes seriously to these techniques, he will save investing time in superficial practices. He will not have to run about physically, since he can take lessons in the astral world. Instead of travelling to locate the gross bodies of various teachers, one can take help from these masters in the subtle world without having to relocate. In addition one can take help from yogis who do not have physical bodies but who are available for instruction in the astral world.

Just recently Yogesh showed another technique, where one can go to the edge of the causal region, where the subtle disappears into the causal. One can take help there from yogis who have long gone through the causal region, giving up subtle mundane existence. Thus in technique yoga, one can break the limitations of having to find teachers physically. One can side-step those spiritual masters who state that one cannot advance unless one has a teacher with a physical form.

April 21, 2001

Lahiri

He said, "This is what I meant by vajroli. It is when the semen no longer stays in the groin area but is distributed through the body by a thorough hatha yoga practice. A vigorous full practice gives this. No cheating, just treating the practice as sacred. This is called sadhana puja or the worshipful regard for practice.

Remarks

In technique yoga, the student is asked to be concerned about the practice, and not so much about the grace of the teacher. That grace is there but it is not the precipitous factor. The student's effort for practice is the very thing which accelerates him. Practice is what he should be most attentive to. The grace of teachers only becomes permanently functional if the student maintains the practice.

April 21, 2001

Shiva

He said, "People do not understand the value of Skanda over Ganesh. Skanda took the instruction at face value and went on pilgrimage but Ganesh was focused on cultural advantages. Skanda won the prize of freedom from responsibility. Even though he became distraught and then angry by Narad's instigation, still he won that prize due to his good son-nature. Ganesh wanted to be a husband, a provider. You should follow Skanda."

Remark:

As the story goes, this story is from the Puranas, both Skanda and Ganesh were told to circumambulate the earth, and return to their parents, Shiva and Goddess Durga. Skanda took the instructions literally and did so.

Ganesh who is a more culturally proficient person, took the instruction to mean that he should circumambulate his mother and father, who are themselves the cause of the earth, He circled his parents clockwise with them to his right. After that he reported to them.

Understanding Ganesh's accomplishment, Shiva and Goddess Durga blessed him and married him to Siddhi and Riddhi, the two most desired females for family life. Sometime, long after, Skanda returned from the long journey around the world. He was surprised to learn that Ganesh had long returned and was happily married. He became distraught.

Somehow Narada went to Skanda and advised him to leave his parents. Narada showed that Shiva and Goddess Durga were not really Skanda's parents since parents usually act in a way to bless their children culturally. They neglected Skanda and make him take a useless journey, while they awarded Ganesh who merely walked around them.

However from this Skanda became like Narada, a leading celibate. Unlike Ganesh, the responsibility for family did not distracted Skanda from the spiritual quest.

Shiva

He directed that I put the astral head into the womb of the astral body, and use the intellect to confront the subtle energy's root during the session when there was a stillness of mento-emotional energy. Here is the posture used while doing this.

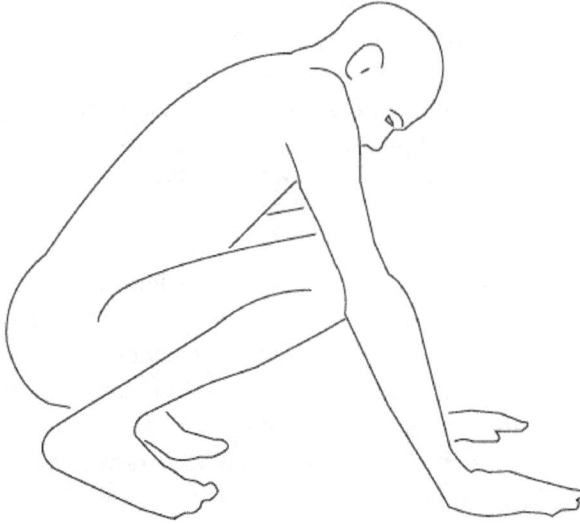

Remark:

When doing breath-infusion, when a certain amount of fresh air and fresh subtle energy is surcharged into the psyche, there may be a place of turmoil or a place of bright light or dark light. There may be a place of stillness or absorption. One should focus within to find these special energy collections. The intellect should be relocated there. Particularly when there is breath-infusion in any posture, when one stops on an inhale or exhale, one should be sure to focus within to discover where the surcharged energy moved or where it is suspended, stirred, suppressed, compressed or expanded. It may convert into sparkling light or heated or cooled feelings. Regardless, one should track it.

On May 22, 2001, a student inquired about keeping the locks when one stops while doing breath-infusion. I explained that when one stops on an inhale, one should push down the abdomen but pull up the sex and anus locks. If one stops on an exhale, one should pull up the abdomen while pulling up the sex and anus locks.

In either application the chin lock should be applied.

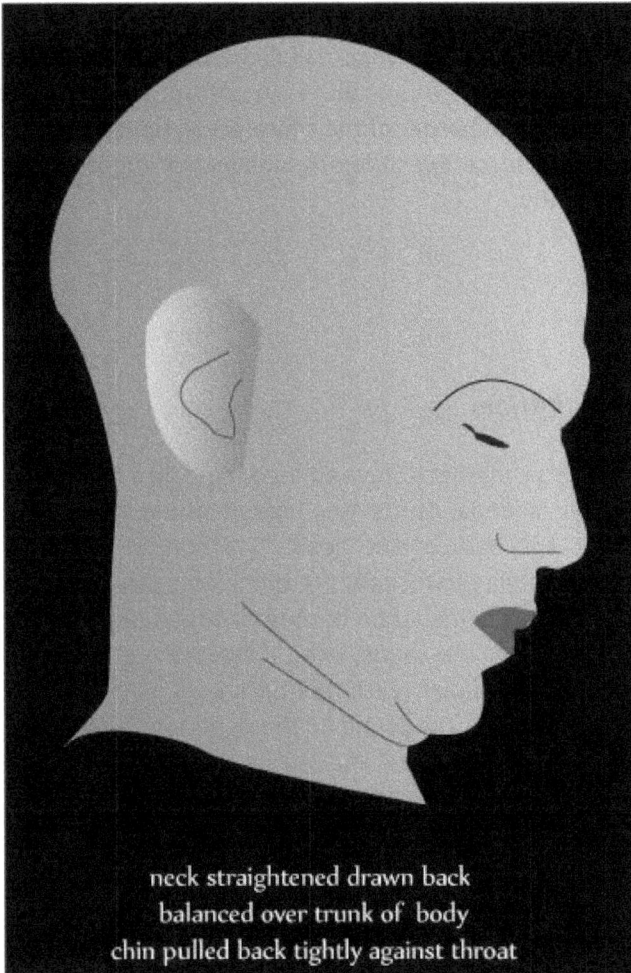

neck straightened drawn back
balanced over trunk of body
chin pulled back tightly against throat

Stopping on an inhale after infusing air by rapid breathing means that one stopped when the lungs were saturated with air. This produces a downward pressure. Keep that pressure without straining muscles in the system. Stopping on an exhale means that there is a certain upward pressure being applied just before you stop. Keep that upward pressure. That serves as a lock. Sometimes when stopping on the inhale one will arouse front kundalini, which is a rare but necessary occurrence for clearing the navel region. This is necessary in advanced practice to remove the impurities in the front of the subtle body.

From the solar plexus many tiny nadis spiral outwards. These have to be blasted by awakening front kundalini. When you stop and focus within make sure that you always take the intellect in the brain to the surcharged energy, wherever it is moving or is stilled or converted into light. According to Yogesh, when subtle energy hits or clashes with fire energy, there is a burst of light. That is called kundalini. Some yogis call it the bhasvara fire, bhasvara agni. Yogesh does not think that kundalini is important but then again, he is a mahayogin living on the border of the causal level. He does not need a subtle body with kundalini force. For others, kundalini has importance. It should be aroused consistently.

April 23, 2001

Shiva

Afternoon meditation.

After resting the intellect, Shiva advised that I do a meditation which was introduced by Shivananda. At first one hears a sound in the right side of the head, nearer to the back of the head. One may hear it now and then, according to one's ability to focus at the time. Sometimes the sound shifts to the left side. Or it may be heard on both sides simultaneously.

If one cannot hear the sound, even if the place is very quiet, one may hear it if one bites the molar teeth, the back jaws. One may bite down and then release and listen for the sound on the right or left side. Biting draws the mind to the back of the head and may cause it to be attentive there. Shivananda told me years earlier in the astral world, that a working man should rest his intellect at the end of the day. The advice is this. If the body and mind are not too tired from a day's work, one should do yoga exercises as usual and then meditate. In fact, one should do a short meditation immediately after the exercises, then take bath, then meditate again. This last meditation after bath is done before resting the body. However if one comes home from the day's work and is not inclined to do postures and breath-infusion, because of feeling that the body and mind are too exhausted, one should take a short rest, to give the body and mind some recharge of energy, then one should exercise, meditate, take bath, and then meditate again.

This diagram shows where the sound may be heard. It is similar to the sound one hears when listening to the echoing vibration in a conchshell. It may also be a sharp shrilling sound, similar to a continuous *Eeeeee* being resounded in the head.

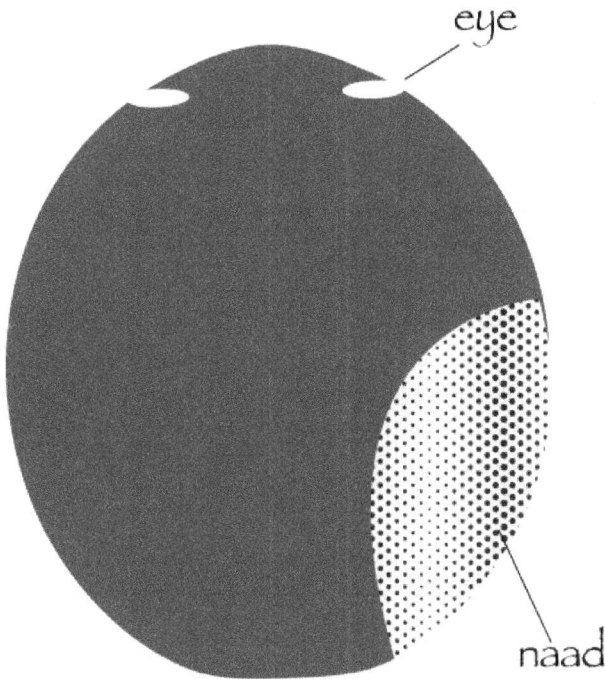

On the same day, Shiva explained that the elementary purpose of yoga is to kill the physical body. He said that this did not mean a forceful killing but rather it is like wanting to go through a locked door, being there behind the door just waiting. Then suddenly one hears that the door latch is released. One gives the door a slight push and it opens.

He said, "You do not kill the body. You do not fight providence, which is time and the supernatural rulers. You let them act first to kill the body, but since you are prepared to escape, you take the opportunity to depart wondrously."

Pointing to my abdomen, he continued, "Look at this. Transfer from the gross to the subtle body. Say, *'Om Vishnu,'* in the back of the head. As soon as the distracting thoughts go away, put your attention in the back continuously."

April 24, 2001

Shiva

A tongue procedure.

He explained that with the tongue curled back to the soft palate, the breath is mostly a top lung one, mostly related to the brain. When the tongue is in the front on the hard palate, the breath goes down to affect the life force.
Remark:
To determine where to hold the tongue during an exercise with breath-infusion, one should begin by always trying to keep the tongue curled back. Then after gaining more progress during the infusion, one should merely observe where the tongue is naturally positioned in the mouth, and see how its location in various postures increases the breathing action or deters it.

April 30, 2001

Durgadevi

She explained that she was the first great yogini except for Ma Sarasvati, who later became known as Arundhati. Ma Durga is the expert for feminine techniques. She inspired Yogi Harbhajan Singh.

Yoni nerve technique.

This one concerns the nerves in the vaginal passage. There are many such techniques.

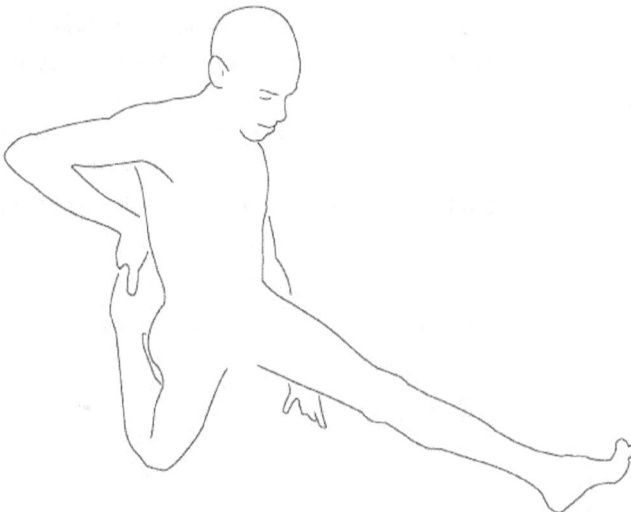

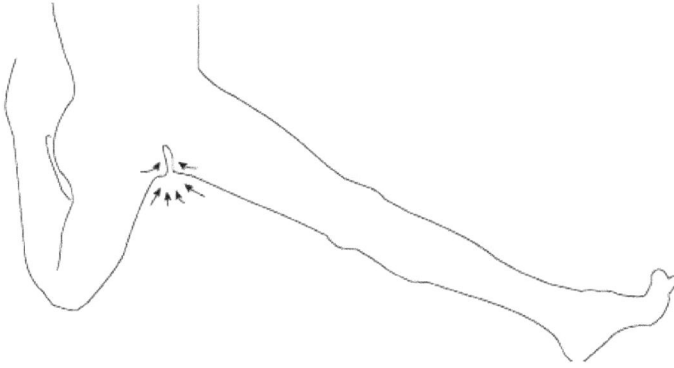

She showed a breast technique.

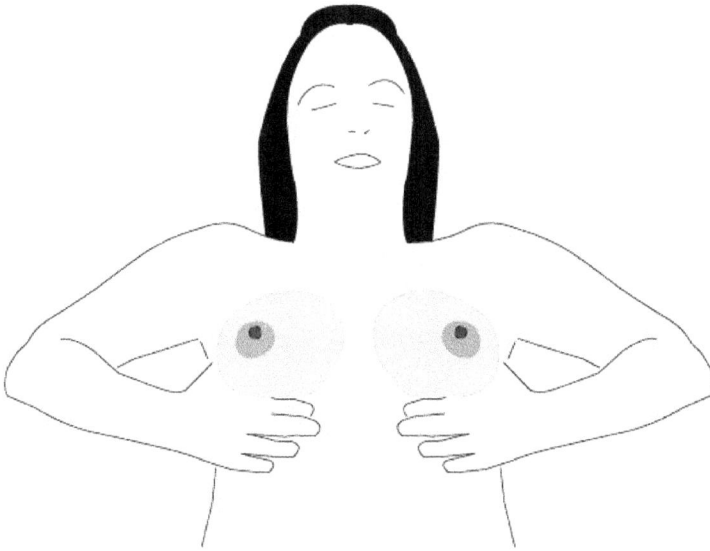

The breast technique is done while standing, breathing rapidly, pumping air into the breasts. Even though men lack breasts they can do this. They do however have a duct in the subtle body which could have produced a breast. In some men, there is a swelling of soft flesh around each nipple, almost as if the body has breasts.

Yoni/lingam procedure.

This one was given by Ma Durga. Yoni means vaginal passage. Lingam is the male sexual organ. This technique pertains to the subtle body. If it is done with the gross form intending to affect the subtle one, it is done in tight lotus. When this is done a vaginal passage appears in the subtle body. Sometimes a yogini places her subtle vagina over the subtle male organ of a yogi. If possible a yogi should prevent this. If however this happens one should not reject the yogini. Her arrival indicates that one is not advanced enough to do this practice. This is how one can gage the progress.

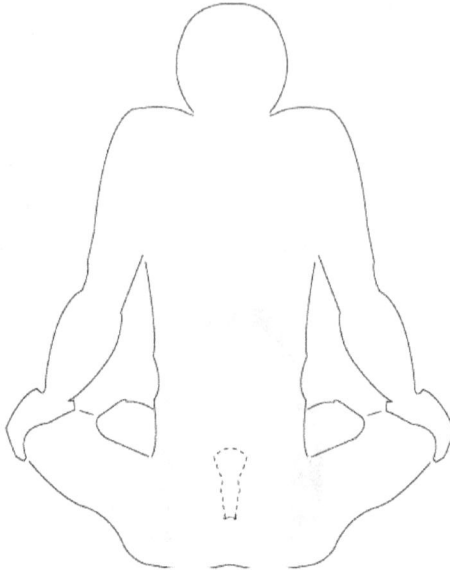

May 2, 2001

Ma Durgadevi

She said, "Work in your body to reimburse for the damage to this one. See those feminine postures. Work on this and this (pointing to breasts) and this (pointing to the vaginal passage).

Remark:

Ma Durga gave postures which I may show females for attaining celibacy. I was instructed by her to work on those postures in my male body to reimburse for damage I caused in those parts of Ma Durga's body.

The question may arise of how I could damage her form. The answer is that during sexual intercourses and during taking births and being a baby suckling mothers, for centuries while transmigrating, I may have intentionally or unintentionally done some harm. Since this damage is on the log of my activities, I am liable for it. This is a chance to atone and reimburse by practicing healing restoring procedures.

In this regard Babaji said that there is a necessity for many yogis to worship Vaishnava Devi, a manifestation of Ma Durga. They have to do that to reimburse damages and to get freed from inherent responsibilities, which have to do with righteous responsible life as family men.

May 3, 2001

Ma Durgadevi, Ma Kali and their associates

They showed female procedures. This makes it valid for me to teach females tantric yoga. However, I am not interested in doing this, because it gives me a bad name and causes foolish people to insult me. Around the year of 1999, a woman wanted to learn tantric practices. When someone heard that I would teach her his opinion of me depreciated. He regarded me as a perverted womanizer.

In another case, a man's wife wanted to talk to me but the man objected. Later on the lady saw me and presented questions. However the man's objection was valid because beneath the whole thing was a sexual adventure. As it is in these cases, one ancestor of the lady plotted for her to leave the husband and make me into a lover for the sake of begetting children.

Ma Durga gave some procedures on this day. She explained that some of those techniques were inspired to Yogi Harbhajan Singh, my teacher of the bhastrika breath-infusion process, which he called the breath-of-fire.

As Ma Durga left, Yogesh came and made some remarks. He was in my brahmrandra, like a person in a nearby room over-hearing everything. He said that he did no female techniques but that they would be effective for me.

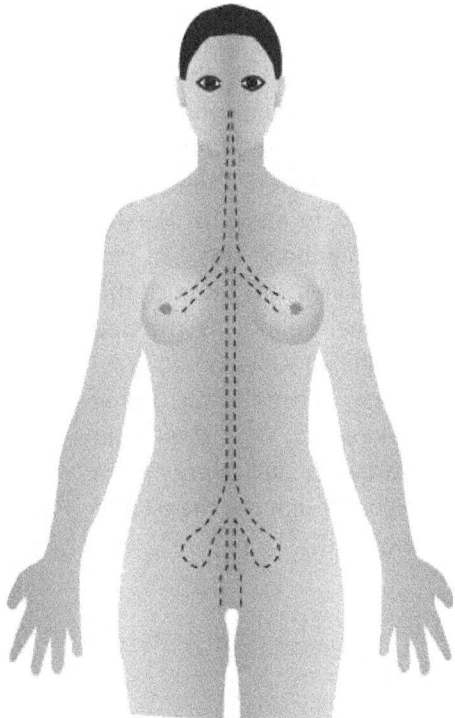

May 4, 2001

Yogi Harbhajan Singh

He said, "Those techniques are given for the ascetic's personal use. Even though I taught them to females, they were given to me by Devi for my use."

Remark:

Somehow Yogi Harbhajan, master of kundalini yoga, came. An unusual visit!

Regarding those female methods, in my case, I got them for both purposes, my personal use on the feminine parts of my body and to show females in the future. Of course because of the underlying sexual implications which are always there lurking in the background, it is risky to teach females. Some techniques were put into my body by Devi for storage, for her retrieval at a later date. This also I do not like because if the Goddess has some idea that my subtle body will be staying on for a long time, that may prohibit me from relinquishing that body, and would limit what I can achieve in yoga practice. As it is in the case of Babaji, he was restricted by Shiva, only to go so far as to develop a yoga siddha form. Yogesh went further and got rid of his kundalini altogether. In any case, being limited, there is not much I can do about it. Here is that technique. This is for females. Males may practice this for personal benefit as stressed by Yogi Bhajan. One should draw up breast energy while doing breath-infusion. One should do down-draw to pull energy from the thigh through the breast and into the head.

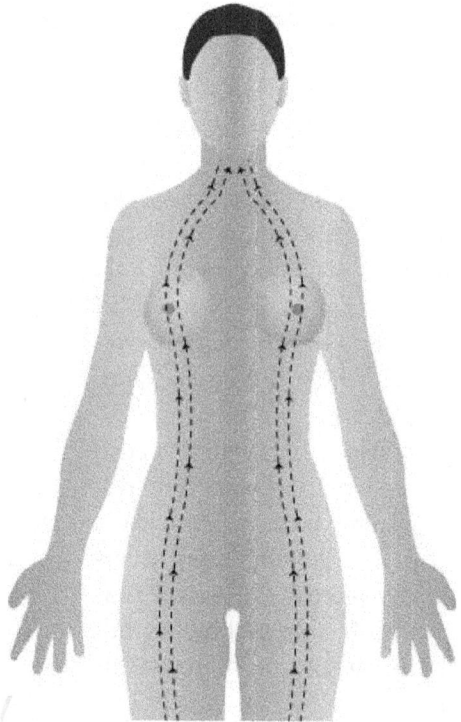

When doing this with breath-infusion, if the subtle body was fully charged with fresh subtle energy, the breasts will be shining bright like two lights. Some apsara heavenly women may come to catch the exuding light. They will see it. In the subtle world it will attract them.

When I did this, I was on the physical side, doing it in my gross body. Since the subtle form is interlocked into the gross form, the subtle body began to exude the light. Shiva alerted me to a risk. He said, "Do not do those exercises for too long. The angelic girls may come in thousands. When they discover that you are male, what will you do? If they become attracted under those circumstances, their sisterly moods will be converted into sexual attraction. You may be force into sexual acts. Be careful when doing those postures, so as not to attract them. Cover the breast lights."

May 4, 2001

I got a realization that the feminine techniques done by males, nullify offenses committed with females. These include faults of childhood and youth, as well as errors committed in elderly years. These methods can cause a reimbursement of the energy which was unduly taken previously from females. When the reimbursement is made, the yogi will have slight or very revealing memories of the past faulty events.

May 7, 2001

Ma Durga

She gave a vaginal passage procedure, a yoni technique.

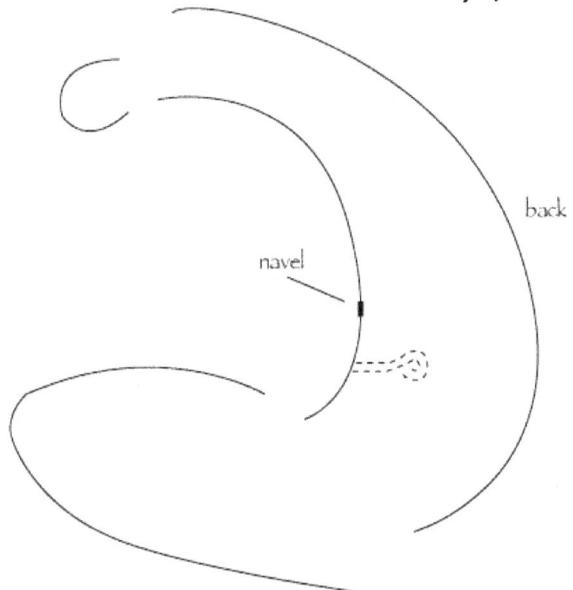

back

navel

May 11, 2001

Ma Durga

She gave a down-draw breath technique to be done in a certain posture. This is mostly for women and for men who are at the terminal stage of their efforts at celibacy.

It is only in the advanced stages of celibacy when one's masculinity is somewhat curbed that a man can perceive the feminine parts of his subtle body.

In this technique, one stands, with hands on hips and feet slightly apart. One does the down-draw breath, which is a pulling breath, with one, two or three draws of breath, then a pause, during which locks are applied. As this is done, one pulls up in the woman's organ. This is done by males by pulling up the male organ and using the wetness of a woman's organ to pull up all fluids which usually abounds there, flushing around, stirring lusts and emotions in the woman's sexual part.

This is not an imagination, one has to use his developed subtle perception so that he can see the actions in the subtle body.

May 11, 2001

Ma Durga

She said, "Some girls practice this."

Remark:

She caused my body to assume a posture. In cases like this, my body is maneuvered by yogini teacher. That posture was with insteps locked behind the head with hands grasped together under the buttocks. The body balances on the curved back.

When this is practiced by advanced yoginis, they extend their subtle tongue into their yoni (vaginal passage), completing a circle of sexual energy (vital force). In the cases like Goddess Kali and some of her associates, their tongues are elongated as is sometimes seen in pictures which artists draw on the basis of statements in the Devi Purana and its related tantric texts.

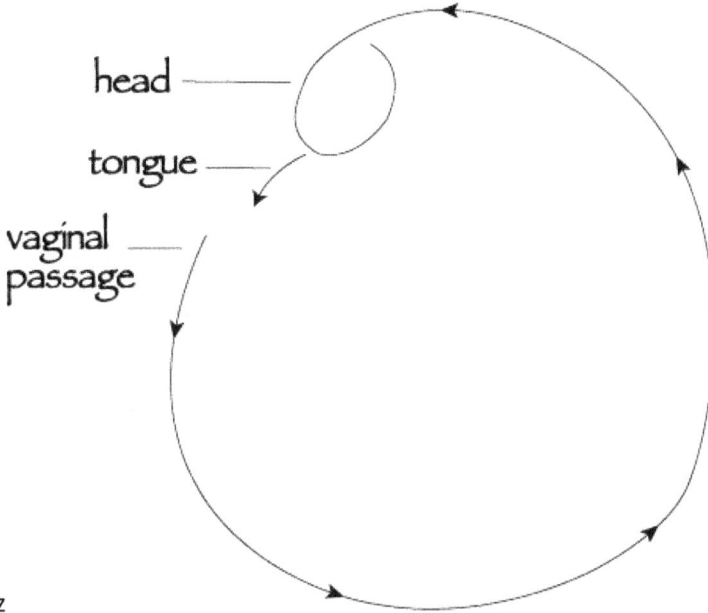

head

tongue

vaginal
passage

z

May 12, 2001

Yogeshwarananda

He instructed that I balance on the side like this.

May 13, 2001

Ma Durga

She said, "I did these procedures when I did austerities. Vak did many of them even before I practiced. I taught these to Kali Ma, Chandika Ma and others. The front kundalini is more prominent in females due to the breasts and womb. However some of the force is spinal. Back kundalini extends to the front. It is mixed with the frontal force. In men the frontal force is more distinct than in females, Vak alone has the best record of yoga austerities."

Remark:

Vak is the daughter of Brahma. At first when he produced her subtle body, he mistook her for his wife. He desired a woman when she appeared through his contemplating energy. She did however reject him. Analyzing her motives, and condemning herself and Brahma, she took to yoga practice. She did not have proper celibate techniques. Brahma took compassion on her. He asked his son Vasishtha to teach her. Vasishtha complied. Subsequently Vak successfully changed the sexual tendencies in her body, such that the body never did exhibit the tendency for intercourse with anyone who was her social senior, brother or dependent. Later by breath-infusion mastership, she killed her gross body and took another form as Arundhati who became the wife of Vasishtha.

May 14, 2001

Ma Durga

She said, "Some postures cannot be done with the physical form. However all postures can be complete with the subtle body."

Remark:

Ma Durga showed some yoni configurations and yoni-curbing mystic actions. Yoni is the vaginal passage.

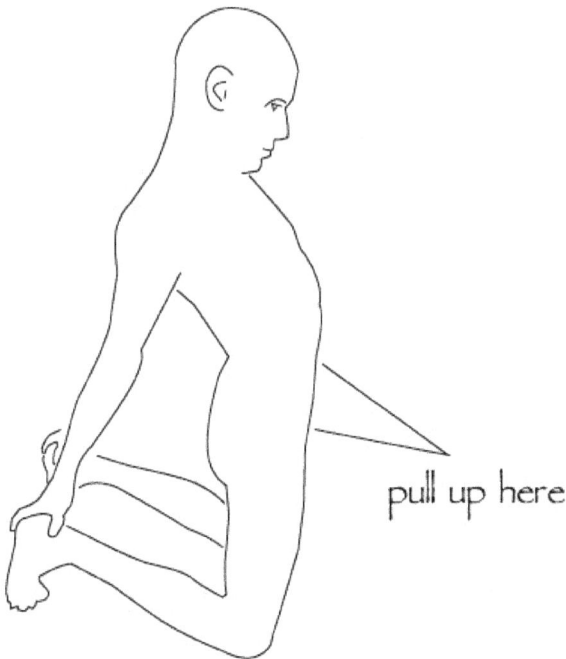

pull up here

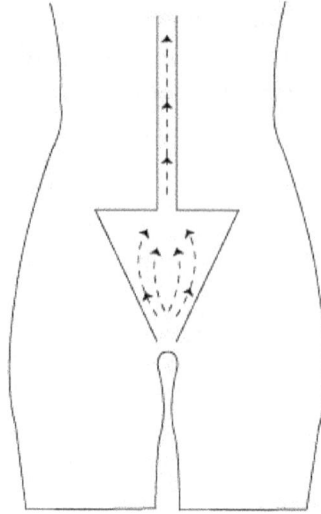

May 15, 2001

Yogeshwarananda

He showed a coordination between the perineum pulling-up pad and the top palate of the mouth. While doing rapid breathing with periodic down-draw breaths, the two areas are coordinated mystically.

May 21, 2001

Yogeshwarananda

He showed a top neck chakra which is a coordination of the bottom end of the sushumna column. These coordination points are self-discovered. Or they may be shown by a yogin in the subtle world. This neck zone may be cloudy or it may be cleared with a hole in the center.

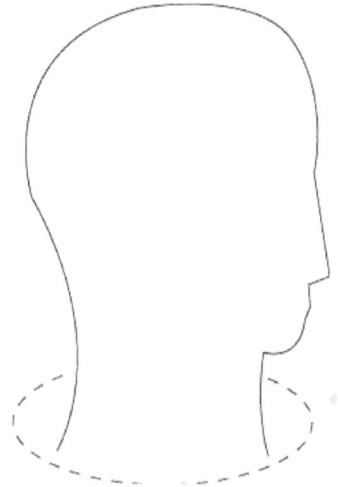

May 25, 2001

Shiva / Ma Durga

This is a female procedure which she inspired.

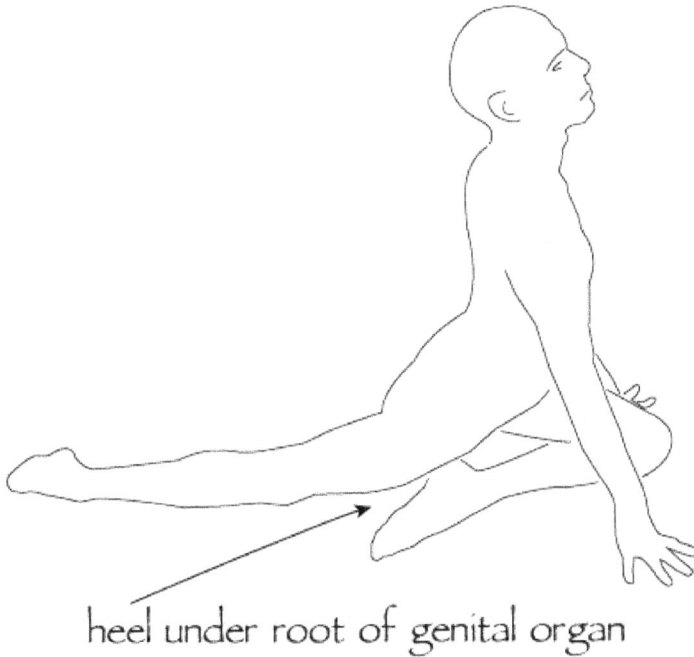

heel under root of genital organ

May 30, 2001

Shiva

He told me to explain the female part of the male body and the male part of the female form. This pertains to the exercises given by Ma Durga. This, more or less, confirms Yogi Bhajan's statement that the exercises inspired to him by Ma Durga, were for personal use. Primarily one should be concerned with self-development. This is yoga at its best. One should not be attached to assisting others. For a male, he should curb the male and female part of the body.

May 31, 2001

Yogeshwarananda

He showed a technique which clears a female blood tube. This is shown below.

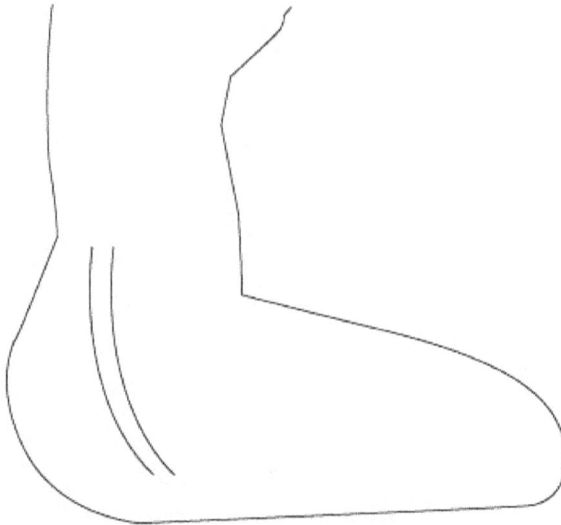

June 1, 2001

Yogeshwarananda

A female procedure

This takes blood out of the thighs and the female organ.

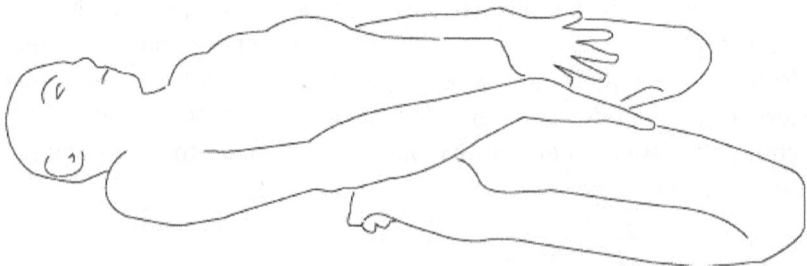

On this day Yogesh showed another reality, namely that in the lower astral form, there is kundalini force but on the higher astral level, there is only the intellect organ, the sense of initiative and the core-self.

June 2, 2001

Ma Durga

She said, "Do these postures as if you exercised my body. In that way repay me by returning a good body, free from lower urges. Part of each gross and subtle form, is mine. The other part belongs to Kailashpati Shiva."

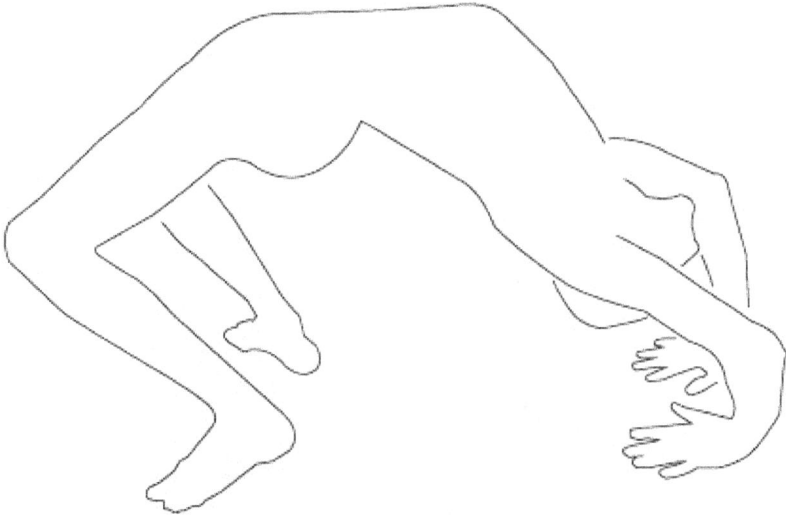

June 3, 2001

When a body is tired from strenuous work or from many hours of being awake, it should be rested for at least one half hour. Then one may do the exercises. This applies at the end of the day. One should be sure not to fall asleep nor forget to do the late afternoon session of exercises. An important exercise which requires little effort but which brings many advantages for the yogi, is to place the feet on a chair, while resting on the back on the ground. If one is tired, this is done before doing the exercises, otherwise it may be done before resting. This causes the blood in the legs and thighs to return to the lung for removing carbon dioxide and other polluting gases. In turn, in the subtle body the fresh subtle energy displaces polluted, used energy.

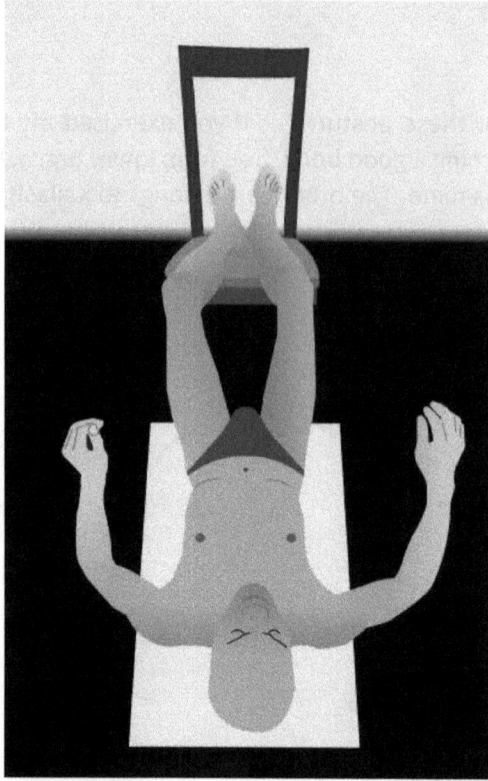

June 6, 2001

Yogeshwarananda

He explained supreme dispassion. This is termed para-vairagya. According to Yogesh, one cannot become liberated without exhibiting this. He explained it to be a total non-interest without aversion or attraction. It is important not to be attracted, nor to hate nor despise nor be repulsed from any item or person. One checks this by changing the attitude of the mind towards various objects, particularly towards objects which were very much liked or disliked.

The mind or the intellect should not think or try to present the object by the way of visualization, memory, inner sounds or expressions. In addition, if the mind senses an object, or picks up an impression or message which came from an object either casually or forcefully, the intellect should be refrained from reacting. It is just like receiving a letter and never opening it.

The life force cannot act unless it takes assistance from the intellect. All the same that assistance usually comes automatically. One should practice to end the automatic approval system which transpires between the intellect and the life force.

One must improve the life force by feeding it a higher grade of energy. Elementary religion means to control the life force by trying to indoctrinate it into higher cultural habits. This however is not a yogic technique. We desire to change the quality of energy the life force feeds on. If it gets a higher energy, its tendencies will change accordingly.

More sincerity is required. More sincerity means that we become more attached to the practice. We understand that our progress hinges on practice. We should be responsible and act in a way to successfully terminate social obligations, so that we can increase the time for practice.

June 9, 2001

Ma Durga / Yogeshwarananda

Under their combined influence, I did this female posture.

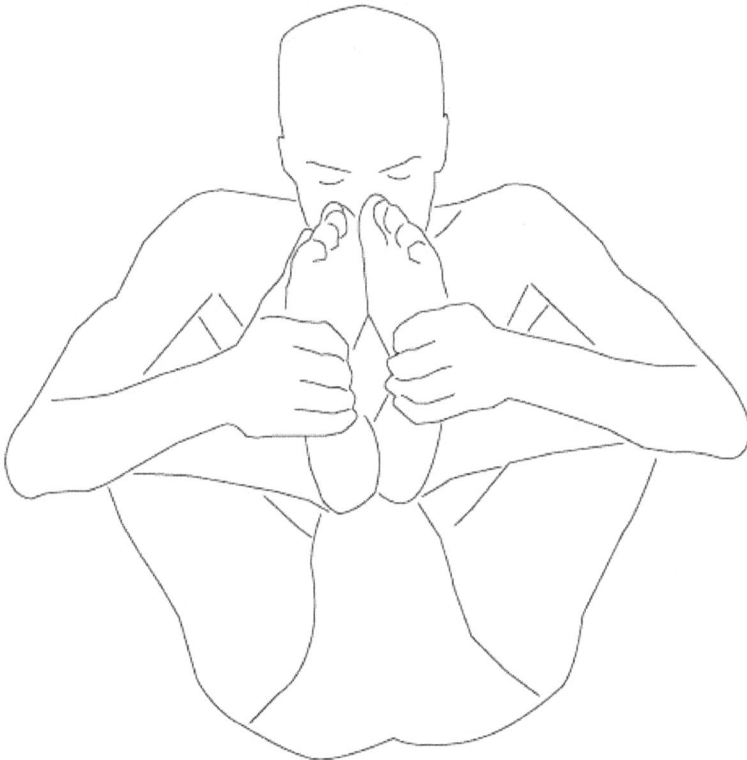

July l, 2001

Yogeshwarananda

He said, "The breasts correspond to the testes. The energy which is used in the breasts of females goes mostly to the testes in males. In the male organ this energy causes a thrusting force. Part of it is used for physique in the chest of the male form."

July 6, 2001

Yogeshwarananda

He said, "First observe. When doing postures, see the thin lines of pain. After looking and looking, one develops nadi vision. The stretched nerves, tendons and muscles show the path of the subtle energy transfers. This shows where to direct the inner vision."

Remark:

This is a big secret for those who practice asanas sincerely. Many critics of hatha yoga, have no understanding of how subtle vision is developed through doing postures.

July 7, 2001

Yogeshwarananda

He said, "Purification of the nadis brings about realization of the intellect lights. Then the lower system of kundalini can be eliminated and energy connection to the kundalini cut off so that the intellect can be explored and realized as it is. This is merely part of the pratyahar interest interiorization, which is the 5th step of the eight stages of yoga.

July 9, 2001

Yogeshwarananda

He instructed that I go around the intellect.

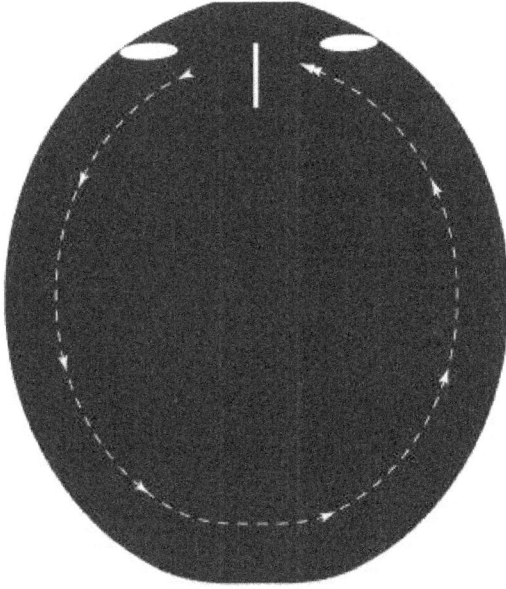

July 10, 2001

Yogeshwarananda

He gave an intellect-light coordinate. In this mystic action one feels the base chakra, the touch sense in the intellect and the subtle material elements which are known as tan maatras.

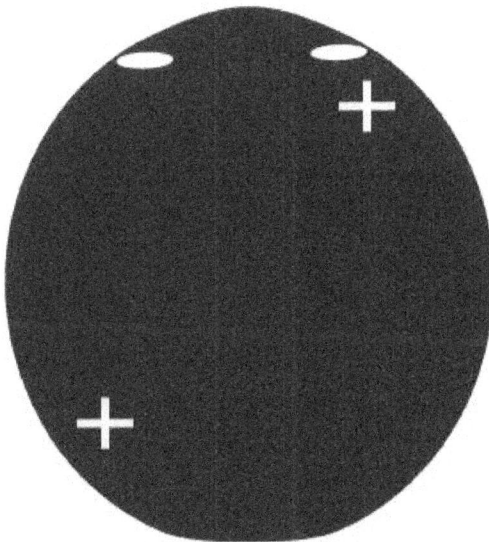

July 11, 2001

Shiva

He said, "The physical brain and the intellect are different instruments. When doing intellect location meditation, do not mistake one for the other. The difference is subtle, with the intellect having subtle lights.

July 12, 2001

Yogeshwarananda

An intellect-kundalini loop energy action.

In this practice, the subtle body does more than the gross one. Hence if someone observes physically what is done, he will not perceive the entire procedure. This has subtle actions which I may or may not explain. One should know that such subtle actions, though unseen to physical perception are performed. Look at this posture.

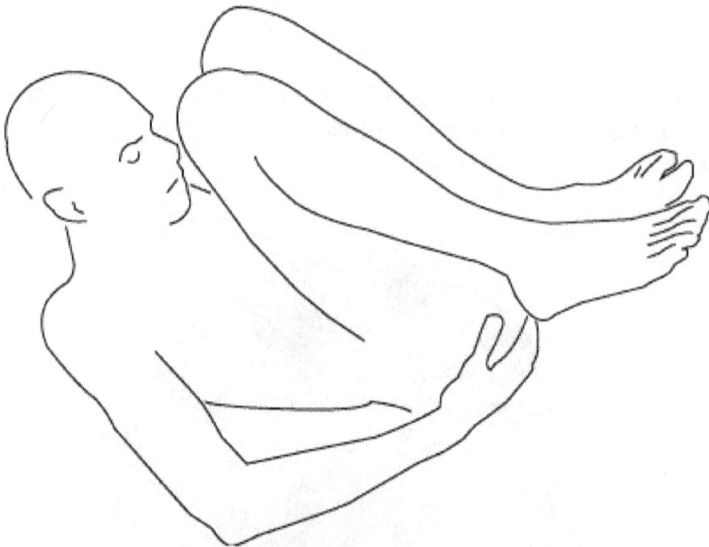

While doing that, the yogi should push his subtle tongue around the back of the body, so that it is stretched around the outside of the spine. On the gross side, the physical tongue is stretched out as far as it can be protruded.

Yogesh reminded me to note that persons doing breath-infusion or postures or a combination of these, which cause the physical body to sweat, should wait until the body cools and stops sweating, before taking bath, or before entering very cold places like air-conditioned rooms. It is a practice of yogis to rub the sweat, spreading it over the body.

July 13, 2001

Yogeshwarananda

He showed some orbs in the intellect. Please see this diagram. These are the controlling points for the special functions labeled.

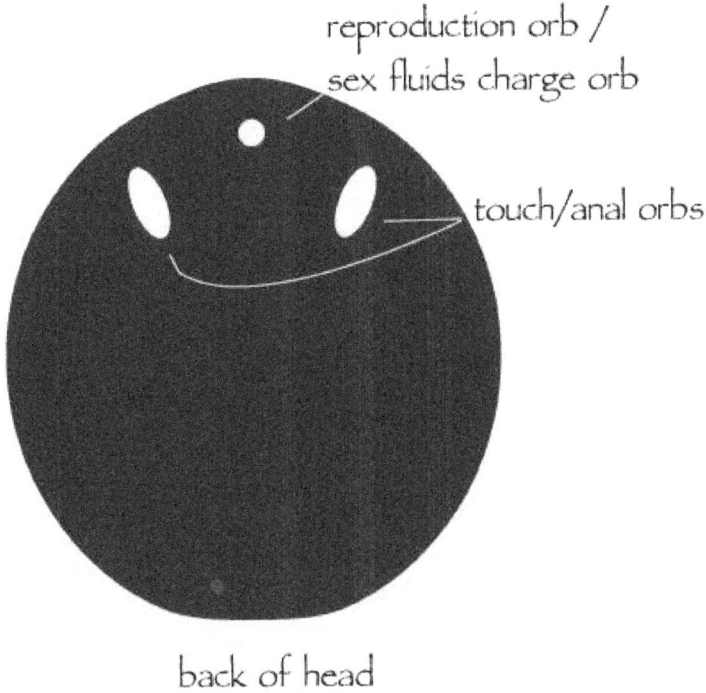

reproduction orb /
sex fluids charge orb

touch/anal orbs

back of head

Yogeshwarananda

Eating-tube clarification

He showed that when there is no late eating for some years, the eating tube in the astral body turns crystal clear. It feels empty in the early morning during exercises. Such accomplishment cannot be attained over-night. This takes time with much sincerity.

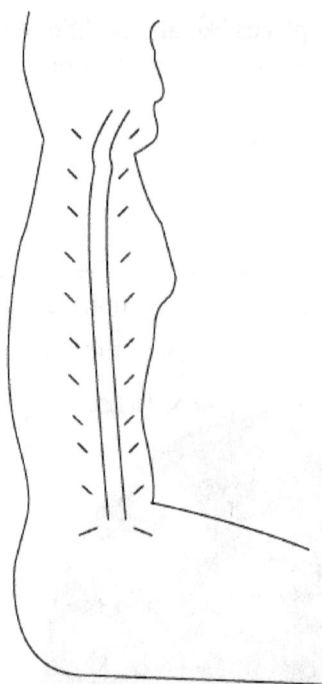

Part 3

Yogeshwarananda

He explained, "The energy from the cosmic background vibration makes one fulfill many desires which the Complete Whole Existence will have to work out as soon as there is opportunity and agents available."

The only way to avoid becoming an agent, is to become supremely detached by the practice of disinterestedness in the social and cultural affairs of the gross and subtle world. The back and forth, exchange of ideas causes the activation of multiple desires in a continuous display of manifestation on the basis of the said desires. Since the energies are supersensitive and super-responsive, God need not supervise this.

July 17, 2001

Yogeshwarananda

An action for the subtle body which is done with the gross form. Set the body in the posture below and do breath-infusion. When the system feels sufficiently charged and filled with fresh subtle energy, take an inhale and apply the locks while pushing down on either side of the abdomen inside the form, but pulling up the sex and anus locks. Then push out the subtle body only. Arch the subtle spine. The gross body should remain as it was.

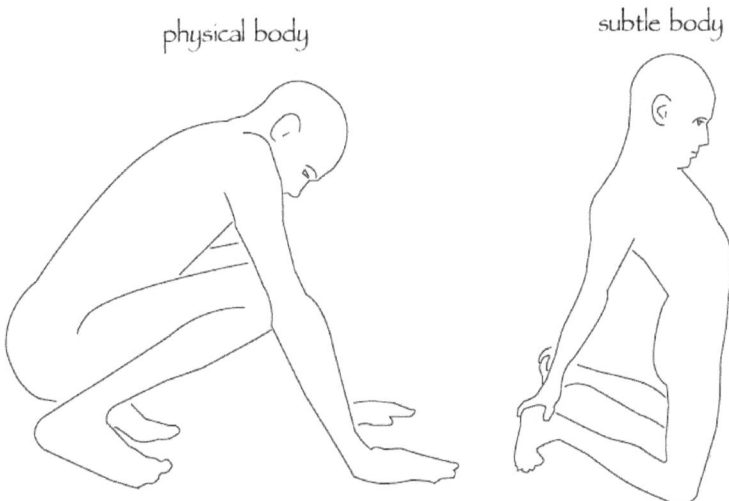

physical body

subtle body

July 18, 2001

Yogeshwarananda

He showed how to perceive the pool of cosmic causal energy from which our individual cosmic forms were derived. I suspect that there is only one such pool, for all beings in our zone. It seems to me that formerly, I used to see other cosmic pools in other regions. In any case, the others are not relevant to our existence here. We cannot switch to some other place. We cannot re-assign ourselves to another creation. We must stay with the Personality of Godhead from whom we emerged initially. I did meditation sitting near to Shiva as I usually do each morning.

Usually Yogesh stays in my brahmrandra, especially at that time. He directs me in various ways. It seems that he stays in my brahmrandra of his own accord. It may be because I am compatible to him or because I have some sincerity, enough to encourage him to assist. I do not know for sure. He is however one of the primal sons of Brahma, one of those Creative Agents who started up the generation of human species on this planet. In this life he became known only as a great yogin.

Sometimes he regards me as an associate. Sometimes he sees me as a student, and sometimes as a beginner yogin. This is because my progress is slow. Compared to some others, I am a great yogi, but compared to him I am not much of anything. For some reason, recently, I was bogged down in the cultural and social life. My practice slowed terribly. Efficiency is lacking because of being involved with many people.

Yogesh, after showing the location of the cosmic causal reservoir and the great light which it emanates, instructed that I return some excess energies to it, as well as some cultural assignments which it gave me long ago. These cultural objectives forcibly adhered to me.

July 20, 2001

Yogeshwarananda

An open-end buttocks nadi

One value of practicing subtle body yoga is the aspect of realizing that all of the body has to be purified. It is not the head alone which is important. All parts of it add up to what we call, consciousness of the psyche. So long as we have this psychology, it should be purified.

Later as the yogi advances, he may reach a stage of getting rid of the subtle body and the kundalini, just as Yogesh did. Until such a time, it remains a priority to purify the psychology. This makes for a cleaner way of passing stools and a more organized and efficient way of eating and digesting.

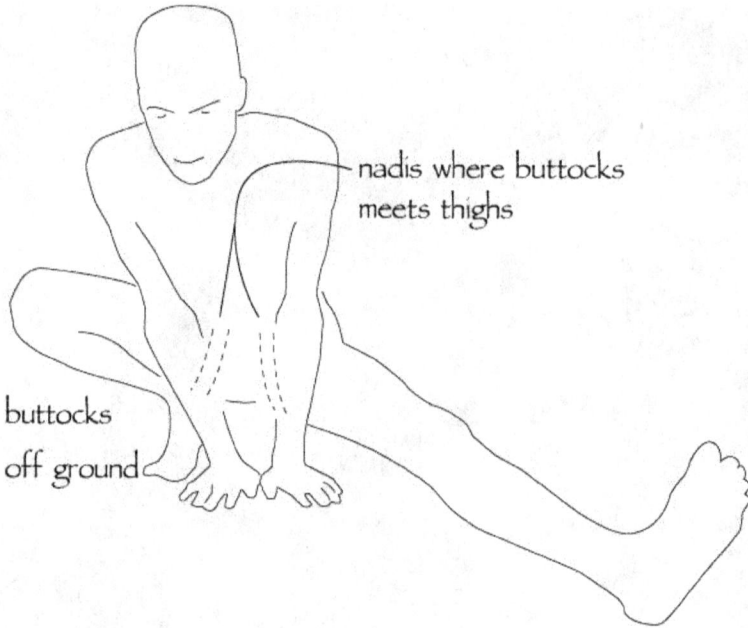

nadis where buttocks
meets thighs

buttocks
off ground

July 20, 2001

Yogeshwarananda

A celibacy choke-lock.

This posture was taught to me years ago by Yogi Bhajan. When one has difficulty with sexual desire and cannot control it, this posture is useful. However Yogesh showed a totally different way of doing it.

Yogi Bhajan's hand grip

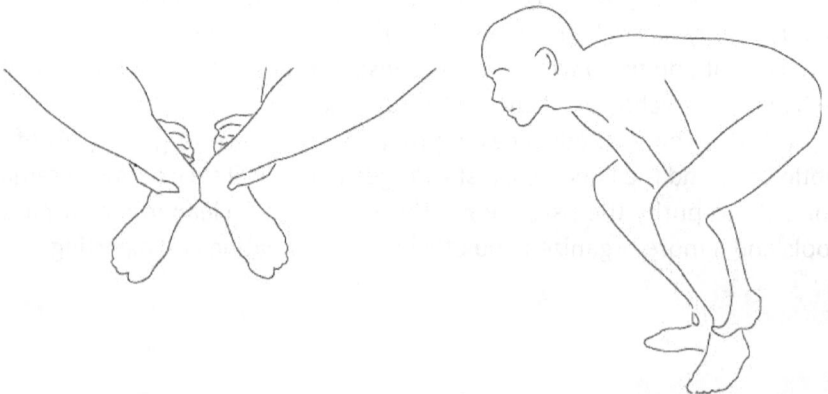

Yogeshwarananda's hand grip

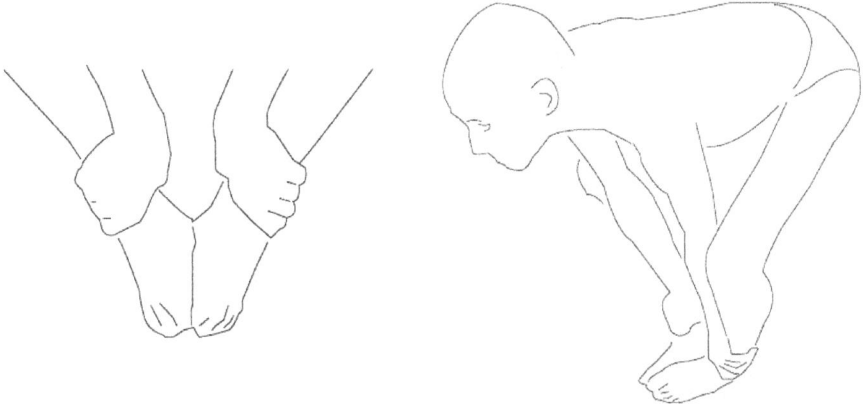

Students should carefully study when the locks are applied in these poses, particularly the sex and anus lock. This should be studied by observation inside the body with eyes closed and the mind being attentive to the genital and anal areas, to known which gross muscles and subtle powers are tensed or pulled inward.

July 21, 2001

Yogeshwarananda

He said, "To evacuate early, eat a piece of fruit early. Use a large orange or any fruit that must be chewed."

Remark:

This was an instruction to observe the connection between the eating operation of the throat and the trigger for passing stool. The two operations are related. If one eats he may derive from the action, an urge to evacuate. In turn, if one evacuates, an appetite may be produced. The two are related.

Citrus fruit is helpful for celibacy but one must be sure to get organically grown fruit. Citrus fruit which is grown in artificially fertilized soils may harm the organs in the body. The chemicals which comprise fertilizer may be irritate the human body.

Chemical irritants are dangerous to any human body but they are especially harmful to yogis. In addition many farmers routinely use chemical pesticides and very harmful herbicides. These are ingested into the plants. When a human eats such plants or fruits, he or she runs the risk of cancers and other ailments.

July 22, 2001

Yogeshwarananda

Location of a touch sensor in the intellect.

He showed where that touch sensor was. I saw the shape and color.

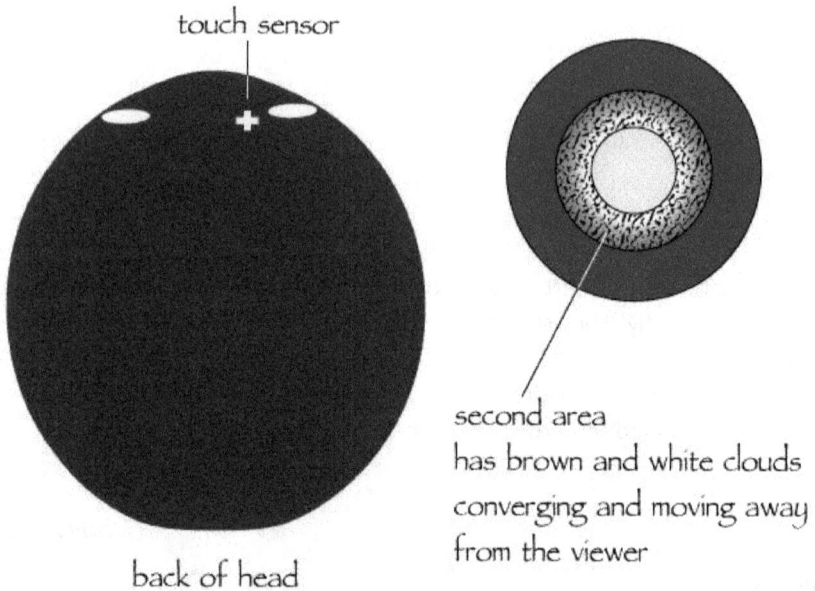

touch sensor

back of head

second area
has brown and white clouds
converging and moving away
from the viewer

July 22, 2001

Swami Shivananda

He instructed, "Do the neck exercises first. This allows the kundalini energy to pass into the brain."

Remark:

I have difficulty with postures where the feet are thrown over the head. Postures may strain tendons in the back and shoulders. In doing hatha yoga, one may find that certain exercises cause a strain that keeps recurring as long as one does an exercise. Such postures should not be done or should be done with great care.

All yoga postures have their usage and advantages. One should not condemn a teacher who recommends an exercise that causes a strain, but rather one should realize that one picked up a defective physical body which cannot do all postures. Each posture gives a particular advantage. It is not a teacher's fault that one picked up a body that is unable to do a posture or that strains when assuming one.

Shiva

He directed me, "Sit here as before. Resume duties."

Remark:

Shiva directed me to continue some duties I performed before I took this body. Since taking this form and being preoccupied with the social and cultural concerns of it, I left aside previous obligations. Now I may resume them. This is the main reason why I hide from most people and why I do not have time to think of my body's relatives.

An evacuation trigger.

This is a procedure for offering one orange to Babaji. This is done early in the morning after exercises and meditation. One does this. One waits to get a mental signal from Babaji to take the offering which is placed before his picture or sculptured form. One then eats the offering. This helps to trigger early evacuations.

Early evacuation however is actually based on early eating. One should eat very early in the morning. That should be the main meal. Later in the day before noon, one may eat something that is not heavy. This is how one accelerates hatha yoga and breath-infusion. Correct diet, correct time of eating and prompt evacuations are accessories of yoga.

Yogeshwarananda

He said, "Counteract telepathy by not responding. Do not allow the intellect or mind stuff to shift once something is detected or even if something comes through space and attaches itself to the outer layer of the mind. That is the way to control telepathy. Without this control, it sabotages the endeavors."

Remark:

Yogesh taught this during the years of 1999, 2000 and 2001. It may be inquired as to why an advanced yogi like the writer recently learnt this. However that is not the issue. The fact is that many disciplines have stages of learning, where one learns the practice, and then learns it again at a higher stage.

When doing mathematics one begins with arithmetic. The student learns to add and subtract. Later, when he studies algebra he must again learn how to add and subtract even though it is done in a different way. In yoga, one learns and then again, one learns, but in a slightly different or greatly modified way. Thus even though I advanced, still I remain a student.

This is why I have little time for others. I have to be concerned with my lessons. I can help you by keeping myself as a successful student of my teachers. Observing this you may get the idea and become sincere. If all of a sudden, I leave aside studentship and pretend that I have the culmination of advancement, my example would mislead others. For safety and honesty, I should remain as a student.

Babaji

He assisted me in regulating the evacuation process. There are many people going down the road of spiritual life but most of them are idiots. This includes many teachers, even some who start big missions and are successful at it. I say this, because to be successful at a big mission, may depend on the ignorance of the mass of seekers. Since such seekers have no mystic perception, their ooos and aaahs to a guru are much of a loud noise. They cannot judge if he is advanced. For instance, suppose the guru passes from his body, then how can the followers ascertain his spirit's destination? They cannot know if they have no mystic perfection. Hence they can be easily fooled.

Ignorant seekers can always form a large membership in any spiritual organization. They can give a guru the idea that he is the only worthy teacher.

In hatha yoga, the evacuation process is important but some teachers disagree. They feel that we should not be concerned with mundane bodily functions. However in hatha yoga, we understand that the evacuation process in a seeker's body tells us everything about the quality of his spiritual practice. It is similar to the medical field. If you go to a doctor he may take urine, blood or stool samples. After getting a report from a laboratory, he forms a diagnosis. From that he treats the disease.

Babaji does not eat physical food. Around the year of 1973, I saw him eating sunlight fruit. These are fruits which are grown on subtle trees. Because he uses a yoga siddha body, he can do that. However he allows me to offer him medicinal food which is needed by me for increased purity in the gross and subtle bodies. I used to offer this to Swami Vishnudevananda and to Shiva, but the Swami, after leaving his physical body, went somewhere in the astral world in isolation. I no longer see him. Every now and again he used to send a subtle message, but I hardly hear from him. I feel that he hides somewhere in the astral world. Shiva who used to accept the offerings, diverted me to Babaji. Since then, Babaji supervises me personally but he has nothing to do with physical food.

I offer Babaji the food, then I wait to be called. He taught me how to wait to be called and how to wait for the eating impulse to stir in the subtle body.

Recently in April 2001, I taught this offering procedure to two persons who were interested. Sometimes a person shows an interest and then he peters out and does not follow. This is natural. Due to complexities of destiny, one is distracted from practice. This is because of acting in such a way as to offend the supernatural rulers who regulate responsibility. If we offend these persons, it does not matter who we are, we will regret the errant behavior.

July 24, 2001

Yogeshwarananda

Evacuation apparatus toning.

In this technique, in the posture given below, one pushes if one was to evacuate. One pushes to the left, to the right, to the center, to the back and front with a slow gradual pushing force, without strain.

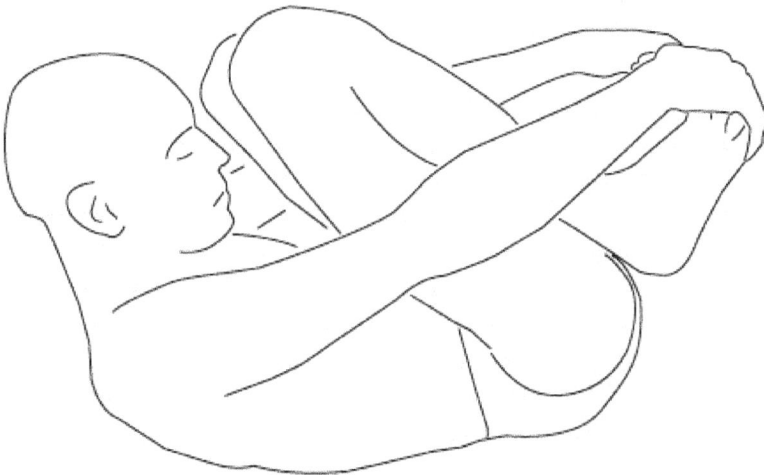

July 25, 2001

Shiva

He said," Do not take a position as a teacher. Sit as a student."

Remark:

This was a reminder not to become a guru but to stick to being a student. I need to complete myself as a student and son, rather than as somebody's husband or somebody's father or guru. There is much fulfillment in being somebody's guru or somebody's father or somebody's sweetheart or husband. But these aspects are distractions. These involve giving attention to others. However, it is best for me to attend my teachers.

Persons who desire to be students should assume a spiritual practice and if possible fulfill their cultural lives. I do not need to be the guru nor to approve of the cultural involvements.

July 26, 2001

Sadashiva

He said, "Sit it here. Let us discuss a topic. What is the importance of dharma in yoga practice?"

Remark:

Here Sadashiva induced me to realize the importance of socially-useful actions. Strictly speaking, such beneficial work has no importance in yoga but it is indirectly related in such a way that it has relevance. So long as the yogi has cultural or social affiliation, he should act responsibly. If he neglects responsibility, he will be unable to practice technique yoga. Supernatural persons will obstruct him.

A technique yogin should note that Krishna induced Arjuna to fight for dharma, to defend and establish righteous conduct and to let the entire world know that if righteous conduct is offended, human society will be inconvenienced by warfare, with women and children crying when their male supporters die in battle.

In the time of Krishna, Jarasandha, the king of Magadha, was not too particular about righteous conduct or responsible living, and so Krishna took Bhima to split Jarasandha's body into two. It appears that Krishna does not like people who neglect responsibilities. He engages His universal form in inconveniencing such persons.

A person who is irresponsible cannot be successful on the path of technique yoga. The supernatural people will make certain that he is disrupted on the physical and psychic planes. In the case of Arjuna, when he wanted to go for yoga austerities in the forest, Krishna brought it to his attention that:

कर्मेन्द्रियाणि संयम्य
य आस्ते मनसा स्मरन् ।
इन्द्रियार्थान्विमूढात्मा
मिथ्याचारः स उच्यते
॥३.६॥

karmendriyāṇi saṁyamya
ya āste manasā smaran
indriyārthānvimūḍhātmā
mithyācāraḥ sa ucyate (3.6)

karmendriyāṇi — bodily limbs; saṁyamya — restraining; ya = yaḥ — who; āste — sits; manasā — by the mind; smaran — remembering; indriyārthān — attractive objects; vimūḍhātmā = vimūḍha — deluded + ātmā — self; mithyācāraḥ — deceiver; sa — he; ucyate — it is declared

A person who while restraining his bodily limbs sits, with the mind remembering attractive objects, is a deceiver. So it is declared. (Bhagavad Gita 3.6)

This means that if one avoids social responsibility when one tries to meditate, one will remember objects to which the mind is attracted, objects towards which one has responsibilities. In that way one's time will be disrupted and one's technique practice will not be completed

July 26, 2001

Shiva

He explained, "The experience of sexual pleasure is similar to that of kundalini, except that sexual pleasure is triggered by the pubio-coccus muscle and by sex stimuli. When kundalini rises, it draws energy from all bodily cells just as when there is sexual pleasure."

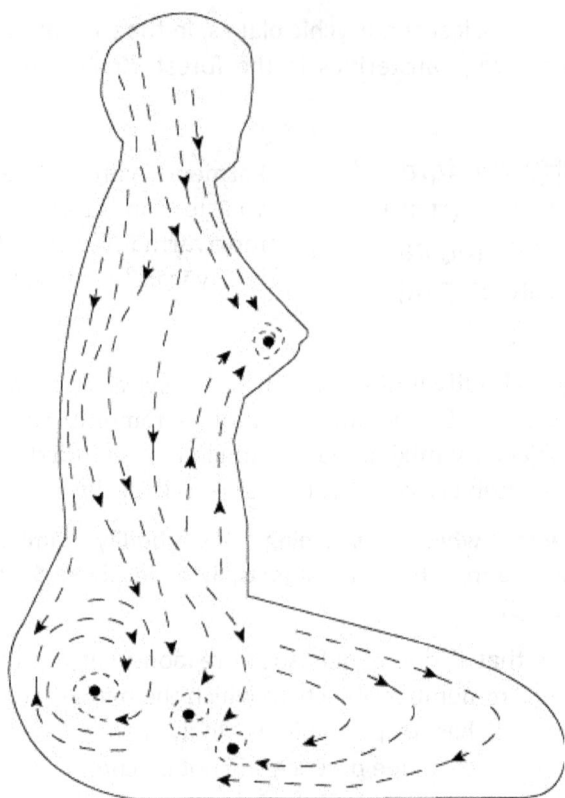

sexual movements

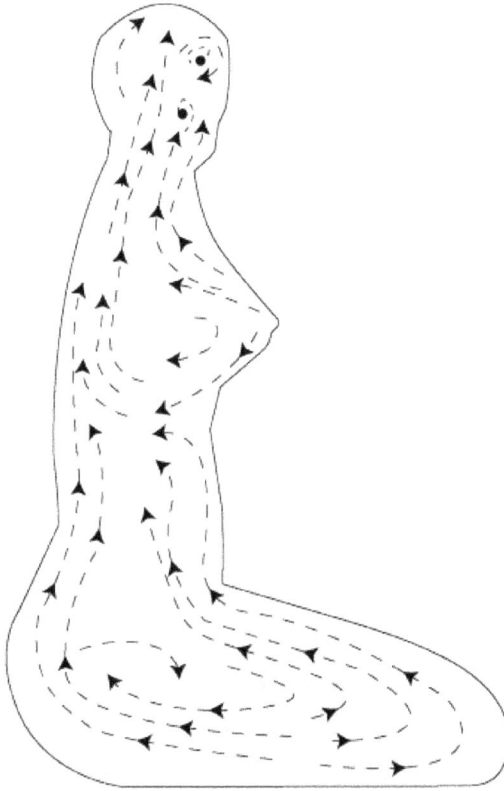

kundalini transits

July 27, 2001

Sadashiva

This Sadashiva is the form of Shiva which Krishna worshipped when he was requested by one of his wives to petition that deity for a son. Subsequently Lord Krishna, playing the part of a family man, went to the Himalayas, took instructions from Rishi Upamanyu and performed the appropriate yoga austerities to invoke this Sadashiva (Mahabharata Anusasana Parva 14).

People generally feel that there is only one Shiva but they are mistaken. In the Puranas, it plainly states that even though initially one Rudra or Shiva appeared, some eleven of them were seen later. There is the supreme one called Sadashiva. In all cases, with the Shivas, Brahmas and Vishnus, there is more than one.

I had a sculptured form of Babaji but generally people call that form, Shiva. I had a form of Agastya Muni and people also call him Shiva. Merely because a sculptured form has the usual symbols of Shiva, like the crescent moon in the hair, the cobra around the neck, does not necessary mean that it is Shiva.

Sadashiva said, "Return to the position as a practicing student. Do not act as a guru."

Remark:

This advice is clear. No one should approach me except with due regard for my studentship.

July 28, 2001

Yogeshwarananda

During a session of breath-infusion, he instructed in such a way, that my sushumna nadi remained open with crystal clear space, without any multi-colored lightning bunches or spots of dark energy. I remained centered from the base disc to the intellect.

This does not mean however that this state of clarity of the kundalini power in the central spinal column will remain like this forever. According to Yogesh, whatever is achieved, can be undone. Another factor is this, even though a student of technique yoga may make some advancement, it does not stick with him initially. He must strive repeatedly to make it permanent.

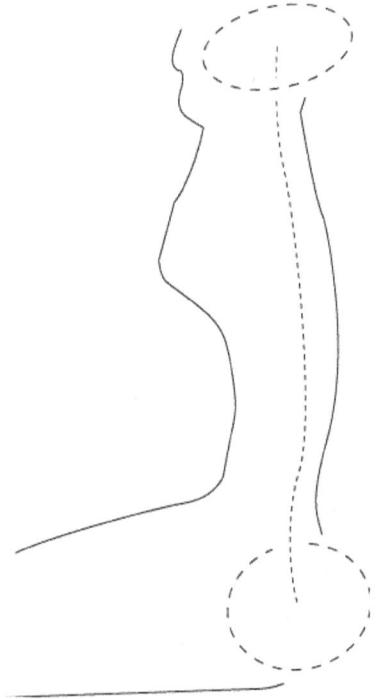

July 28, 2001

Babaji

He used my abdomen to change my subtle and gross digestive systems. He also used my body to instruct others. In such cases, he is their guru. There are times, on rare occasions, when I take a position as someone's teacher. This is usually when Babaji wants to say something or wants me to convey a message. Otherwise for others like Yogi Bhajan and Yogesh, I may instruct someone on their behalf.

By eating through my body, Babaji helped me to see how to change my diet in order to move myself in the direction of assuming a yoga-siddhi body. Babaji Mahasaya rarely eats, even subtle food.

Sometimes he takes sunlight fruits from the angelic people. However he may enter a student's body and direct that person in how to purify the psyche.

July 28, 2001

Evacuation techniques

These exercises which cause the evacuation process to be more efficient. These are helpful in curbing the life force and making the subtle energy cleaner and more efficient.

In this regard Babaji recommended that I take two oranges, eaten with the pulp, without juicing them. These are eaten early just after exercises and meditation about 4 am. After this, one should eat an early morning full meal around 5 am or 5.30 am. By eating the two oranges early, one may cause stool to move into the anal pouch earlier. The throat is an evacuation trigger point. When one eats, a signal is sent to the nerves in the anal pouch to collect and release stool from the body.

push-pull anus

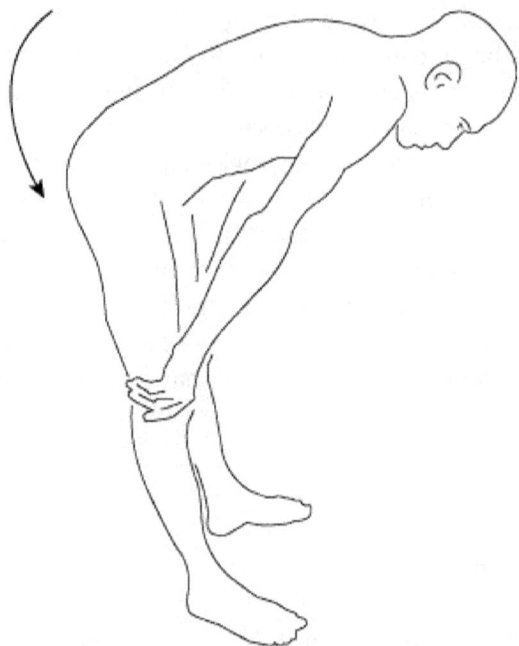

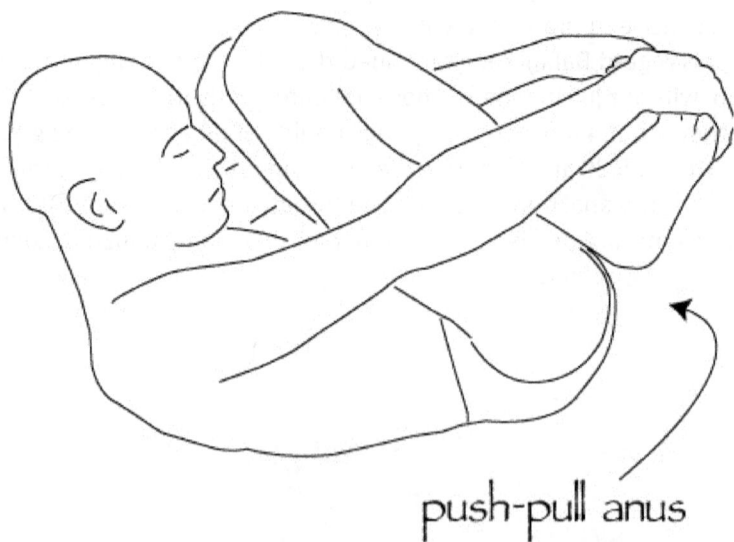

push-pull anus

July 29, 2001

Sadashiva

He said, "Be more the disciple and less the teacher. Be a student. The person is the same in either case. He can be a teacher and simultaneously exhibit the student position humbly. However his natural posture should be the practicing student only. He may be the teacher, occasionally, but he should not feel comfortable in that role."

July 30, 2001

Yogeshwarananda

He said, "The causal energy holds in reserve all resentments and longings. Even if it has to wait millions of years for fulfillments, it fulfils these partially or fully when there is opportunity.

Remark:

A yogi should avoid being in a position where resentments towards him are formed. He does not want to be located as a victim when the causal energy vents hard feelings in the future.

July 30, 2001

Shiva

He said: "You are responsible for the exposure of your psyche. Isolation is a necessity"

Remark:

Exposure of one's psyche causes an unfavorable attraction, indifference or repulsion in others. One should minimize such exposure or be prepared to be responsible for the actions and reactions which are caused by it.

Shiva.

On this day he gave instructions for drawing-in sexual energy which was sent or offered by the forefathers of my body. Departed spirits send energies to their descendants who use physical forms. An ascetic cannot in all cases reject that sexual energy. Sometimes even if he mentally rejects, still their force affects his subtle and gross bodies.

Shiva instructed that during breath-infusion, I should pull the sexual energy sent by them. This energy may be a lusty urge or an embodied lust force in the form of a sexually- attractive human being.

Such forms usually appear to be appetizing or sexually desirable to the senses of the person being victimized. From the subtle realm, departed spirits who are eligible for new bodies, see sexually-attractive human beings as a food source.

On this side however, when we see such forms, we interpret them as being sexually desirable. The underlying basis is the nutritional value of such forms. Departed spirits see that they can acquire nutrients for making their new baby forms from sexually-attractive bodies.

Shiva instructed that when the energy is strong and when I am unable to avoid it, I should draw it in while doing breath-infusion. It moves upward as the kundalini force rises.

July 31, 2001

Shiva

He said, "Hatha yoga pain shows the mind, the location of the nadis. It diverts the mind from other painful but non-beneficial responsibility-carrying objects."

Remark:

Hatha yoga is the gateway to true celibacy. It allows for the bodily cells of the gross and subtle forms to release their sexual energy on a regular basis in an orderly controlled way. The responsibility-carrying sense objects are those which cause an ascetic to enact cultural and social activities in the near or distant future. The near future is in this life. The distant future pertains to future times. There are many single priests, monks and the like who have no gross sexual contact with any persons of the opposite sex. Still such persons may be amassing volumes of cultural and social responsibilities by their involvements with sexually attractive persons whom they preach to. These priests and monks are involved under the caption of religion and spirituality but such a caption will not prevent the formation of sexual responsibilities in their future.

Yogeshwarananda

Backward abdomen flexes.

These are exercises which Yogesh showed. He took control of my body and did these. These are different to the forward over-bending standard nauli pumps. When these are done, they affect the lower intestines and rectum area which has the anal porch. For women these pumps exercise their ovaries, uterus and fallopian tubes.

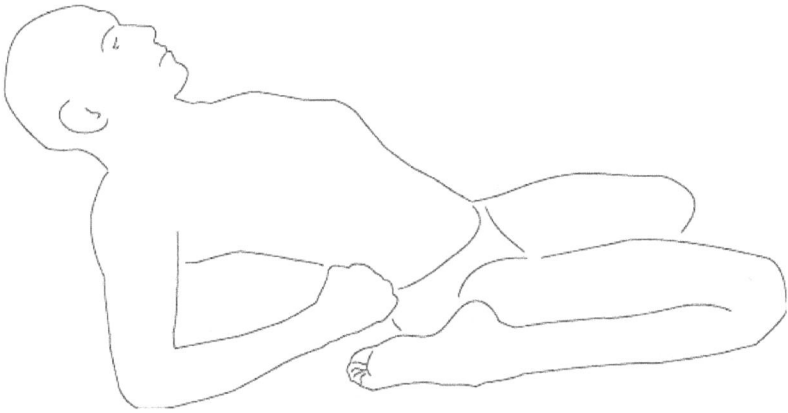

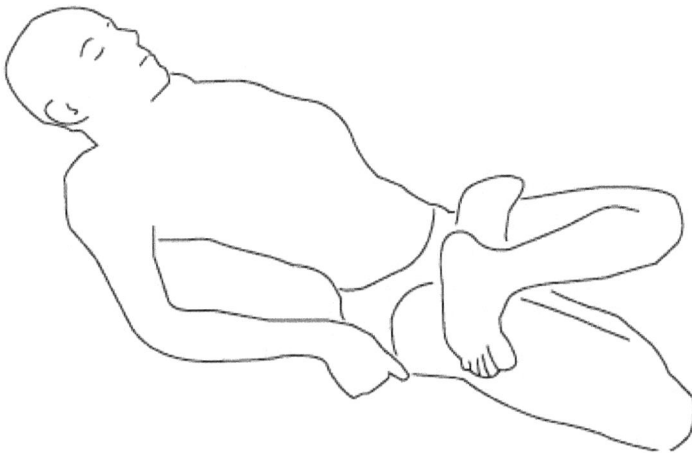

Shiva / Yogeshwarananda

Kundalini lights.

These were lights from the bottom of the trunk of the body, shining up to the intellect organ, but there was some darkness in the middle portion of the body. As the kundalini light increases, that darkness is gradually dissipated.

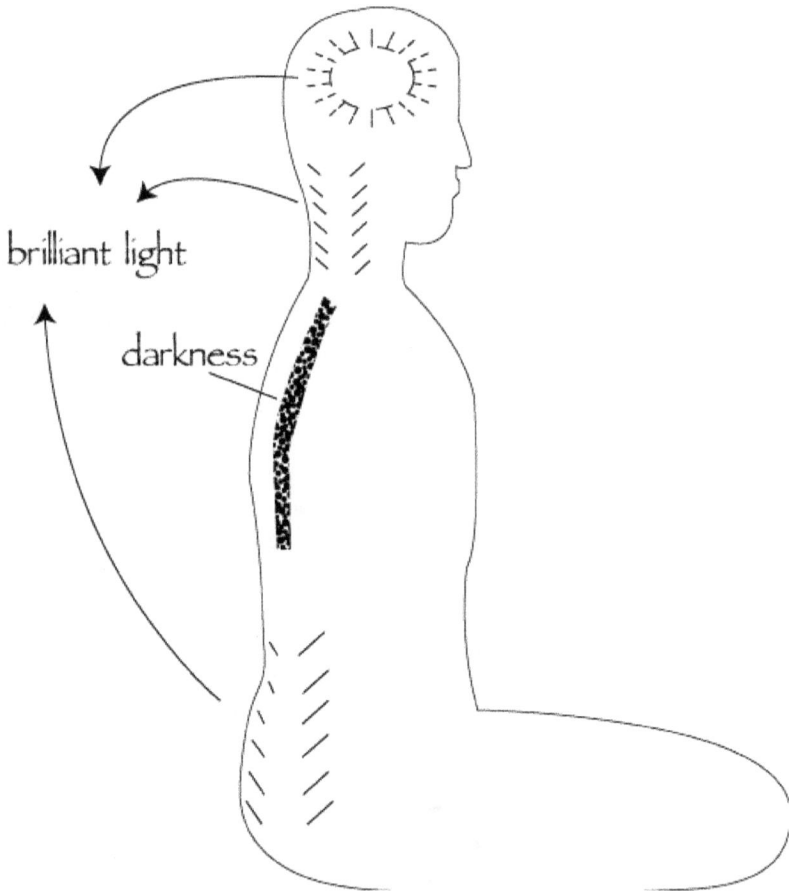

brilliant light

darkness

August 3, 2001

Yogeshwarananda

He said, "Yirk back in the hand-supported headstand. Find the nadis from the chest to under-abdomen."

Yogeshwarananda / Shiva

This is an abdomen pull-up exercise which they supervised. In this practice one makes sure that the contractions and muscular releases go deep under the abdomen, affecting the lower intestines, anal pouch and sexual apparatus. This posture is especially beneficial for women, since their sexual apparatus is in the trunk of the body.

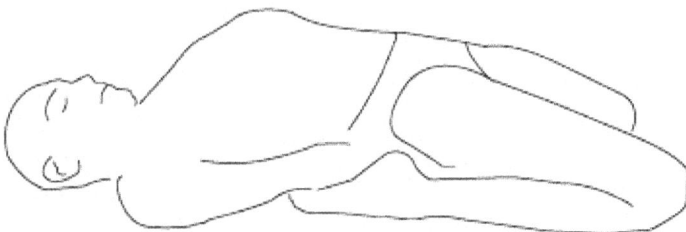

August 4, 2001

Shiva / Yogeshwarananda

Yogesh said, "When in a certain posture the breath is stopped after a rapid breathing session, if you find that the psyche wants to move under the influence of the generated energy, allow that force to move the subtle body. Do not stop it merely because the physical one cannot perform the movement.

"Let the physical system remain as it is with the locks applied. Let the subtle form continue the action which the infused energy initiates. Eliminate the mind's tendency of stopping the psychic movement.

"By the practice of allowing the subtle body to complete the movement, while the physical one ignores it, one develops absorption. There will be short duration absorptions."

Shiva / Sadashiva

Shiva said,

"Meditation is destroyed by mental weight which is due to unfinished tasks and too close a proximity to humanity."

August 5, 2001

Yogeshwarananda

He gave a bowel-stomach pump.

This is done while sitting on heels, leaning backwards. Form fists with the hands and place fist on the small of the back, where the back curves just above the buttocks. The buttocks are lifted slightly off the ground.

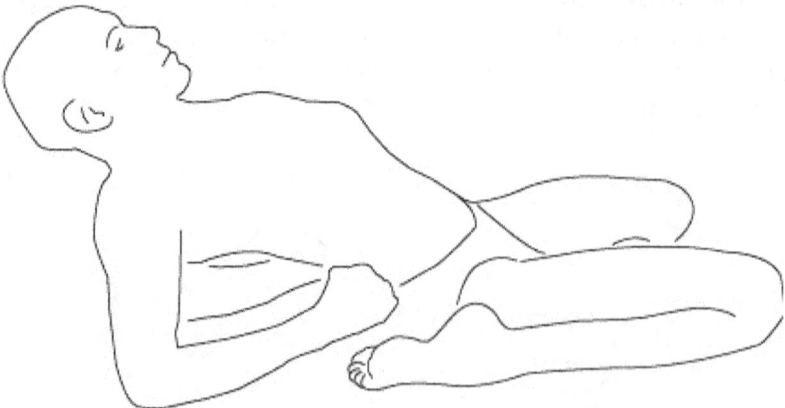

Shiva

He gave a special instruction, "Sit here as a parallel existence."

Remark:

I sat to Shiva's left. This was an instruction to sit without making demands, even the inquiries made upon a teacher by a student.

Sometimes, Shiva or other supernatural beings desire not to be pestered with questions, nor humorous relations.

Yogeshwarananda

He instructed, "Start with that. Bring that up. When it is lost, bring it again. It is lower but it can be brought up by training. The others cannot see it."

Remark:

This refers to the brow chakra orb, which should be lifted within the intellect. This orb is not the same as the brow chakra on the outside of the intellect. This orb is within the intellect. Yogesh spoke from within my intellect. He assisted in lifting that orb.

So long as we have many social and cultural concerns, the subtle instruments seem to be heavy or they seem not to exist. Otherwise they become perceptible and easy to maneuver.

Yogeshwarananda

He instructed, "Lean back on hands, fingers should point away from the body. Do up-and-down flop-abdomen flexes."

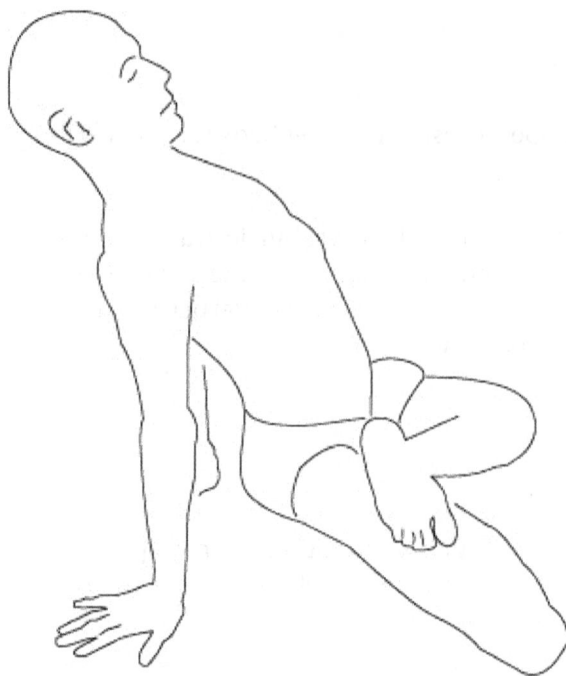

August 7, 2001

Yogeshwarananda

He said, "Take it. Gather the scattered light and darkness of it. Do this until it becomes focal and organized. Gradually take hold. Re-focus it."

After five minutes, Shiva made a remark.

"Do you understand what the Swami said? By practice each yogi develops himself."

Remark:

This pertains to the visual sense in the intellect organ.

August 8, 2001

Vishnudevananda

He instructed that I should wet my arms to push them through the thighs and legs for doing kakutasana. This posture is shown below. If one uses silky fabric for pants, the hands may slide through easily.

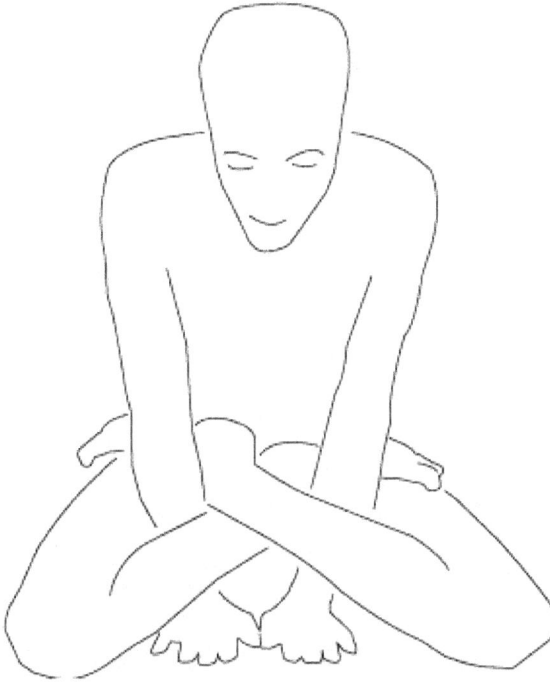

Yogeshwarananda

He said, "Do this daily. Gather these colors. Then repeatedly move them."

Remark:

He spoke of the scattered visual power in the brain and mind.

August 8, 2001

Yogeshwarananda

He said, "Memory is part of the feelings-energy, not part of the core-self. When separated from it or from a part of it, the core cannot use it. It is the same with social conscience. The core is stainless, which means that it can be duped again. In dreams it may forget one type of existence and accept another, just like that, totally leaving aside the discrimination from the previous existence. Its memory from one world may not be transferred when it goes to another dimension. This is one disadvantage of being stainless. Nothing adheres to it permanently."

Remark:

Such information is useful for a technique yogin who is aware of his astral experiences and who keeps track of dream activity while his gross form sleeps.

August 9, 2001

Pubio-coccus technique

This posture below helps the yogi to find the sex nerve which operates sexual pleasure. This nerve needs to be brought under control. Its tendency needs to be inverted inwards, so that it releases its energies into the body up and through the spine or through the frontal kundalini. As it is, this nerve which is circular, is oriented towards releasing sexual energy outwards through the head of the male organ. By releasing the sexual energy in that direction the male gets oriented to sexual intercourse either by linking into a woman's sexual part or a male anus or even by self-stimulation.·

The physical location of this pubio-coccus muscle is shown in a diagram below. The yogi can locate the muscle-nerve physically by tracing his penis where it enters the body. The muscle-nerve is located underneath, just where the penis disappears into the body.

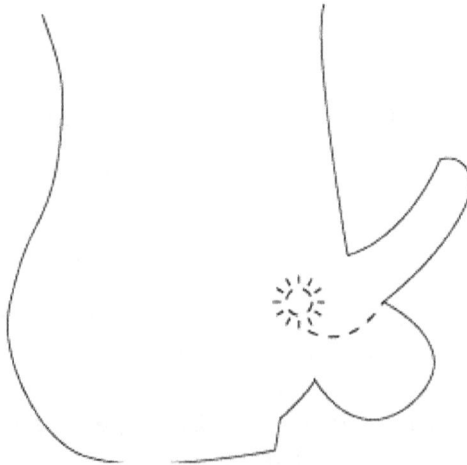

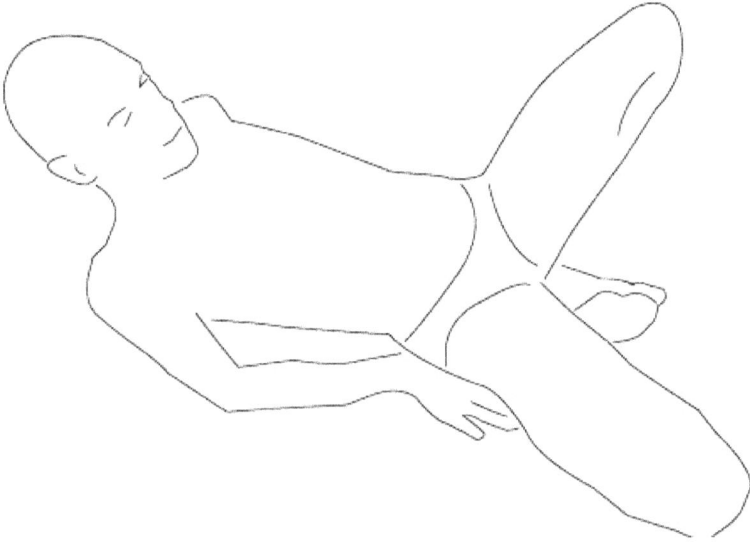

August 9, 2001

Yogeshwarananda

Three touch-points.

He showed these points which are electrically and psychically connected. They are the soft palate, which is pushed in the mouth by the upturned tongue, the pubio-coccus muscle and the brow chakra. When the yogi is in lotus posture these are held together by mental contact.

August 10, 2001

Yogeshwarananda

He said, "After breath-infusion, when holding the breath in or out, allow free movements of the subtle form, even if the physical body remains immobile or is incapable of carrying out the actions which are dictated by the aroused subtle energy."

Remark:

Here, the teacher reminds me not to impede the movements of the subtle form when it is prompted into postures which are impossible for the physical body to perform.

Yogeshwarananda

While my gross body was in lotus he helped me to assume a special subtle posture.

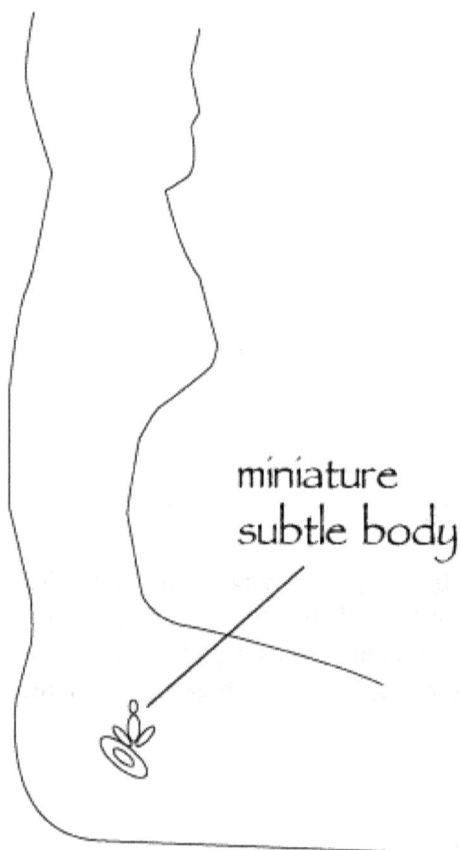

miniature
subtle body

August 12, 2001

Yogeshwarananda

Touch-points for the pubio-coccus muscle

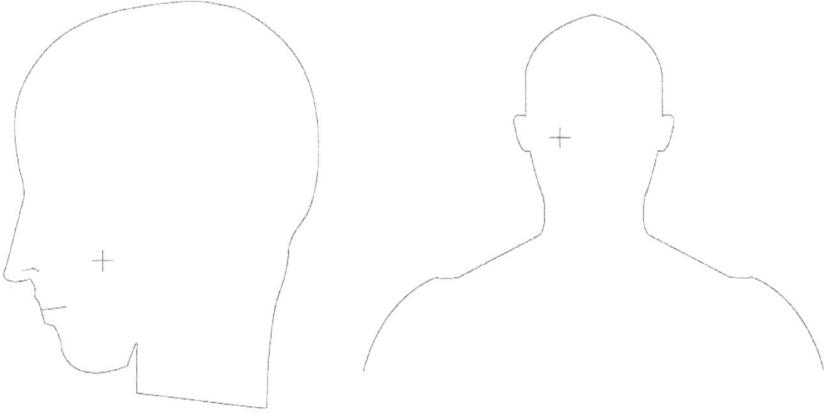

August 13, 2001

Yogeshwarananda

He said, "A total lack of interest is the supreme detachment. Without it, liberation is impossible. Any slight interest draws the yogi back to social and cultural affairs."

August 14, 2001

Babaji

An experiment with sugar.

Babaji had me take a small quantity of sugar by eating apples and taking honey.

He said, "Hatha yoga begins with diet control as prescribed in Chapter four of Bhagavad Gita. Sugar is counterproductive. Witness the effects from the plane of clarity. See what it does."

Remark:

This is the verse from the Gita.

अपरे नियताहाराः
प्राणान्प्राणेषु जुह्वति ।
सर्वेऽप्येते यज्ञविदो
यज्ञक्षपितकल्मषाः
॥४.३०॥

apare niyatāhārāḥ
prāṇānprāṇeṣu juhvati
sarve'pyete yajñavido
yajñakṣapitakalmaṣāḥ (4.30)

apare — others; niyatāhārāḥ — persons restrained in diet; prāṇān — fresh air; prāṇeṣu — into the previous inhalations; juhvati — impel; sarve — all; 'pyete (apyete) = apy (api) — also + ete — these; yajñavido = yajñavidaḥ — those who know the value of an act of sacrifice; yajñakṣapitakalmaṣāḥ = yajña — austerity and religious ceremony + kṣapita — destroyed, removed + kalmaṣāḥ — impurities

Others who were restrained in diet, impel fresh air into the previously inhaled air. All these ascetics whose impurities were removed by austerity and religious ceremony understand the value of an act of sacrifice. (Bhagavad Gita 4.30)

As advised by Babaji, I took two apples but I did not eat the pulp. I sucked the juice and spat the pulp. This was for the purpose of not putting any bulk food matter into the intestines, since that disturbs the next morning's yoga practice. I used bulk foods at a large meal once per day in the early morning. After this I did not take bulk foods. I may chew nuts and spit the pulp or take some water, milk or fruit juice during the day. I avoid solid or bulk foods after I take the early morning meal. I took the two apples, chewed on them and took about three teaspoons of honey.

Ingestion of sugar during the day, has an effect on activity later when the gross body sleeps. I noticed that my subtle body shifted to lower astral realms, going where worldly beings enjoy just as they do on this physical side. The sugar makes the physical form sluggish after it has slept sufficiently. It causes the physical form to crave excess sleep, causing a reluctance to rise from bed. It makes the muscles of the physical body ache. It causes the intellect not focus in meditation. It prevents the association with higher yogis. Overall, sugar intake discourages higher yoga practice.

August 16, 2001

Yogeshwarananda

He said, "Appreciate small kundalini urges and small infused energy movements. Love all. Be attentive to all."

Remark:

In doing bhastrika, the yogi should be keenly aware of any slight awakening of kundalini or movement of infused energy. He should not be spaced-out but should pay attention to any small adjustment in the psyche. Small changes are important.

August 20, 2001

Yogeshwarananda

He said, "While on the back of the body with hands outside the feet and legs gripping the toes and soles, exercise the anal system. Push-pull the anus and rectum. Be sure you pull in firmly.

August 20, 2001

Yogeshwarananda

While pointing to causal energy which was energized in the causal cove, he said, "Work from here, the actual source."
He also said, "That is a subsidiary central distributor."
He pointed to the kanda.

Remark:

As he said this, Yogesh, in a miniature form in my psyche, dropped something like a small pill. It moved down into my kanda and dissolved. Just after this I moved with him to a light in the causal cove. The cove was full of frosty light.

The kanda is a small bulb in the pubic area of the subtle body. This bulb holds subtle sexual fluids. In a yogi who practices celibacy yoga, the subtle sexual fluids are not stored in the kanda but rather they are distributed from there throughout the body through tiny subtle tubes.

Yogeshwarananda

He instructed, "Do the kanda-release technique on the back. Knees should be pulled to the ground, with hands grabbing the insteps. This changes the base energies from the base chakra to the perineum which is the end of the kanda. The touch points are the perineum, kanda bulb, the back of the neck, the big toes and brow chakra."

Remark:

This is a complicated technique which can be done at advanced stages. Generally the base chakra which is near the anus is considered as the base point of the life force. When this technique is done, the base shifts. The kanda, then acts as base.

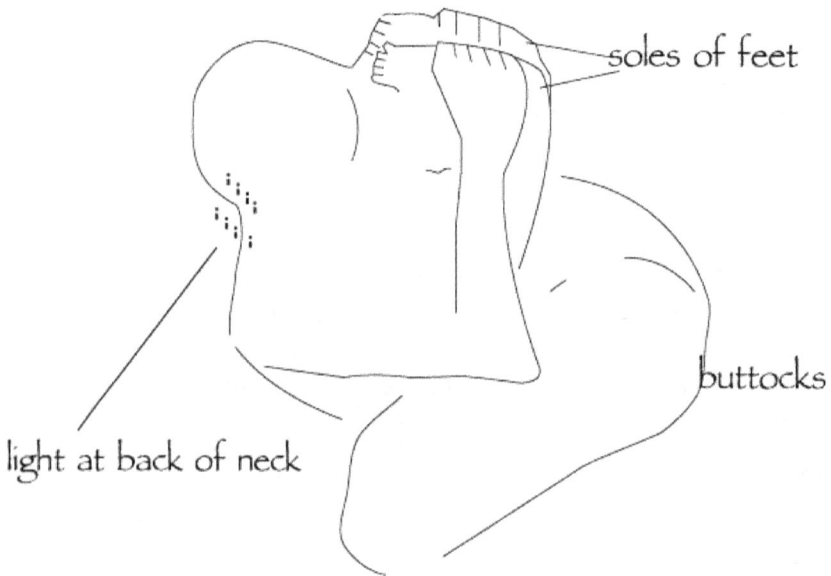

soles of feet

buttocks

light at back of neck

Yogeshwarananda

He instructed, "Exercise the abdomen. Go back while between the heels. Do middle abdomen pumps, pulling up and down.

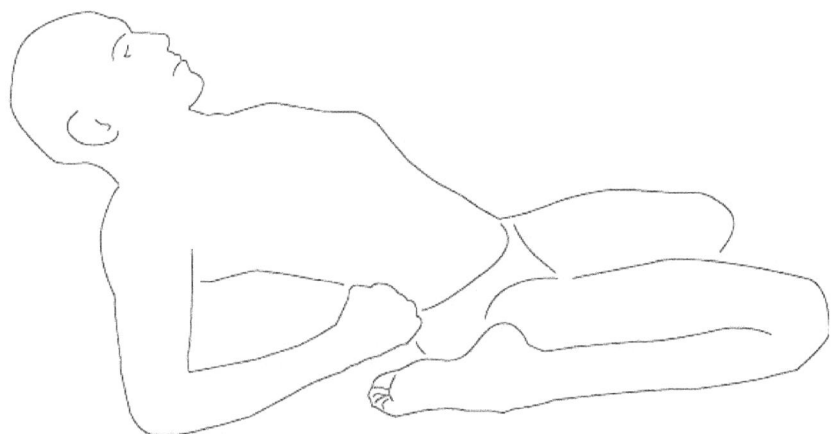

Part 4

Yogeshwarananda

He instructed, "Hold the visual power which is in the front of the intellect. Gradually you can control it. As a scattered energy, it will take a tubal cylindrical shape. Then after a time you can focus it."

August 23, 2001

Yogeshwarananda

He said, "Do not bother. Some siddhi perfectional skills function involuntarily as they express themselves in the subtle form. This particular manifestation is a dimensional transfer from an apsara angelic girl who is on another level. Sometimes these ladies try to reach me but they are unable to."

Remark:

This was a said to me while I read one of Yogesh's books. I smelt an agreeable subtle odor. Knowing that it was not from the physical side of existence, I tracked it. It originated where Yogesh stayed in my brahmrandra. At first I did not form a conclusion of it. However I felt that as an accomplished yogi, he produced the odor. Knowing my incorrect idea, he showed the origin of it. An angelic woman heard of him. She became attracted and desired to reach him. Since he was not maintaining a subtle form, which she could perceive, she could not reach him but since he was in my psyche, her body odor penetrated to reach him.

August 24, 2001

Yogeshwarananda

A middle region bowel exercise.
He said, "Bend backwards while doing easy pose. Do muscular flexes with hands behind acting as back support, placed on the small of the back.

August 27, 2001

Yogeshwarananda

He instructed, "Cup it. Keep it contained until you get it settled. Then work to focus it."

Remark:

This refers to the visual power which is in the front of the intellect. In this case, this energy was chaotic. This chaos or scattering of it, is based on my lack of disinterest in social and cultural affairs. In addition, one develops chaos if one associates with others who are enlivened by social and cultural contact.

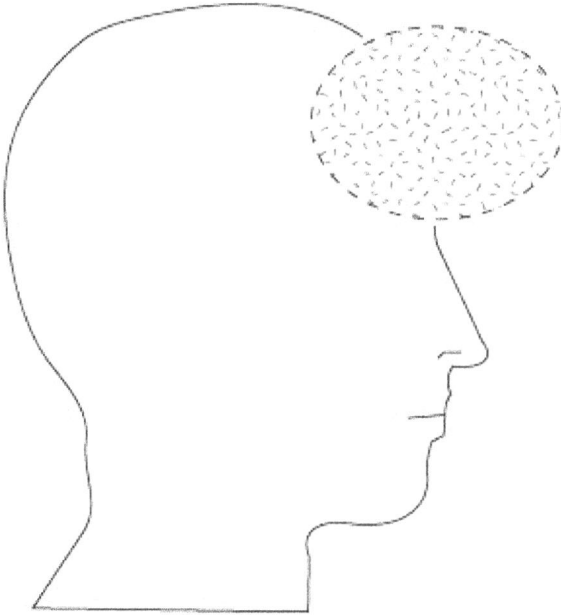

August 28, 2001

Yogeshwarananda

He said, "If there is no night or late afternoon eating, there will be no digestion at night. Thus there will be no undue abdomen sweat and no resulting staleness nor stink of body in the morning."

He taught me a sushumna nadi exercise. Doing this one breathes into the vee-groove in the back

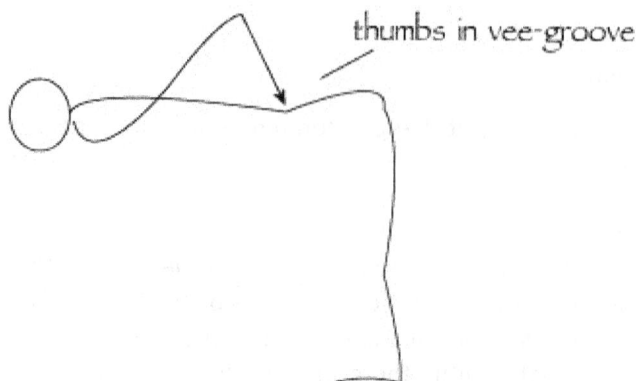

thumbs in vee-groove

Yogesh insisted that I bring pranavision and intellect vision together at all times. He said that the intellect vision may not be focused. It may be energy in a random cluster or energy in a capsule-like containment. But it should not be kept separated from the pranic energy which comes up from the lower part of the body.

August 29, 2001

Yogi Bhajan

He said, "Always stay on the mat."

About ten minutes after Yogi left, Shiva said, "That is not that important but his interest in you is beneficial. Adhere to him. He will reset your timing for the exercises and make them more efficient.

Later on Yogeshwarananda again instructed that I bring intellect vision to be with pranavision.

Remark:

Here is a case of getting an instruction from one teacher and taking that instruction even though a higher authority states that the instruction is not that important. Shiva explained that Yogi Bhajan's interest in me was useful. Even though the interest came with an instruction which was not so essential, I will observe it. In fact, since that day I have carefully followed that instruction.

A long time ago, when I first learned breath-infusion from Yogi Bhajan's disciples, his explanation for using mats was told to me. It is this: The kundalini energy will leak into the earth, if one does not use a mat. Subsequently the energy charge will not build up as one does the rapid breathing. Thus, the kundalini power may not accumulate sufficiently.

It is an old tradition that yogis use a mat. Some use the traditional tiger skin. Yogi Bhajan used a sheep skin in 1972 when I stayed at one of his ashrams. At that time, the students used sheep skins. There was some objection about this especially by some of Bhaktivedanta's disciples, who once told Yogi Bhajan that he indirectly contributed to the violence of killing animals by using a skin.

In any case, Shiva is reputed to use a tiger skin. Many great yogins did so. I used a cloth, made out of polyester batting and cotton. When sitting for meditation, I use a folded blanket. Once Yogesh showed how to make a tight lotus where the body is balanced and cushioned on the intertwined thighs and legs. Since then I do not feel the necessity to be on a soft material, but I do use a mat.

I should not disobey the instruction of Yogi Bhajan. I became carefree in following his instruction. Once when Yogesh chided Yogi Bhajan in the astral world, about the slow progress of his kundalini yoga method, Yogi Bhajan came to see me. At the time I did exercises early one morning. From the astral world, Yogi Bhajan said, "You brought me undue criticism. Please from now on use a mat. If you do so, progress will be quicker and I will not be ridiculed."

Shiva said that Yogi Bhajan, by his interest, would reset my timing and to tell the truth, I do not understand how the yogi would do that. I can say this much. I am in his favor.

Recently I had occasion to speak to Yogi Bhajan. While taking, he said, "I do not recall having initiated you at any time but some yogis feel that you are my disciple. I do not mind. Now tell me how did you become a disciple?"

In reply I explained to him how I lived in his ashram in Denver, Colorado in 1972 and 1973. I also lived in his Kansas City, Missouri ashram. I worked at two of his restaurants, one in Denver and another in Kansas City, Missouri.

After I explained about this, he still did not recall. I then said, "Once while I lived in the Denver ashram, you came there for one day and gave a lecture where someone asked you about the separation of Brian and his wife. After Brian left, your disciple Prem Kaur took over the leadership of the ashram."

As I explained this, he smiled and then mused to himself. He then said, "I remember you. You were the black boy with the oddly wrapped turban. I recall you because of the black body and unusual turban. In that turban you did not look like a Sikh but looked like a Persian magi. I do remember you. Welcome. I am glad that you maintained the practice after so many years and after I gave you so little association. That is the power of practice. If a person adheres to it, he will progress no matter what. Association is not everything. Practice is powerful too."

August 30, 2001

Yogeshwarananda

He showed some orbs and their interaction.

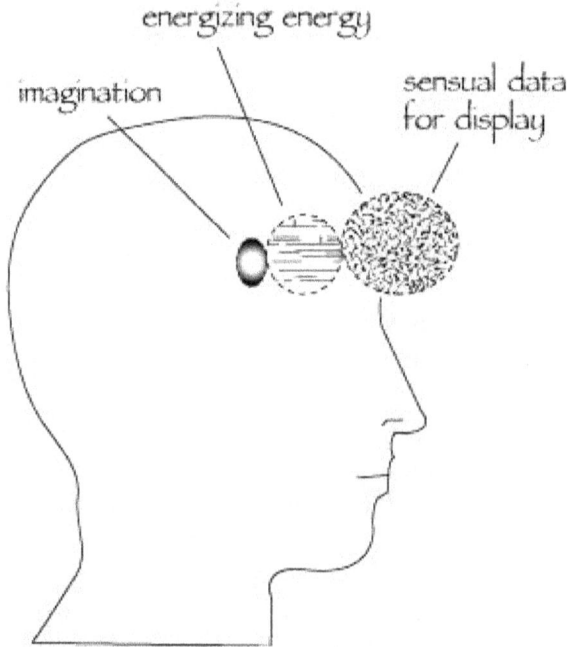

energizing energy

imagination

sensual data for display

Under his instruction. I mixed the intellect orb with the energizing energy orb and then put those two into the imagination orb. This action allows one to see how the imaginative, cognitive and motivational powers work. The motivational force is the feelings-energy which is very subtle and which moves in all directions. The cognitive force is the intellect through which one understands and analyses correctly or incorrectly. The imaginative force is the one used in day dreaming and in creating within one's mind, practical or impractical concepts.

Of the three forces, all are impulsive. All mislead and waste energy. The imaginative force is the worst of all. Yogesh showed in slow motion, how my sense of initiative is captured and used by the imaginative force which can use the intellect and feeling-energies to conceive of something practical or impractical.

Normally one cannot see any of this in slow motion. The spirit has only his initiative invested in this creation. By that, his radiating energy is captured by various forces. This is how he is tagged for acts committed by his psyche, even though in fact, he does not at all initiate activity. He is merely a witness but that does not free him from liabilities. However, by extreme detachment, he develops a waiver which frees him from responsibilities. Extreme dispassion however is not a state of mind nor is it something he can conveniently induce merely by reasoning out his position. He has to develop actual mystic resistance and clearly perceive the parts of the psyche, just as Yogesh showed, otherwise it will be impossible for him to get the waiver and be liberated.

Yogesh demonstrated that when the cognitive and feeling-energies are unified and then taken into the imaginative orb, the impulsive conceptions cease. At first he showed this by doing it himself with my faculties. Then he instructed that I do it. After that I practiced this repeatedly, for about three weeks twice daily. On this day while I did some exercises, Yogi Bhajan came. He told me that if one does not use a mat, the energy currents do not stabilize nor build up properly. The electric fields do not align properly for raising kundalini. He instructed that I stay on a mat. Persons doing breath-infusion should follow this instruction.

September 3, 2001

Yogeshwarananda

An advanced pratyahar procedure.

He showed an alignment of the cognitive, motivational and imaginative force orbs, which causes the psyche to reduce its sexual polarity and to greatly reduce its exploitive tendencies. This procedure if practiced in meditation causes the senses to turn away from desirable objects which ruin the psyche.

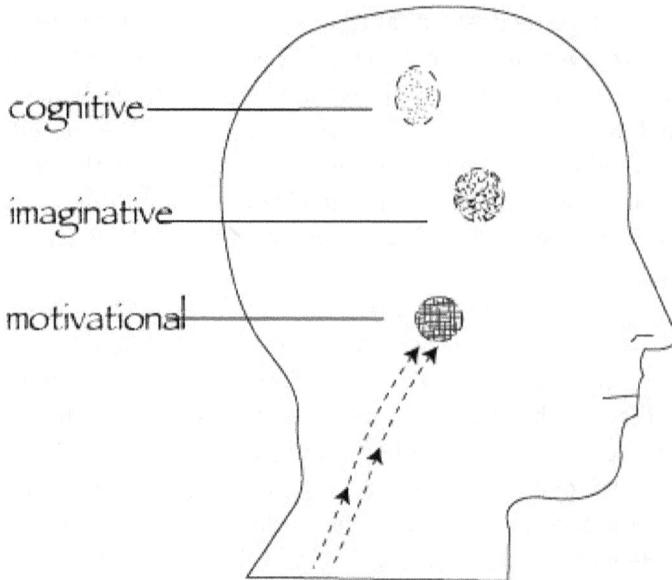

By causing the intellect and the motivational force to be unified with the imaginative force which is in the middle of the diagram, one causes these forces to stop their irresponsible and whimsical psychic activities.

This technique yoga takes time but even with time, even if one has much free time, still he will not be able to master it if he does not free himself from social and cultural complications. One must rid himself of disturbing associations and all sorts of people related and unrelated who retard practice.

September 5, 2001

Yogeshwarananda

He instructed, "Assume tight lotus after doing breath-infusion and surcharging the psyche. Join the index finger and thumb tips. These should be joined on the knees. Take the capsule vision down into the pranic area which is stirred or stimulated. Join the capsule with feelings-vision. Stay in lotus posture for a longer period. Do it daily."

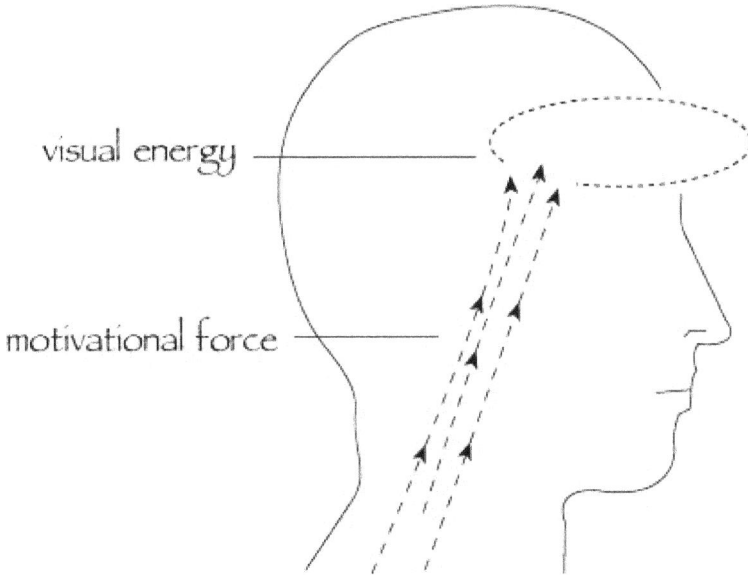

visual energy

motivational force

October 6, 2001

Yogeshwarananda

He informed me, "One cannot do anything about his relationship with the sum-total spiritual energy which is all-pervasive. That is eternal. One also cannot do anything about the feelings-energy. It will remain with many unfulfilled desires.

It will always act as the background for the subtle and gross panorama of activities. By varying degrees of detachment, some negative accords may be sidestepped.

In meditation certain developments occur after a certain amount of effort. Sit for a certain time and certain things will occur. You must deposit its due time in practice.

Yogeshwarananda

He said, "Keep this pace. Forego excitement and sorrow. Remove the self from the everlasting sensuality which brings on responsibility for piety and impiety. It thrives on social responsibility. That is the same in all cases of piety or impiety."

Remark:

Sometimes, we get the idea or someone impresses upon us the view that piety is better than impiety. From a certain angle this is correct. In fact for cultural purposes this is good reasoning. However, from the view of pure spirituality, the piety or impiety are in a sense, irrelevant, since the real problem is responsibility.

One man works honestly for a livelihood. Another one does criminal acts to acquire money. In both cases, the underlying motivation is to fulfill needs. These urges bring on a feeling of being responsible to do this or that, for this or that reason. Ultimately it is responsibility which drives piety or impiety.

September 8, 2001

Yogeshwarananda

On this day, strangely, we both began laughing at the same time. What happened was this. Since he resides in my brahmrandra, he is able to go through my memory and other confidential parts of my psyche. I saw him going through my memory. He saw something I did when I was in Trinidad. Seeing what he saw, both of us laughed.

Actually what he saw was not funny. I will explain. When I lived in Trinidad in the years of 1966 and 1967, I had a girl-friend. I was hard pressed to have sexual relations with the girl but somehow providence prevented contact. A friend proposed to help us. However again the meeting was foiled by providence. Yogesh could see all this in my memory, the way one can see something in a movie theatre on film or even on a television. Then he said

1. 3rd eye / brow chakra
2. up and down ida and pingala
3. sushumna nadi
4. buddhi to jyoti
5. buddhi/ sushumna
6. stabilize buddhi/sushumna
7. atma chakra with ahankara dot
8. atma / brahman dissolution
9. guru mission
10. liberation or loka attainment, which are part of the guru mission

These are what he gave as the techniques. He did not show me how to perform these. He left immediately after. What happened was this. The person who annoyed him, could not get these techniques from him. He left them with me to give to that person at a later date. The fact that he did not explain the details of those techniques, means that when the time was right he would send a message with details or he would return to explain. I state this to prevent any reader from asking me about it. I certainly know some of the methods but that is beside the point.

September 15, 2001

Patanjali

He gave what he called a shitakarshana breath-infusion. He said, "After intense breath-infusion, when there is heat and hot air energy in the body I sit immediately in tight lotus, with hands cupping knees or in another hand gesture, according to the attitude of the surcharged energy. Hold the front sight intellect and the intellect as a whole, to check memory. Breathe hot air out through the lips which are slightly puckered. Blow a constant stream of air out. Inhale through the nostrils. Keep this sequence until the body cools.

"The usual shitakarshana breath-infusion is done in the opposite way inhaling through the lips. Breath-infusion of different types occur naturally by intense sincere practice.

"Memory is a problem. Look at this."

He showed a scene in my mind. It was a scene from a television program which I viewed for only a minute, while working at someone's house. Patanjali opened up a section of my mind where that information was stored. He said, "Stop this or you will not be successful. Keep this memory closed. Protect the mind from this filing system."

He later said that the ahankara itself is the problem. He ordered, "Control that bija."

After this he suggested that I translate his Yoga Sutras and give a commentary. He told me that in the second sutra a complete checking of the intellect from its thinking and imagining ability is required.

Remark:

Up to this date of April 6, 2002, I had not translated the Yoga Sutras. As far as the Sanskrit to English rendering is concerned, there are many reliable translation. The problem is, however that most translators have not entered absorption. This is why I have not attempted to translate it. Right now I am preparing to relocate to Guyana to develop the absorption disciplines. Perhaps if I am allowed the time, I would translate the Sutras. Patanjali is a mahayogin. Only another great ascetic can effective explain his sutras. Yogesh did on occasion elaborate on them but he did not leave a full translation. Perhaps in consultation with him I may write a commentary.

September 15, 2001

Yogeshwarananda

He instructed that I get the intellect to go with pranavision. He showed postures which facilitate this.

Yogeshwarananda

He said, "It is focused here. He showed the imagination corner of the intellect. Finding it, one can limit the memory impressions."

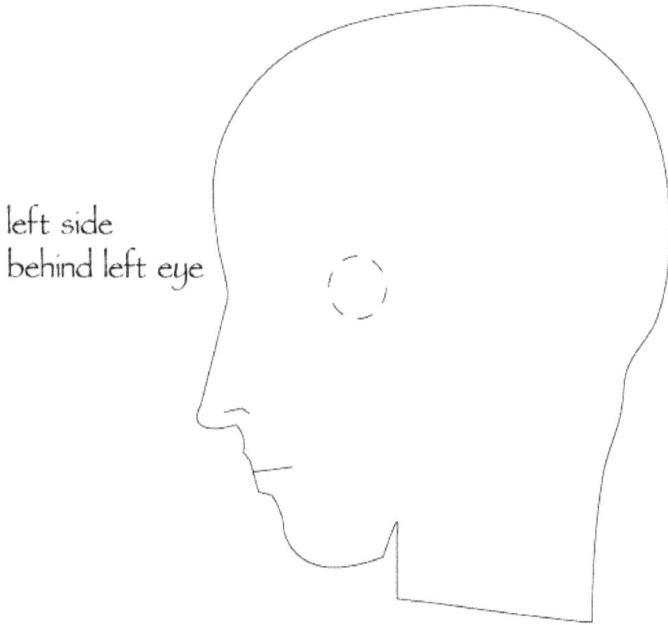

left side
behind left eye

September 18, 2001

Yogeshwarananda

He said, "Get stillness now. Why do you think yogis remain still for hours, isolated from excitement? If it were merely a matter of focus, they would have done that only. It is based on stillness."

September 19, 2001

Yogeshwarananda

He said, "Get a focus. Hold it while pulling the visual sense. Do not release the focus. Patiently hold it."

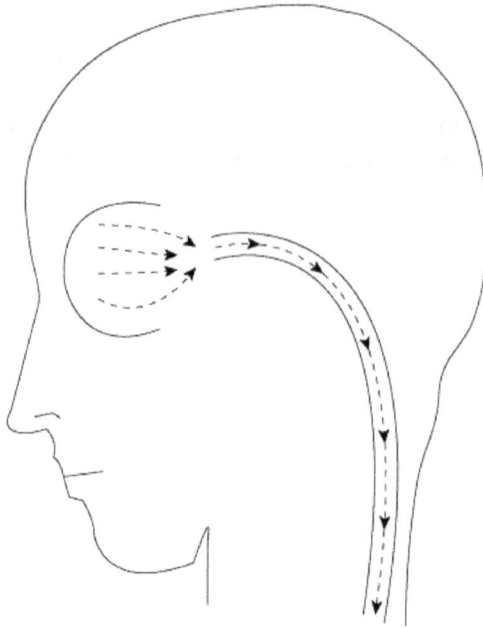

He also said that a spinal twist exercise when done in the lotus pose helps to keep the sushumna passage open. He explained that sometimes the astral body does a spinal twist on impulse from the cleared sushumna.

September 22, 2001

Yogeshwarananda

He explained that the dot seen in the feelings-energy is the core-self's sense of identity reflection. That dot has spatial rays. Seeing it is seeing the core-self indirectly.

October 2, 2001

Yogeshwarananda

He observed my posture and breath-infusion practice. He said that when there is no food boost to the navel heat, the kundalini disappears.

Remark:

The kundalini chakra functions according to eating habits. From food energy it gets fuel to operate. It blazes up on the basis of food supply.

October 3, 2001

Yogeshwarananda

He suggested that I take the intellect down into the psyche; first to the kundalini chakra and then to the causal body. To take it to kundalini, one should have a cleared sushumna passage. To take it to the causal body one must subdue kundalini chakra.

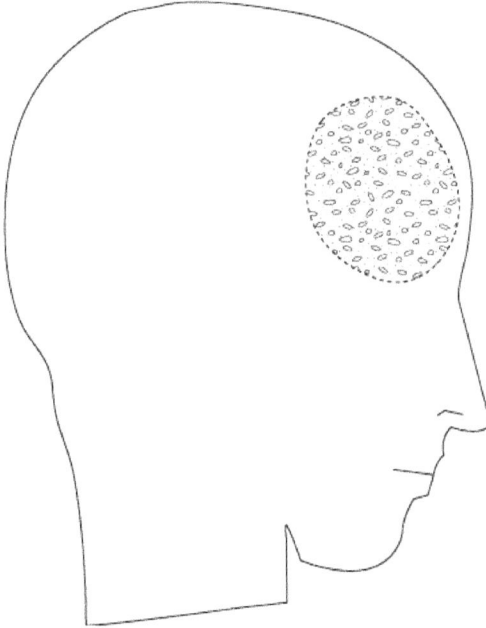

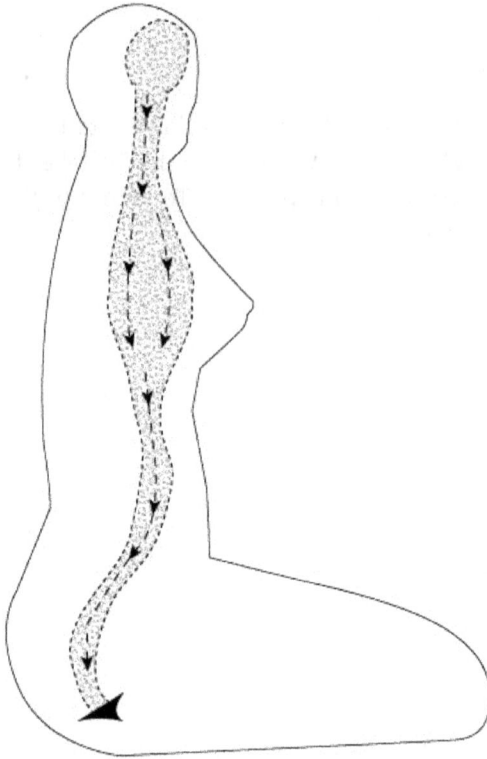

October 11, 2001

Yogeshwarananda

He showed how to grasp the imagination orb. This organ focuses slowly on ideas and daydreaming conceptions. Since the core-self is hypnotized by it, it appears to move rapidly. The power to grasp it comes from paravairagya mainly. That is a complete disinterest in cultural development.

October 12, 2001

Yogeshwarananda

He showed that the imagination orb is the same subtle instrument which converts pictures into impressions and sounds. It takes impressions from objects and converts these into signals just like a digital machine. It has to be curbed before I can practice the absorptions.

Yogesh said that when it is curbed, it is called ritambhara buddhi or the reality-perceiving vision.

Oct 15, 2001

Yogeshwarananda

He told me that by tapping the finger tips and nail tips, one can decrease mischievousness and cynicism. When this is done, it sends sharp sensations back into the energy in the causal body. This exercises the stimulant-hungry feelings-energy.

If there is no exercise like this, the feelings creates urges in the subtle body, a need to bring compressed experiences, of various sorts. That drives the subtle body to act in irresponsible ways.

Yogesh said, "Find that spot where it was last imagined. Go to that spot. Meditate there. If it imagines again, find the location again. Go where it acted last. Take the vision and intellect mechanism there."

Remark:

This is a technique used when one first begins to practice the 6th stage of yoga, that of dharana focus. As one tries to focus as recommended the focus is diverted by the imagination orb, which has a way about it, where it compels the core-self to give up the desired focus and to accept another idea or another series of ideas. When this happens, the core gradually realizes that he was shifted from the objective. He should then implement the advice given above. All this is preparation for reaching the 8th stage of yoga, full transcendence absorption practice.

October. 22, 2001

Yogeshwarananda

He showed some lower abdomen flexes. Asana postures though only the 3rd stage, and though considered elementary and mundane, is continued through higher stages. It has value all the way up to the time of death of the physical body. Unless one's body becomes crippled or incapacitated, one should keep doing it at least twice per day.

Abdomen flexes are important for prompt evacuation and for preparing the body for absorptions. These helps considerably to influence the body and life force to reduce food cravings.

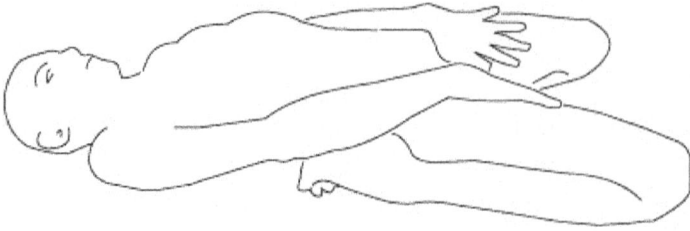

rotate abdomen in direction of arrows

do one side, then other side, then center

take deep breath, blow air out,

rotate abdomen with air out

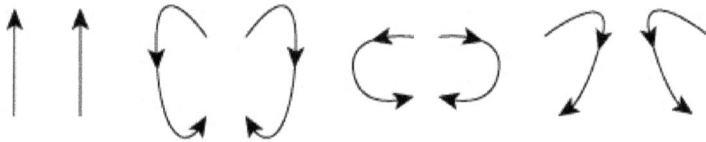

October 23, 2001

Yogeshwarananda

He gave a technique for curbing the imagination orb. That curbing process is the key to perceiving in the sky of consciousness, the chit akash. Unfortunately many persons who say that they are interested in technique yoga, are addicted to the imagination which they regard as a private compartment, and as a place for enacting unrealistic pastimes, acts which reality will not accommodate but which the imagination enacts in mental motion. However such addictions prove to be great impediments in the quest of technique yoga.

Yogesh instructed that I put the I-sense in the center of the psychic location where the imagination occurred. The imagination orb usually interlocks with a specific sensual orb. From that linkage, it absorbs an impression or idea, which expands into a motion show, which is spellbinding to the self.

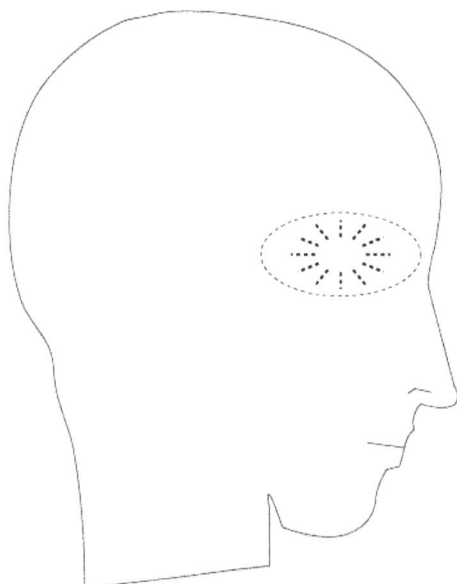

Yogeshwarananda

He gave a special stomach flex. This, in addition to the one described in the recent entry, is part of the absorption practice preparation.

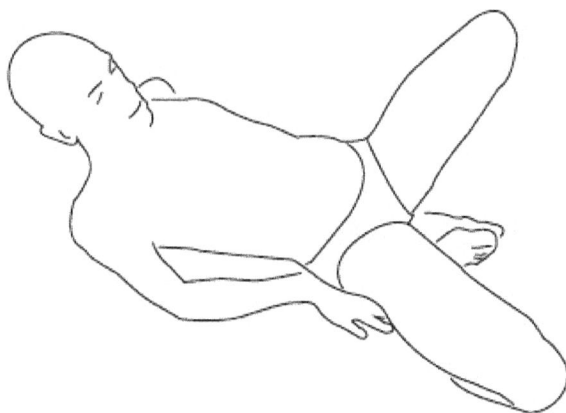

soles together, sit on soles

lean back on eldows

October 25, 2001

Hanuman

He said, "Track the imagination. Station the self in it. Do not look at it or at what it presents. Enter and remain in it, until it ceases the presentations.

"Notice how the self is hypnotized by it. Do this as a habit to curb it. Notice its activities; memory, invocation, idea expansion, reference and conception."

Remark:

This was spoken to me by Hanuman just after I assumed a tight lotus posture in preparation for meditation. I had just finished a session of postures with breath-infusion.

October 27, 2001

Shiva

He said, "See this."

Remark:

He showed that when the left nostril is open, the left front kundalini lights show many tiny tubes on the left side of the subtle body.

Under his influence I realized that after several breath-infusions one gets the ability to attentively introspect. After in-focusing on the introspection, one gets the ability to do transcendental focus. This cannot be attained without sustained practice.

October 29, 2001

Yogeshwarananda

He advised that to stop the mind from conceiving of thoughts I should go where the thoughts occurred and reside there. This was a mystic terrain in the intellect of the subtle body. This is a process used in transcendental focus when one sits to meditate after doing the postures and breath-infusion.

If one tries to meditate without doing postures and breath-infusion, one is unable to do this effectively, because the psyche is not surcharged enough with fresh energy to cause the self to have the required speed of perception on the subtle plane.

Thoughts, ideas and picturizations move very fast on the subtle level. One must energize the system, so that one can perceive them in slow motion.

One must control thought reception and responses, otherwise one will not meditate.

B.K.S. Iyengar / Hanuman

They showed how to do some asana postures perfectly with proper body alignment.

Remark:

Many persons who do asana postures, feel that these are the full course, but yoga is an eight part process, of which asana is the 3rd stage. One needs to get advice from an expert to understand what perfect alignment is and what the final forms are. In the beginning it is not important that one do it perfectly but it is important to know if one is not doing an asana correctly, so that as one's body becomes more capable of flexing, one may adjust it to do the ideal postures.

Does yoga take time? It certainly takes time to practice, just as anything else which you may learn. Therefore you will not have the time if it does not seem important to you. Some begin yoga and then find that it is time-consuming, and does not give quick results. They begin with much hope and then cease the practice with the feeling that it is not what it seemed to be.

This is due in part to modern yoga teachers who advertise yoga as a gracious and easy course. Yoga was never easy nor gracious because formerly yoga was done by forest ascetics, the majority of which were hard men who endured a rough life in the forested areas. Yoga was not done in air conditioned buildings with pretty shapely women stretching their elegant sexually-appealing forms.

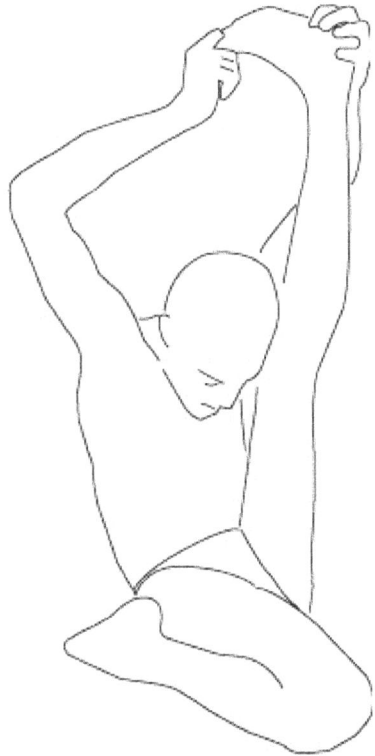

The commercialization of yoga by Western teachers, conveys the idea that yoga is for everyone and that it is very easy to practice, and that it will award the practitioner a shapely body, peace of mind, easy living, health, and existential superiority. But this presentation is based on a desire for financial success by selling yoga as something other than what it really is. Somehow, yoga masters like B.K.S. Iyengar are victimized by their students who first learn yoga postures and then travel here and there in the developed countries and subject yoga to commercialization.

Yoga in its true form has nothing to do with finances. There is no history of any proficient ancient yogi who sold yoga to the public or who used yoga teachings as a means of livelihood. That is a purely Western invention.

The story of Vasishtha Rishi and King Vishvamitra shows this. Vishvamitra heard that Vasishtha Rishi had a wish-fulfilling cow, but when Vishvamitra went to the forest hermitage of Rishi Vasishtha, he observed that it was just an ordinary animal, because the Rishi lived in very poor surroundings in a very simple cottage made of crude forest materials. In any case Vasishtha Rishi felt that King Vishvamitra should be respected. He gave the king a royal greeting.

Rishi Vasishtha, that great yogin, went to the cow and got royal facilities from the animal's udders. It was so fantastic, that King Vishvamitra decided to procure the cow. He could see that from that cow's body, one could have palaces, attendants and whatever wealth, one may desire.

King Vishvamitra then proposed that since Vasishtha was not a king, he should donate the cow for the country's upkeep. The Rishi said that he could not give away the pet animal. However since the King persisted, the Rishi went to the cow and explain the request of the king. The cow however refused.

After this King Vishvamitra decided that he would take the animal by force. In trying to do so he was ruined because from the cow's arse soldiers were created which destroyed his army.

The point is that yoga is not for commercialization. It is not for making a livelihood. If one uses yoga in that way, he will not be successful, even if may become famous on videos, television and computers. In real terms he will be a failure. And so will be his students.

Just as in the final chapter of the Bhagavad Gita, Lord Krishna laid down a stipulation about anyone teaching the course of the Gita, so there are stipulations about yoga. If one violates these, he will not be successful and the persons whom he influences, will not get the benefit of yoga. No one can force yoga to give itself to anyone, just as we may see that even though many commentators squeeze the Bhagavad Gita, to give it to their followers, still the actual meaning remains in its own time and place and does not move forward to suit modern conditions and needs.

Let us see what Krishna said about explaining the Gita, then we will consider the prerequisites for teaching yoga.

इदं ते नातपस्काय
नाभक्ताय कदाचन ।
न चाशुश्रूषवे वाच्यं
न च मां योऽभ्यसूयति
॥१८.६७॥

idaṁ te nātapaskāya
nābhaktāya kadācana
na cāśuśrūṣave vācyaṁ
na ca māṁ yo'bhyasūyati (18.67)

idaṁ — this; te — of you; nātapaskāya — na — not + atapaskāya — to one who does not perform austerity; nābhaktāya = na — not + abhaktāya — to one who is not devoted: kadācana — at any time; na — not; cāśuśrūṣave — ca — and + aśuśrūṣave — one who does not desire to hear; vācyaṁ — what is to be said; na — not; ca — and: mām — me; yo — yaḥ — who; 'bhyasūyati = abhyasūyati — he is critical

This should not be told by you to anyone who does not perform austerity or is not devoted at anytime, or does not desire to hear what is said or is critical of Me. (Bhagavad Gita 18.67)

Despite this stipulation, many modern missionaries from India, teach the Bhagavad Gita to audiences who do not perform the austerities mentioned in the Gita. That is the first and foremost violation. I heard their excuses many times. It is that no one would learn the Gita if that person has to first master those austerities. But actually no one learns the Gita who does not master those disciplines. This is because if one is cynical of Krishna, one will naturally disregard his regulations and minimize them in the name of preaching his glories. That cynicism will bar one from understanding the Gita. It is something subtle but it is so effective that one will study what one considers to be the Gita but which in fact is not the textual meaning. In other words, one's intellect will misconstrue the meanings of the Sanskrit terms.

We can say then, that Krishna issued a curse over the Gita, such that anyone who slights his regulations about teaching the text, will not understand his teachings, even if such a person is in the disciplic succession from Krishna or even if such a person feels sincere about Krishna. Such a person will not desire to hear what Krishna actually told Arjuna because he would be under the influence of his personal needs for certain meanings. His mind will polish over Krishna's words to make them confirm to what he feels he requires for salvation. Such a person will think that he is devoted to Krishna, even though in fact, if he were in Arjuna's place he would vehemently refuse to fight as a valiant soldier, doing bodily harm to people merely because he was destined to be an agent of the corrosive supreme will which eats away at anyone and anything which does not conform to it.

The secret of the prerequisites for yoga practice is hidden in the same verse of the Bhagavad Gita. There is a slight difference. While for understanding the Gita, one has to be devoted to Krishna, for doing yoga, one has to be devoted to the practice itself. This practice is described in chapter 4 of the Gita, from verse 24 through 30. And the basis details are given in Chapter six and elsewhere.

Before teaching yoga, a teacher should introduce students to austerity. When the students are habituated to that, then the teacher can begin to teach yoga. This is by virtue of the fact that yoga thrives on austerity the way a plant thrives on soil. If there is no soil, the plant dies, naturally. If there is no austerity, yoga is finished. Even though today, people want to do yoga amidst opulence, formerly we hear of many such stories in the Puranas of kings who left aside opulent conditions to accept the hard life in the forest for doing yoga. This is what King Vishvamitra eventually did to master it. Why did he not stay in his palaces and engage a teacher to teach it a fee.

Nowadays, out of every five books on yoga, three or four are illustrated with a female doing yoga. Why is this? Why is it that an art which was practiced mostly by men under very harsh living conditions is now being demonstrated mostly by women? Why the change? What caused this? It is because they are doing something which looks like yoga but which is quite distinct from it. Yoga does not give itself over without austerity.

Yoga in luxurious conditions is indeed one of the biggest jokes of our time. Yoga without stringent austerities with people sitting on foam mats, using invented stretching aids, with music being heard via stereo devices, computer discs and state of art technology, with foods created in electric blenders and juicers, by people who have sport cars and when live in fashionable buildings in San Francisco, Los Angeles and New York, is ridiculous. The whole scope of modern yoga is disgusting.

But that does not mean that such persons cannot do asana postures and cannot sit quietly to calm their troubles minds. They certainly can. But still that is not yoga. They missed the essential point of it.

Somehow yoga masters like B.K.S. Iyengar, were providentially drawn into situations where their teaching were misused. Such is this life. However these masters of yoga, teach the superficial part of it and remain silent about the deeper directives. This protects the teachers and yoga from abuse.

One lady who was used to illustrate yoga postures and who mastered the superficial part of it, in terms of being able to make her material body do the final forms, did ask me in the astral world about her inability to remove from her body, the sexual focus of it. I smiled because I was not destined to help her overcome it. She is a disciple of my hatha yoga teacher, the late Swami Vishnudevananda.

The lady under discussion can do more final forms than I. Still, she does not understand the true purpose of yoga. Still in the Western Countries, she is regarded as an expert. To help her I would have to get authority from Shiva. Unless one has such authority, he cannot effectively subject a student to the rigors of the practice. In addition, to help a female, a male yogin would have to absorb her sexuality. And that requires caution.

Only a foolish yogin would want to do something like that which more than likely would terminate his yoga progression. Sexuality and yoga do not harmonize nicely with one another. There are diametrically opposed. Brahmrandra and sexual chakra cannot exist together. It is either one or the other.

Any person who masters postures and feels that it is yoga, cannot have an operative brahmrandra, if the sexual chakras is not completely closed. It is not possible. But nowadays people who know nothing of these matters become famous as experts of yoga.

October 30, 2001

Yogeshwarananda

He showed how the intellect operates. In the center of it is a bright-white bluish light. That is the imagination orb. This is actually an object but if one has no mystic perception, one experiences this as the part of the mind in which one imagines or the part of the mind where one finds oneself projecting ideas and day-dreaming. It is hard to understand that such a psychological place is an object but it is. In advanced yoga, one sees this visually.

Yogesh showed how that central light, the imagination orb, moves about in the intellect. It moves from one sensual orb to the next, detecting any impressions which these orbs picked up by their sensing capacity. In the intellect, there is also the memory conversion compartment. It is a highly sensitive organ and is mostly imperceptible except after one reaches the 7th and 8th stages of yoga practice.

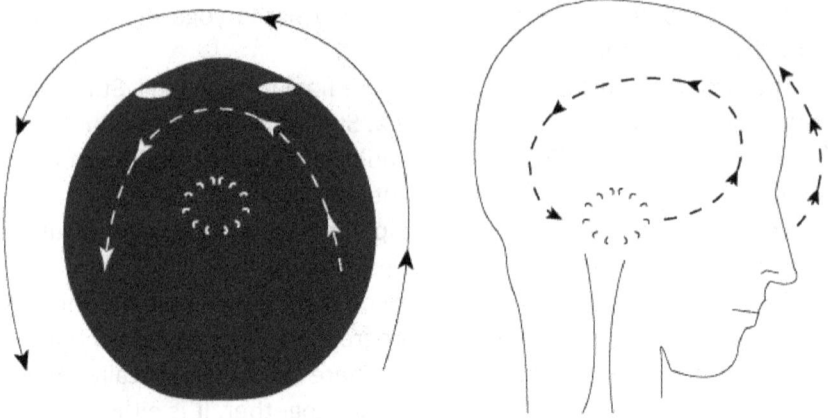

arrows show counter-clockwise sweeping action of buddhi

October 31, 2001

Yogeshwarananda

He showed how the imagination orb works as a sensing ray which sweeps through the mindscape. I used the word mindscape as we may use the word landscape. The mind has an environment just as we see in the physical world outside.

If one could see how this intellect mechanism operates, one would see that the intellect imagination orb projects from itself a ray of white light which sweeps around in a circular fashion. This ray hits the sense orbs, one after another. If it senses information, the ray expands. When Yogesh showed this, he used a miniature subtle body. It was just about one-fourth of an inch in height. In that way he entered those subtle zones which were in microscopic compartments.

The imagination ray moves in a counterclockwise direction, like a large searchlight sweeping through the night sky. When it hits impressions, it magnifies and expands them. This is experienced as imagination, conception and visualization. ·

Yogesh explained the necessity for the imagination orb to convert the impressions. He said that the senses first convert experiences into impressions. These he said cannot be made into intelligible information directly. They must first be reconverted into ideas, pictures and concepts, just as when a tape recorder converts human voices into magnetic signatures. After that, the signatures are reconverted into sounds. The reconverted sounds are not the original human voices, but they represent that accurately or inaccurately, according to the degree of distortion developed in the recording device.

November 3, 2001

Yogeshwarananda

He instructed, "Do this. Retrieve this energy which is a lightning-fast blast from the intellect."

Remark:

This was an alternate procedure. It is used during meditation sessions in the effort to stop the intellect from its impulsive mind sweeps. Instead of the previously mentioned action of positioning oneself where the imagination expands in the mindscape (terrain inside the mind), one may repossess the attention-power into the intellect. This causes a reserve of energy which stabilizes the intellect and discourages it from creating imagination.

November 5, 2001

Yogeshwarananda

He had me do several uddhiyana bandhas with the stomach drawn under the rib cage. This is done after doing breath-infusion with intensity. Sometimes this is called the fly-up technique. It works only if one has got the kundalini to a responsive stage. When one draws the stomach up under the rib cage, then sometimes, the kundalini energy feels that it has to rise through the spine, because it is prohibited from expanding its energies through the abdomen. One should master diet and greatly reduce eating.

When one does these techniques, one has to be attentive to kundalini. If kundalini rises quickly, it may cause the physical body to fall to the ground. But if one realizes that it will rise, one may apply tight locks (bandhas). That causes kundalini to rise in a controlled way and one does not lose track of the material body. Then kundalini chakra does not remove one's objective consciousness. One can experience both the subjective and objective phases of consciousness simultaneously. Such dual experience is the right preparation for entering absorption and for perceiving existence on the causal plane.

November 5, 2001

Yogeshwarananda

We had a discussion of the causal energy. This energy should be studied by a yogin. Yogesh discussed that this energy is the prime mover in this world. In terms of individual acts and universal mundane creation of all sorts, the causal energy is the immediate cause. It is the cause of mischievousness. It prompts activity and receives the impressions from the experiences which the creatures endure.

It is reckless. It does not differentiate between good and bad. It is interested in the impressions which are derived from experiences. It sponsors pious, impious or even worthless activities. In a greater sense, more than we know, we are victimized by it.

November 16, 2001

On this day I remembered Lahiri, one of the pioneers of technique yoga for householders. He stressed that the advanced techniques come naturally in the course of a sincere yoga practice. This is an advanced technique for celibates. This is called vajroli. It used to be done by drawing up a liquid through the penis. The idea was to draw up water and then to draw up a heavier liquid like honey through the tubal organ. ·

After that mastership, the yogi draws up semen so that when he is sexually involved, he could pull up his own and his female partner's sexual fluids. This is part of tantric practice. This may cause the body to change genetically so that it does not use the hormones for sexual purposes. In other words, if a yogi has a body from a rishi family, in which the bodies were genetically coded not to use the hormones for sexual purposes, he had no need for the vajroli practice.

If however he did not, then he should work with the body to change it for the mastery of celibacy, because unless he mastered that he could not do brahma yoga. Many ascetics worked strenuously with their bodies to change natural tendencies. Vajroli became popular in the time of Gorakshnath, who was a mahayogin of repute from sometime around the 12th century after Christ (1100-1200). At that time many young men who did not have sexually-resistant bodies wanted to abandon cultural life to gain liberation from material existence. Once they understood that yogic celibacy was required as a prerequisite for practicing brahma yoga, they experimented to change their bodies. Many failed, because material nature is not that easy to alter.

Lahiri did not agree that one should take drastic steps to gain celibacy but he felt that a steady yoga practice would give a sure grip on celibacy after some time. The drastic methods in hatha yoga, which were used by pseudo-followers of Yogi Gorakshnath, were discouraged by Lahiri. For one thing, many of these persons did not understand mystic yoga. They could not clearly distinguish between kundalini yoga, celibacy yoga, purity of the psyche yoga and brahma yoga.

If one sincerely practices technique yoga and strives consistently and honestly, the methods will be revealed. My practice is the evidence of this.

November 6, 2001

Yogeshwarananda

From in the brahmrandra, he showed a region where there is dissolution of subtle bodies, with only causal existence remaining for those core-selves. For most of us, this dissolution will take place when this universe is terminated. According to the modern astronomers, that may be some fifteen billion years hence or even later.

When I observed that place, it appeared that much energy was in turmoil. There were milky-white and white-bluish lights swirling. Yogesh said, "This is how you will exist then. There will be no body, only a causal configuration."

Remark:

Premature destruction of the subtle body, hinges on whether a yogin can get beyond the causal place before the time of the dissolution. If he cannot, then his subtle body would meet destruction when the visible universe is destroyed.

November 13, 2001

Yogeshwarananda

That great yogin was there as I did exercises in the early morning. Due to consistent anal cleanliness and a lack of later meals for some time, along with persistent asana postures and breath-infusion practice, there was a white fire at the bottom of my spine.

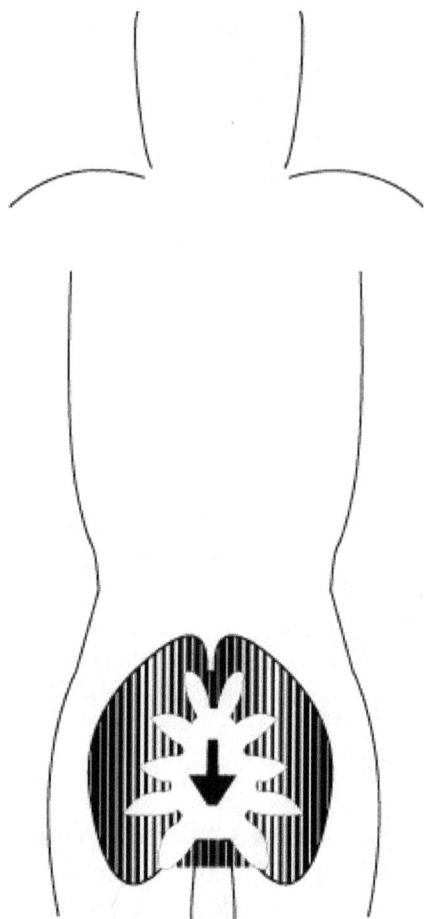

November 16, 2001

Yogeshwarananda

Front kundalini chin-up technique:

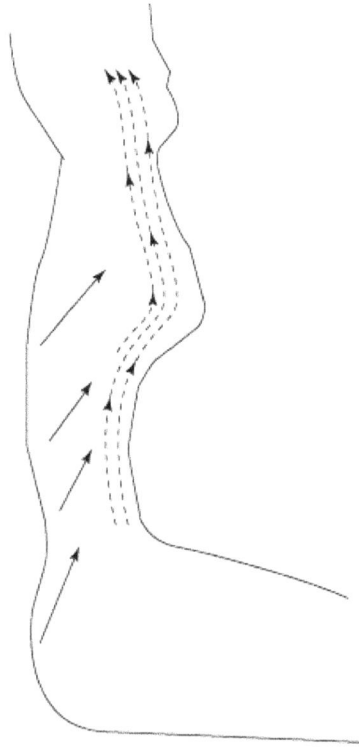

November 17, 2001

Visual vision and pranavision unification.

This was given by Yogesh. This technique may be done without breath-infusion. If bhastrika is done one should stop after sufficient energization and focus on the eyes and on the thigh in-groin muscles and nerves. The eyelids should be closed while doing this.

November 18, 2001

Hariharananda (Kapila sampradaya)

This Swami did a commentary on Patanjali Yoga sutras. On this day he said, "When this becomes the basis, the mind's actions do not deter but rather adds to the function of withdrawal, concentration and absorption. This comes after the student established that.

"In celibate practice, one feels the sexual energy expressing itself upwards. Thus the sexuality acts in that way as a continuity of the flow of energy up the gut nadi. The yogi does not have to repress the sexual energy."

Remark:

Hariharananda is one of the few commentators on Patanjali Yoga Sutras, who have the realization required for an effective translation and commentary. The English translation of his work is not as potent as his original in the Indian language. This Swami spoke to me about celibacy in the advanced yoga practice. Unless there is celibacy as a prerequisite, yoga remains a psychological and physiological game. Celibacy in yoga is the active celibacy which comes about by hatha yoga, breath-infusion, and mystic reform. This is not the passive celibacy which is done without yoga practice.

Hariharananda

He said, "Due to darkness here, they do not meet. By an honest practice due to sincere celibacy and nonattachment, while paying attention to self-faults, this clears away."

In this respect Yogesh revealed that the pranic energy and the kundalini battery force at the base of the spine, do mix with the navel power force (bhasvara agni). This navel force is a fire power in the body. It is a chemical power on the physical side and an astral fire power on the subtle side.

In persons who do no kundalini yoga, the bottom chakra has a little fire going at all times on the subtle plane. This flares up during sexual intercourse and it is perceived by the ordinary humans and by animals, as pleasure energy. After the pleasure of sexual intercourse, the reserve hormones being

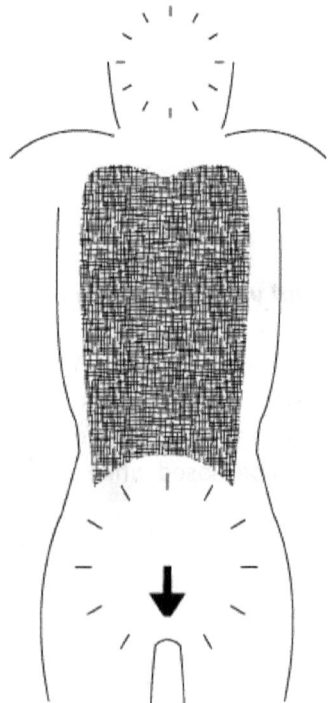

consumed, the navel force-fire is reduced to a warm state. Then again when the hormones accumulate and when there is another sexual intercourse, it flares up. This is how the kundalini chakra is operated in the average human being.

November 11, 2001

B.K.S. Iyengar

He said, "With honest practice comes absorption. Balance both sides. The balance comes naturally from consistent practice."

Remark:

I had recently purchased a book titled *Hatha Yoga Tradition of the Mysore Palace* by N.E. Sjomon. This text explains the lineage of B.K.S. Iyengar. Somehow by mystic means, he knew that I purchased that book. He came to check my practice.

Nov 23, 2001

B.K.S. Iyengar

He said, "Work for the balance. Control form and posture. Serve Hatha Yoga Devi."

Remark:

Hatha Yoga Devi is Sarasvati Ma, a supernatural lady. She is the patron deity of hatha yoga. If one has her blessings, if one comes under her shelter, one will do the postures in final forms. Loyalty in practice to Ma Uma, Mother Durga, Shiva's wife, causes one to master the female techniques. However for me, such a loyalty is dangerous. I advise that males not aspire for this but instead, they should try to stick to the association of the great yogins, to Shiva, Krishna and Balarama. Even if one becomes advanced enough to be noticed by Mother Durga, one should not go over to her side, but one should not refuse her contribution of special self-tantric procedures. It is dangerous for a male to be with the students of Ma Durga. Most of her pupils are females. These yoginis, despite their success with technique yoga, may have residual sexual needs. By such needs, one will be led away from practice. A person as powerful as Lord Krishna's grandson Aniruddha, was led away for sexual purposes by the mahayogini Chitralekha. She procured him for her friend, Usha, whom Aniruddha later married. One should not play games with these yogini women. They are a sure way to wipe out celibate practice. Ma

Durga is detached from any male or female who studies yoga under her direction or under the direction of any of her split-off and parallel forms like Ma Kali or Ma Chandika. Thus if a male associates with her students, he will more than likely be carried off. Invariably that will lead to sexual intercourse and companionship with that female. That will result in taking births in sub worlds in which one will forget yoga.

It is different with Hatha Yoga Devi. Her form, though female, does not exude sensual energies. She gives association without risk. However this goddess is not easy to contact.

November 24, 2001

Yogeshwarananda

He said, "Take the intellect and the visual orb to the pain which is felt during hatha yoga postures. A monkey body is not capable of doing all postures perfectly. Still the effort should be made.

Remark:

One may have a body which will never do final forms and which may never do postures with perfect balance. Nevertheless one should do his best with the practice for as soon as that form is given up at its death, one will resume the subtle body on a full time basis. One can then complete the postures in the ideal way. One should not be discouraged if one picked up a monkey-like body as this writer did.

December 4, 2001

Yogeshwarananda

He said, "Subtle flirtations on the gross level support and cause subtle sexual contacts. Such flirtations weaken the resistance and causes the subtle body to find sexually-enticing realms in the astral world."

He gave a bottom-lip technique. This concerns the passage of energy through that lip in the subtle body. The subtle energy taken in food affects the purity of the energy which flows through that lip.

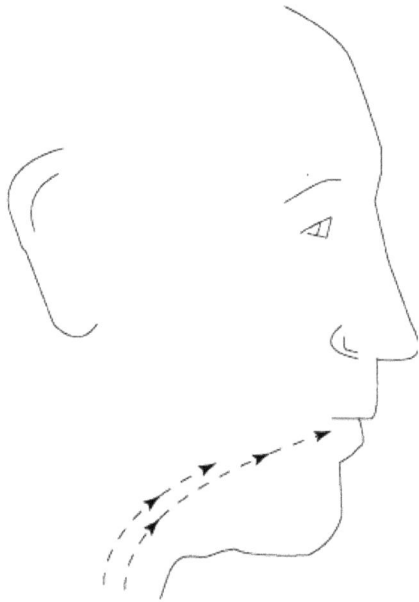

December 5, 2001

Yogeshwarananda / Shiva

Under their influence I experienced a nadi tube which passes from the kanda bulb to the back of the spine, where it emits through a hole.

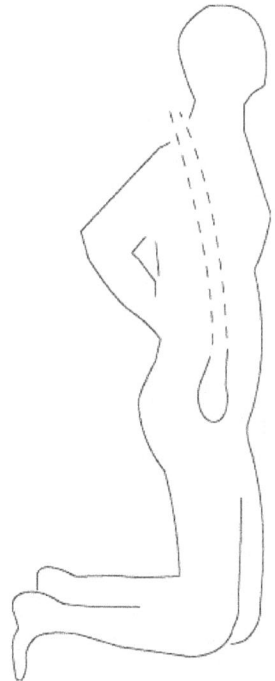

Part 5

Yogeshwarananda

On this day I finished reading a book by an archeologist in which the writer explained the idea of the evolution of the living beings on the basis of observations of fossils of prehistoric creatures. I realized while I read that book that Yogesh was reading it through my mind and eyeballs. In other words he used my psyche to read that book.

Great yogins can do such things which are called perfectional skills or siddhis. Yogesh got rid of his kundalini chakra. That means that he does not have a subtle body like the one we use in dreams. However, for him it is not necessary. He can use anyone else's if he desires. There are many stories of great yogins, entering and possessing the body of another person.

Yogesh's usage of my psyche was beneficial for me since I was able to see his thinking patterns, benefit from his deep insights and his investigation of history on the causal plane.

Yogeshwarananda

He showed the particulars of detachment. The mind and intellect complex engage in attachments whimsically. This results in a lack of detachment. Yogesh explained that sensual investigation and curiosity are subtle phases of attachment which leads to sorrow and a lack of the truth-revealing sight and insight (ritambhara intellect).

The intellect's pursuit of sensation is a direct cause of a lack of yogic insight. The protrusion of energy from the intellect through the forehead into the outer world is the indication of this.

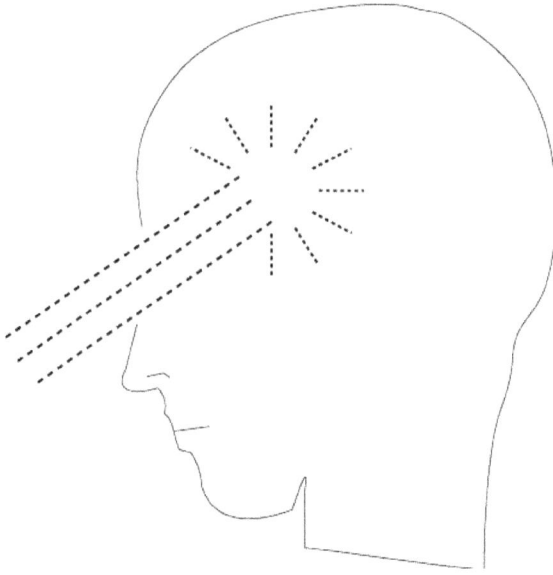

One should do day-time attention retraction, keeping the intellect from verbal, mental and visual inquiries and curiosities. This practice causes the light of the intellect to shine within profusely. It takes practice.

December 12, 2001

Agastya

He said, "When the intellect sends down-rays through the chakras, the rays penetrate only if the chakras are cleared. Otherwise the effort is a waste of time. Work hard to cleanse the subtle energy in the lower regions."

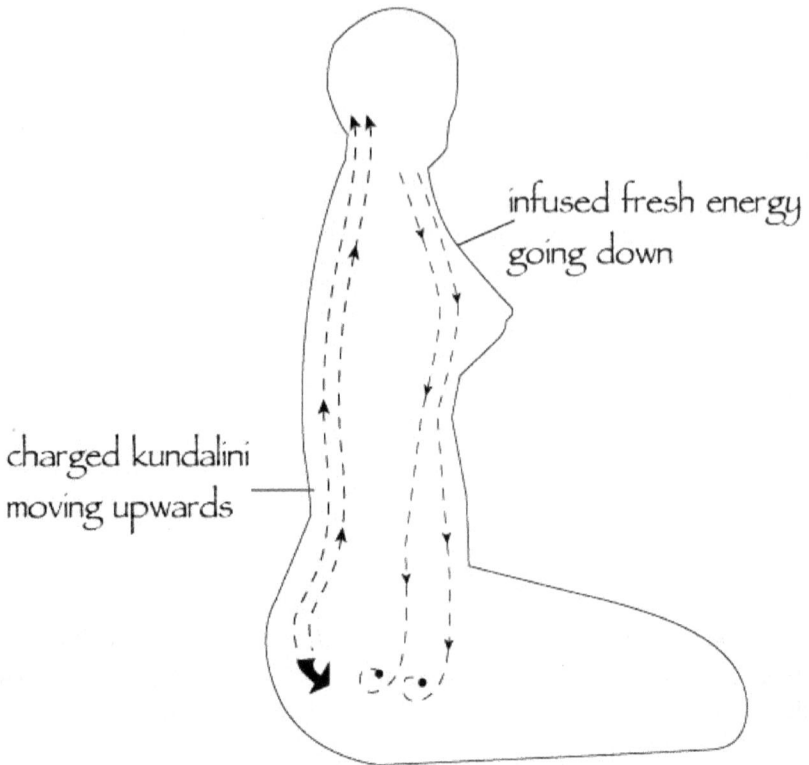

infused fresh energy going down

charged kundalini moving upwards

December 12, 2001

Yogeshwarananda

He said, "That is a standard breath-infusion. Even without being taught many techniques will be discovered in an honest practice,."

Remark:

I did a breath-infusion by discovery. This happens by the influence of higher subtle energy after doing an intense session of breath-infusion. On that day, after infusing with surcharged night energy, I sat in lotus posture. I held the breath for a time without discomfort. Then I exhaled and held the breath out for a long time. I did not use a counting system. During the exhales, I pulled up the stomach tightly until I inhaled again. After the inhales, I held the stomach in tight slightly. The key however is to keep the intellect attentive to the surcharged energy distribution. The intellect must be made to give full attention. It should cease scanning for other sensual information and for any hints from the memory power pore which gives it impressions to translate and illustrate.

lowered intellect

lung cavity

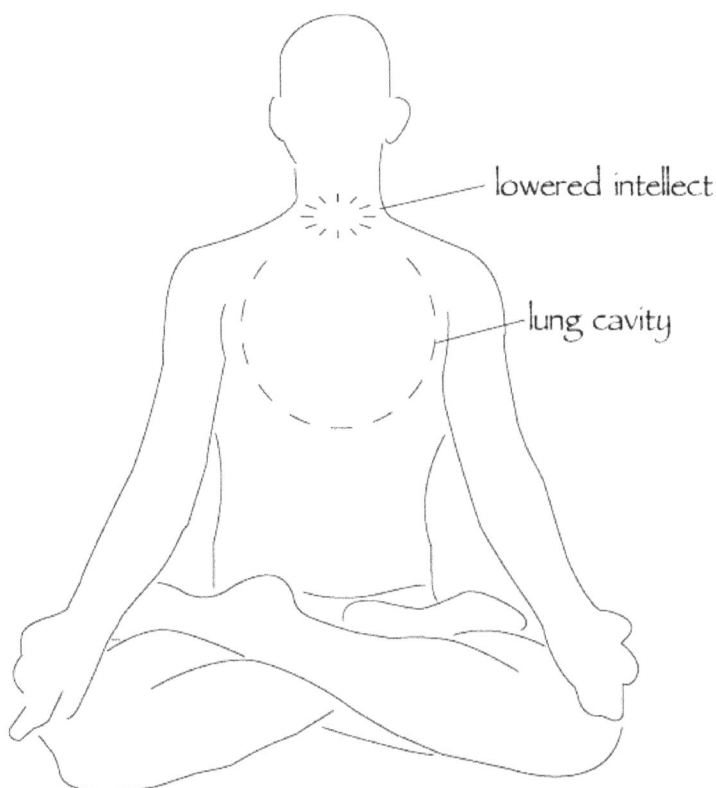

December 14, 2001

Yogeshwarananda

He said, "Stand after intense breath-infusion. Look down with pranavision and see the cleared thighs and feet. Push breath through. See the bottom of the feet but pull up clear energy."

Yogeshwarananda

He said, "Work on the lungs. They correspond to the causal body. Study what it does and how it does it. That will help you get causal awakening."

Remark:

There is a similarity between the lung and the causal cove. Just as the lung absorbs air, so the causal cove absorbs very

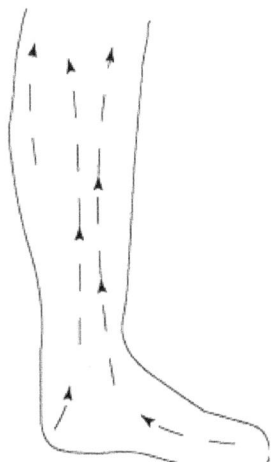

subtle energy. This subtle energy is called chitta. It is the medium of consciousness as we know it on this physical level.

December 20, 2001

Yogananda

He showed how he did a hansa and nadi shodana up-and-down spine routine.

Remark:

This is a standard technique given to some technique students who join the formal successions which came from Lahiri. Yogananda is a master of this. He is still available to teach it in the astral world. Mostly he stays in California on the astral grounds of some communities; those formed by himself while he used a physical body, and those formed by Kriyananda, one of his disciples.

December 22, 2001

Shiva

He showed in slow motion the actions of the mind and intellect. The mind upon commands of the intellect shows an object. The mind then puts the object besides something in the memory which is related. It may be a contrasting memory file. The intellect then evaluates these.

These actions of the mind and intellect are done hundreds of times daily. It works spontaneously. Unless it is stopped there would be no conservation of energy for an effective pratyahar sensual energy withdrawal practice.

The impulsive operation of the mind and intellect occurs very fast, at the speed of light transmission. Unless one can speed up his perception of the psychological actions, he cannot control it. This is why it is futile to do meditation without first doing postures and breath-infusion, which cause the self to perceive much more rapidly. Usually human beings do psychic perception at a slow speed, this is because the kundalini chakra is darkened by its low subtle energy intake.

While the intellect and mind carry out their impulsive functions, the causal energy waits for the compressed impressions to reach it. These go to it automatically. It receives these, processes them by matching them to energies in itself, and then sends out desire energies into the subtle body. These new desires cause the intellect and mind to become enthusiastic about pursuing new or old sense objects. The causal body in relationship to the subtle form is similar to a blind man's relationship to his servants or a prisoner's relationship to a morning guard who briefs him on what happens outside the prison. Because of its dependence on the subtle body, the causal form develops massive ignorance, which cause the spirit to transmigrate haphazardly.

December 23, 2001

Babaji

He said, "At this time, we ask that these be put in the Ganges. What need is there when you have direct perception?"

Remark:

Babaji spoke of the need for materially-formed deities.

This request of his does not mean that a yogi should emerge all deities in a river. It means rather that by virtue of being able to perceive objects in the sky of consciousness, a yogi may get a direct connection in the supernatural world. That yogi does not depend solely on materially-formed deities. He does respect these but he is not restricted to Deity Worship on this side of existence.

December 24, 2001

Yogeshwarananda

On this day, Yogesh beamed a light through my brahmrandra. It travelled through my physical eyes into the physical world. It shine on a young girl and her mother."

Remark:

I did not ask the yogi as to why he shined on the females.

Two days later, he showed the operation of the light. It was the vision of the imagination in the form of a psychic searchlight beam, focusing in and through the mind. It is activated on the basis of whimsical attractions in the case of ordinary people. By supreme dispassion, a yogi learns how to control it so that it works in his interest to research the objects in the sky of consciousness.

December 30, 2001

Shiva

He said, "I chant, *Om Narayanaya namah.*"

Remark:

Agastya Muni then told me to chant, *Om Namah Shivaya.*

December 31, 2001

Shiva

He said, "So long as the sensual energy is in conflict, one will fall away from spirituality repeatedly. It will again disagree with reality and cause false perceptions."

December 31, 2001

Shiva / Yogeshwarananda

Under their influence I did this technique.

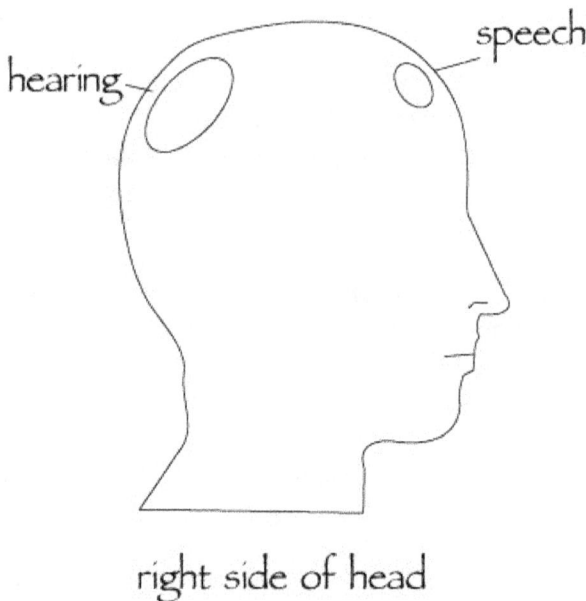

right side of head

January 1, 2002

Yogeshwarananda

He showed that pranavision is used by human beings when they enjoy the climax of sexual intercourse. If during intercourse, a human being focuses on the intense pleasure which is felt in the groin area and which spreads all over the body, that person would be experiencing pranavision.

Yogesh showed this experience through a memory channel in my sexual organ.

January 2, 2002

Yogeshwarananda

He gave a technique for taking the intellect down the sushumna passage. As the intellect descends, the chakras through which it passes shrinks and converts into disc.

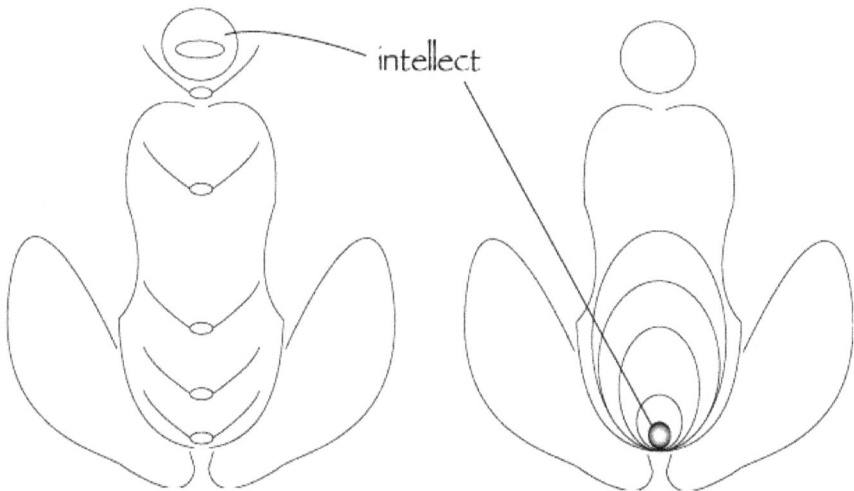

intellect

January 6, 2002

Yogeshwarananda

He said, "First control its whimsical focusing power. Then you may develop deliberate power. When it is exhausted, it cannot be focused, even by itself or its impulsions. It has to be energized. Patanjali suggested the stoppage of its vrittis or usual operations; the process of nirodhah restraint.

Remark:

This has to do with the intellect's control in the 6th stage of yoga practice, that of dharana deliberate transcendence focus.

January 8, 2002

Yogeshwarananda

He gave a technique for the focusing element in meditation. This involved the sense of touch or feeling, which is the most primitive of the senses. This is rooted at the base chakra. At the same chakra, there is a smelling sense. When one descends to that chakra, it does not activate its sensual energy unless one has an odor.

One may sit in lotus posture and focus on the base chakra. After some time one may find that the area where the nose curls under is a coordinate point. If one focuses on the base chakra after sensing this, one will gradually see brownish light.

January 10, 2002

Shiva

This was in the afternoon. Usually I was too tired to sit in lotus posture but Yogesh taught a fatigue-absorbing technique where the pains and aches of the muscles are used to focus the mind into the psyche.

January 11, 2002

Yogeshwarananda

He showed a meditation that is done in the head alone. That is in the head of the subtle body. This is done without involvement of the kundalini. It can be done effectively only if the kundalini was cleared, so that none of its chakras has dark areas. This type of meditation is in preparation for focusing within the developed brahmrandra.

January 12, 2002

Yogeshwarananda

He showed a technique for pulling kundalini into the causal body. This had to do with getting away from the causal body's dominance.

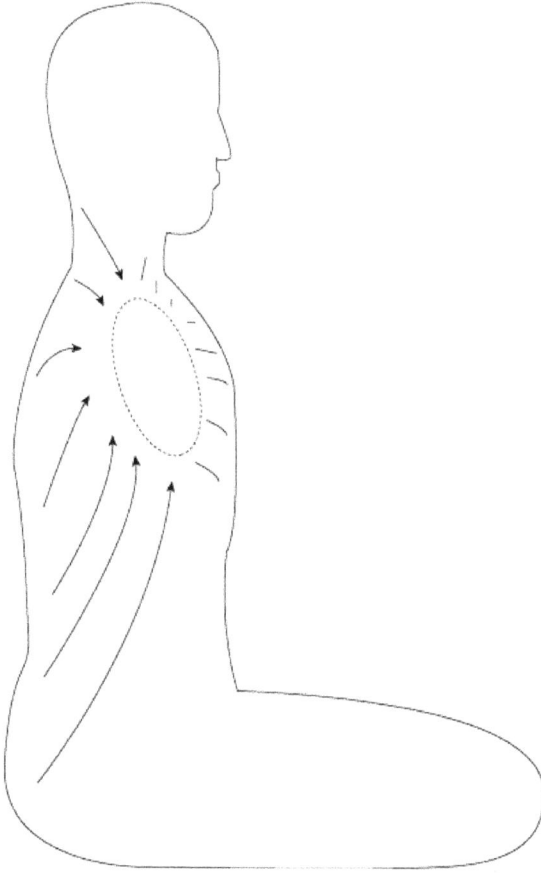

January 13, 2002

On this day I had communication with Yogesh. I lost touch with him because I associated with some non-yogis. Whenever one associates with such persons, one lose focus on yoga, one regresses. Yogesh gave me a practice for banishing kundalini chakra. He indicated that kundalini is derived from the passionate focusing force

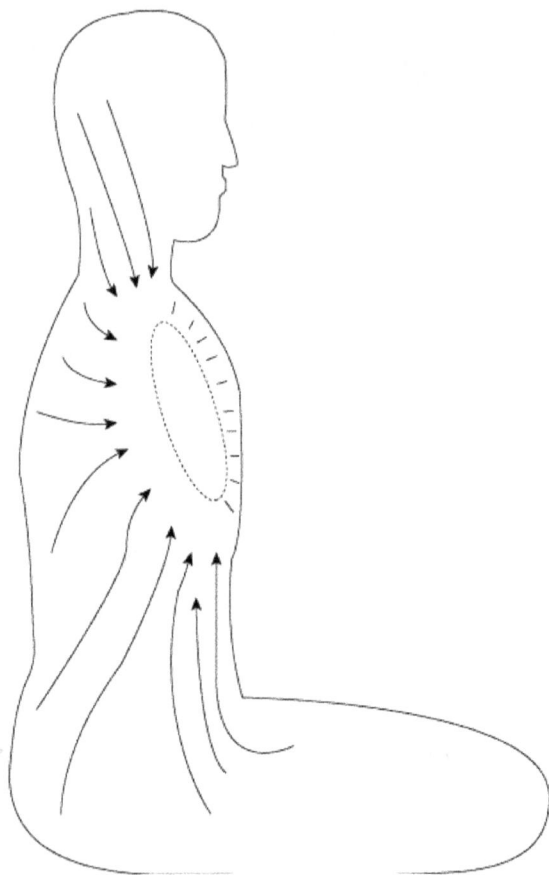

January 13, 2002

On this day, somehow, my subtle body slipped into a parallel world. In that place there were no radios, nor television. There were some primitive cars, one or two, not many.

The women were dressed in brightly colored Indian saris.

Some men drank a liquor but it did not make them boisterous. Some smoked a type of tobacco. There I saw the subtle body of a lady I knew from this earthly place. In that dimension she did not recognize that I was from this world. While here, she usually regards me as a potential lover; there she related to me as her brother.

The place was a parallel dimension, located somewhere in the Gobi desert of this world. There were some deities of Shiva and a few of Ganesh. Most of the people used bodies between 19 and 50 years of age. There were no bodies older than 50 and none younger than 19. There was no written language. The people seem to have no spiritual aspirations and very little political awareness.

Sometimes, after the death of one's physical form, one slips into such a dimension permanently. One loses the memory of the past life on earth, and assumes that place to be the only existence. One then lives there for some time, until one again slips into another world.

January 17, 2002

Yogeshwarananda / Shiva

Under their influence I realized that attachment to excitement results in a slowness in yoga progress and a lack of confidence, due to inability to detect small progressions. A yogi should appreciate small results. If one is habituated to excitements, he will over-look small progressions. His hankering for big results will cause him to be discouraged.

January 19, 2002

Hanuman

He instructed that I bow to the deity of the lotus posture (Padmasana Devi).

Remark:

This is done by assuming easy pose. Then using the right hand to grab the instep of the left foot. Pull the left foot up using hands to pull to the toes. Do breath-infusion. Hold breath when body is sufficiently charged. Bow head to big toe.

This is done first with left leg on right thigh. Then it is done with right leg on left thigh. When right foot is on left thigh, right hands grab right toes and pull them up and breathing is done. Then breath is held and one bows head to touch big toe of right foot.

January 19, 2002

Hanuman

He gave a monkey-body reform posture. This was originally given to Hanuman by Agastya. Jambavan also practiced this to reform the animal form he used.

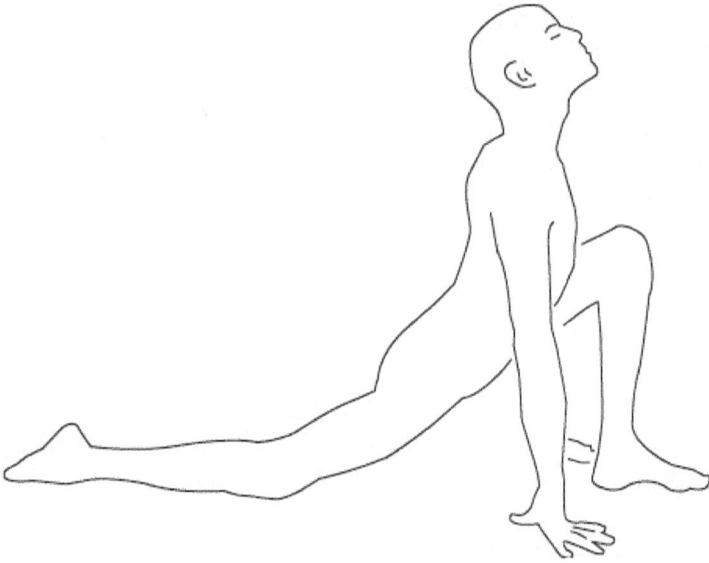

January 19, 2002

Yogeshwarananda

He initiated me into middle kundalini. This was because my celibacy practice reached a stage where the energy from the kanda bulb was reaching up to my neck. The middle passage for kundalini is when that energy travels through the center of the subtle form, as contrasted to moving up the spine or moving near the front of the body. When this energy is seen, it is like looking through a dark tunnel with a tiny hole at the far end.

While I did this technique, I happen to share in a memory of an experience Yogesh had when he used a physical body and did austerities. Once in a cave he was approached by a black bear. He threw fire at the animal. Its hairs ignited and burnt the creature's body to death. I saw this in his memory when I did that exercise. It was due to the sharing of my psyche with him.

Later on Yogesh told me that when he had the encounter with the black bear, he practiced a similar technique and reached the same stage of advancement.

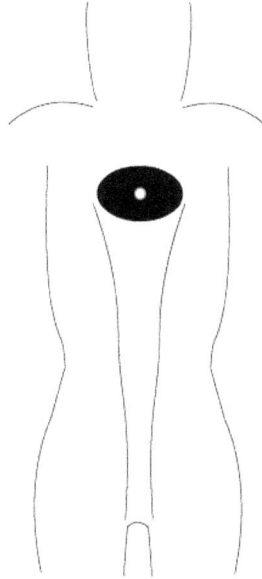

Yogeshwarananda

He showed the chest kanda, which is the source of the nadis that are distributed through the subtle body. Shivananda was the one who first distributed a diagram of those nadis.

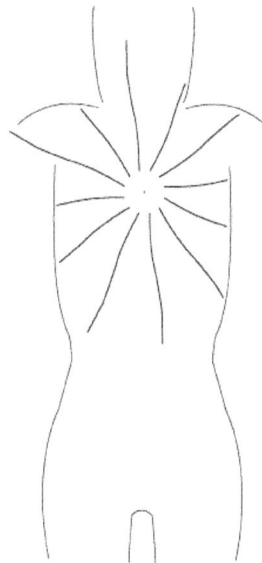

January 23, 2002

Yogeshwarananda

He showed long pranavision, which is used from the causal body. It is beamed through the subtle form and can reach into the physical body.

January 23, 2002

Yogeshwarananda

He said, "Tratak is for this."

Remark:

This was for developing the long pranavision, using the optic sense in other directions and turning it inwards.

January 26, 2002

Yogeshwarananda

He showed a tratak application, which is the moon-dish cosmic energy intake.

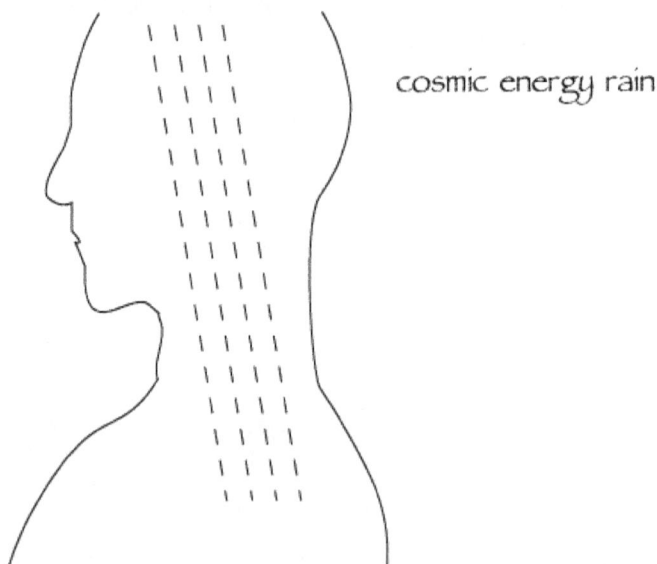

cosmic energy rain

January 28, 2002

Yogeshwarananda

He gave a causal body hand gesture mudra.

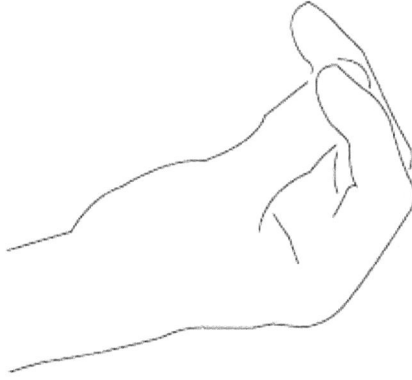

January 29, 2002

Yogeshwarananda

He gave an inside tratak procedure which widens supernatural vision. It is like seeing through a wide beam of pouring light.

January 30, 2002

Yogeshwarananda

He gave a long pranavision used with tratak and directed to the causal level. It is like seeing through a stream of vision energy which is surcharged with subtle energy molecules.

Tratak is a practice of sitting and staring into nowhere. But they are different types of tratak depending on the type of body used and the type of seeing done.

January 31, 2002

Yogeshwarananda

He showed the connection between the causal body and the sushumna.

When one does bhastrika with an intense session, concentrating on the lung, then in the causal body energy spreads and joins with the spinal force, the kundalini chakra. The causal energy is usually blueish. The spinal energy is usually white-yellowish

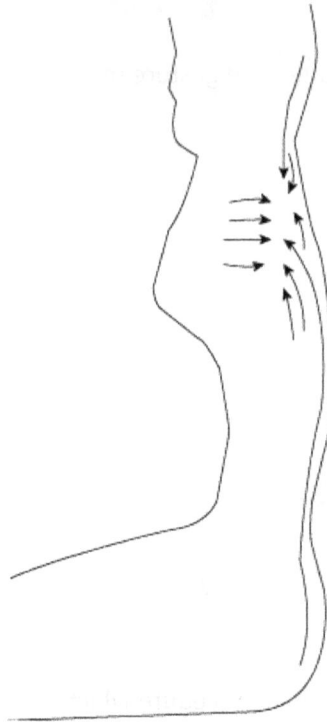

February 5, 2002

Yogeshwarananda

He said, "Control the imagination faculty and the visualization power. Do not allow it free rein. Gradually it can be regulated. Look at how it automatically expands ideas and how it stops by the core-self's influence."

He said further, "The deliberate and impulsive usages of the imagination faculty in reference to the gross level or lower subtle world, is inversely proportionate to its usage in the higher subtle and causal levels."

February 6, 2002

Yogeshwarananda

He showed how the different senses automatically focus regardless of the desire of the self. Usually their actions contravene spiritual progress.

Remark:

One may notice the actions of the senses in all undertakings, in visual perception, in hearing activities, in touching sensation, in smelling and in tasting. A yogi should be observant.

February 12, 2002

Yogesh discussed with me what he meant by a subtle body without a kundalini force. He spoke of how a yogin stayed on the causal level for millions of years, never taking any subtle or gross mundane forms.

energy from
cosmic intellect

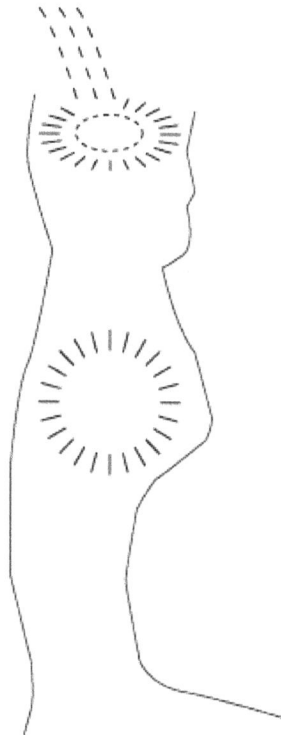

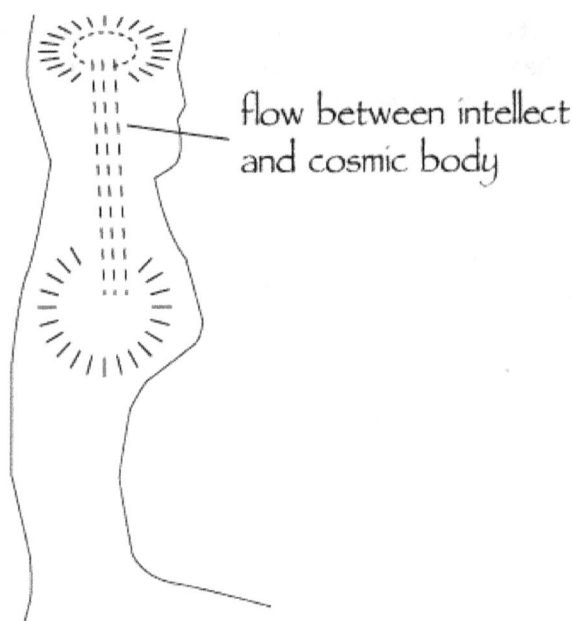

flow between intellect and cosmic body

February 15, 2002

Yogesh showed an anti-social subtle body. Such a body is attained by yogins who have not achieved the causal level, but who are advanced enough to detach themselves from the need for rebirth. Such yogins got rid of their kundalini chakra. They became immune to the course of birth and death.

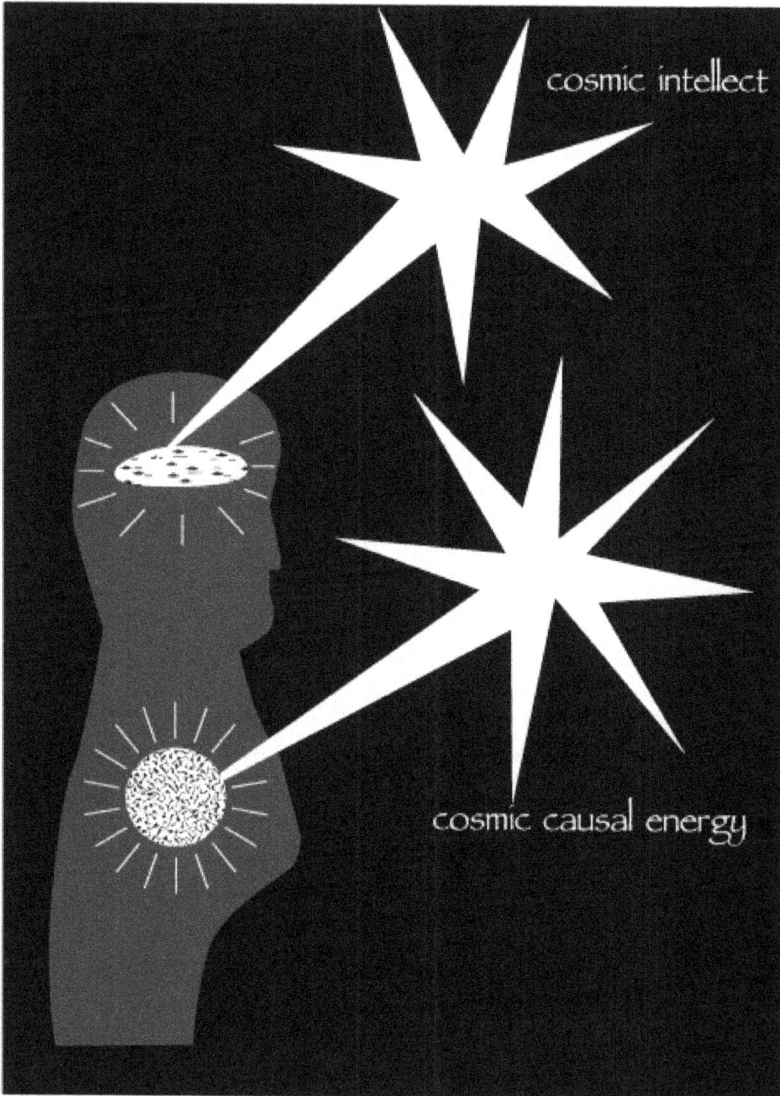

February 16, 2002

Yogeshwarananda

He showed a front thigh pump-in, air clearance procedure. As one does this one uses long pranavision to look through the subtle thigh. Those who did not developed pranavision, need not despair. They should keep the eyes closed while doing postures and focus into the muscles and nerves of the thigh. Over a time, one will develop pranavision as a matter of course.

infuse air into thighs

hands brace under hips

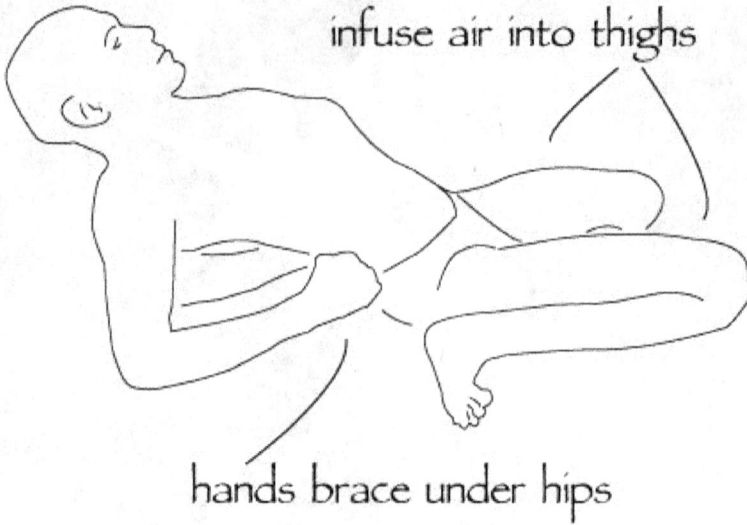

Yogeshwarananda

He insisted that I make this notation: The life force as subtle polarized energy keeps working at all times in a living body, even in deep absorption as he experienced.

Remark:

I noticed that if I work in the later afternoon, after working all day, and if I do not eat around 2 or 3 in the afternoon, there develops in the abdomen a wind pain at about 4:30 to 7:30 p.m. This wind pain may stay in the body all night on occasion. Yogesh explained it in this way:

"Due to energy working on an empty abdomen, it produces air from its subtle activity. By body heat this air expands and causes pain. If the person eats timely, there is no pain, since the digestive energy would work into the food. As soon as one works overtime, the energy senses that and tries to digest food. If there is no food, heated air is created. This expands and creates wind pains."

February 22, 2002

Yogeshwarananda

He stated, "The intellect takes sensual indications and formulated visions on the basis of past experiences. If not checked, this causes the intellect to imagine sensual satisfactions. These contemplations ruin the attempts at mystic focus and meditation. It rules out the possibility of higher yoga."

Remark:

Yogesh said this to me from within my brahmrandra, while I travelled on a small airplane. He trained me in how to deflect the intellect from its impulsive habits which are antagonistic to higher yoga. The situation was this:

I was in a small blue and white plane. After absorbing the impressions of the colors, the intellect conceived of it in relation to a blue sky with white clouds over a landscape. This caused a defocus from reading a spiritual book. It was cloudy. The plane travelled at 10,000 feet in thick clouds. Being low-powered, the aircraft could not travel at a higher altitude. The intellect developed a dissatisfaction because it was cloudy. It could not complete its plan for the vision of a clear blue sky, with some clouds and clear spaces to see the land below.

Instead of abandoning the idea, it prompted the eyes to stay alert for any possible break in the clouds. This required more psychological energy as the vision energy kept pouring out of the psyche in expectation for an opening in the clouds. Yogesh alerted me that this is the way the intellect operates in its impulsive mode. A yogi should change this or be content with a mediocre yoga practice and with little results.

February 22, 2002

Yogeshwarananda

He showed the intellect in an oblong balloon shape.

Yogesh explained that the senses must be quieted by proper rest, breath-infusion and honest practice to stop pursuing objects. If this is done, the sensual orbs do not shoot their hunting energies impulsively. They remain still as little energy balls in dormancy.

He showed how the intellect and core-self reflect on the feeling energy, the emotional force, just as if the feelings were a mirror. This shows as a crystal light like a glistening white star.

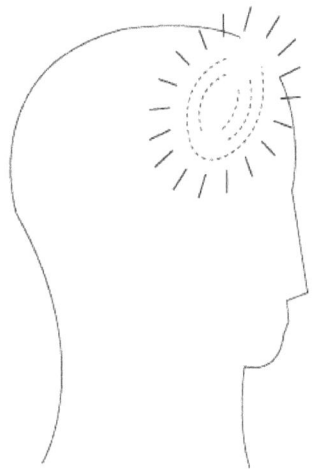

March 1, 2002

Yogeshwarananda

He showed a meeting of light and light. This was my individual intellect meeting with the cosmic intellect.

Remark:

This is an important stage of advancement for a yogin. It occurs after he makes some progress with the pratyahar sense withdrawal. I will explain something about this. Yogesh introduced this but it was something far beyond the much-advertised third eye vision. This has nothing to do with the brow chakra or the vision that opens between the eyebrows. It is an entirely different perception.

As in all cases, even if a yogi helps one to open a higher vision, still if one does not have the advancement to sustain it, it will vanish. One will have to work to establish it. By work, I mean advance further in the austerities and move into a more conducive lifestyle that facilitates absorption practice.

When the intellect becomes quiescent in meditation, and when the entry to sky of consciousness clears, so that the darkness or speckled darkness within the head dissipates and there is supernatural light, then automatically one perceives a bright reservoir of supernatural light which emits a ray in contact with one's individual intellect.

A question arises as to whether the individual intellect remains in contact with the cosmic intellect. The answer is that it does not remain in contact because it is separated by passionate energy, blocked off, surrounded as it was by the passionate force. Krishna called that covering power the kamarupa, which He stated was the perpetual enemy of the living being.

श्रीभगवानुवाच
काम एष क्रोध एष
रजोगुणसमुद्भवः।
महाशनो महापाप्मा
विद्ध्येनमिह वैरिणम्
॥३.३७॥

śrībhagavānuvāca
kāma eṣa krodha eṣa
rajoguṇasamudbhavaḥ
mahāśano mahāpāpmā
viddhyenamiha vairiṇam

śri bhagavān — the Blessed Lord; uvāca — said; kāma — craving; eṣa — this; krodha — anger; eṣa — this; rajoguṇasamudbhavaḥ = rajo (rajaḥ) — passion + guṇa — emotion + samudbhavaḥ — source; mahāśano (mahāśanaḥ) = mahā — great + aśana — consuming power; mahāpāpmā = mahā — much + pāpmā — damage; viddhyenam = viddhi — recognize + enam — this; iha — in this case; vairiṇam — enemy

The Blessed Lord said: This force is craving. This power is anger. The passionate emotion is the source. It has a great consuming power and does much damage. Recognize it as the enemy in this case. (Bhagavad Gita 3.37)

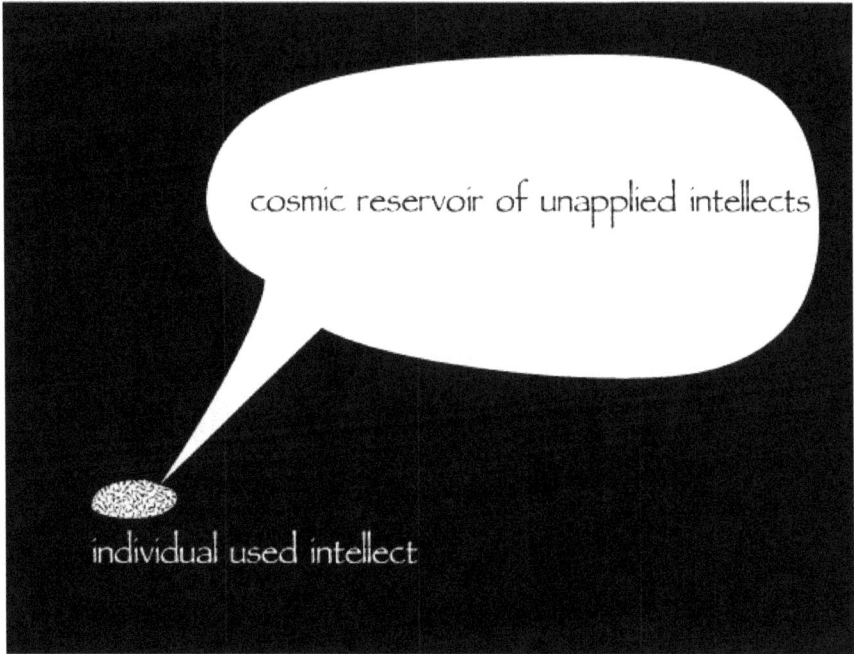

Usually the mind field is surrounded by passionate energy. The intellect and the sensual orbs are contained in that mind field. The ahankara sense of initiative is linked to the intellect.

The passionate energy described by Krishna in those verses is the fine chitta energy which has oozed over into the subtle form. It is not the degraded course passionate force which is felt as lust for sexual indulgence or as greed for objects. That lusty energy is a lower level of the passionate force.

March 1, 2002

Yogeshwarananda

He showed a front kundalini which is spread downwards.

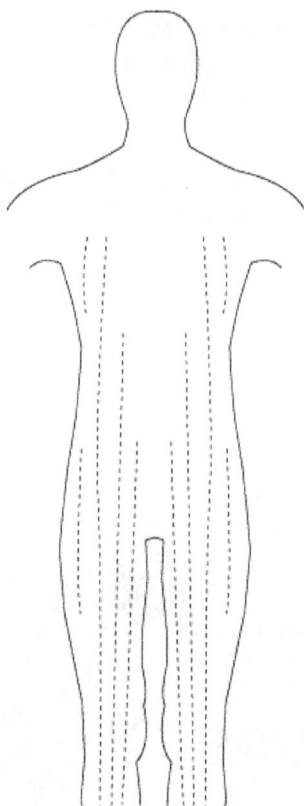

March 2, 2002

Yogeshwarananda

He showed a connection to the cosmic energy. There was a thin partition between the cosmic intellect energy and the feelings-force, which is a more refined form of subtle potency.

intellect energy (buddhi)   feelings force (chitta)

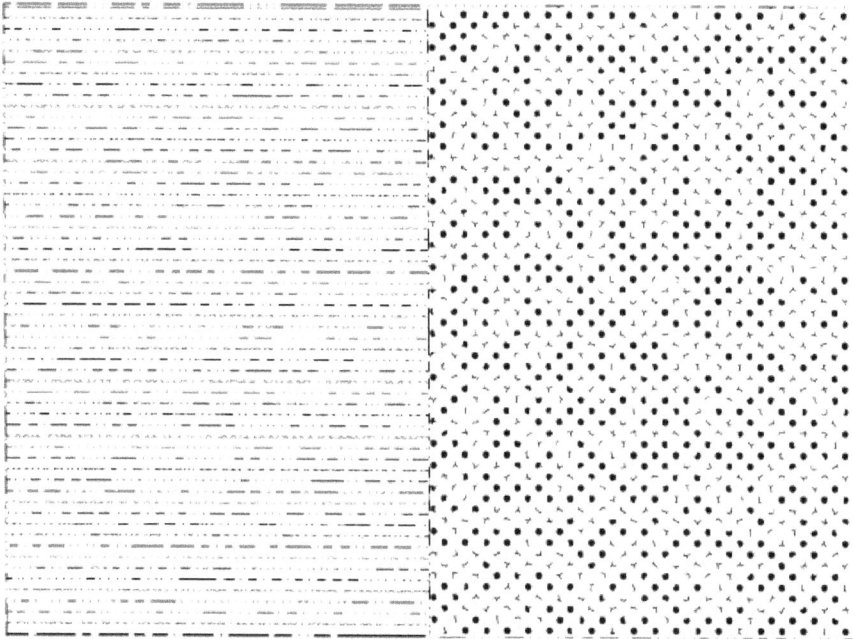

March 3, 2002

Yogeshwarananda

He showed a neck nadi in the subtle body. He showed that the hormonal energy can be pulled directly without having to go through the genitals, without receiving a sexual charge.

When doing kundalini yoga one becomes concerned with pulling up the sexually-charged energy which is funneled through the testes in the male forms and the ovaries in the female ones. However when one completed kundalini yoga, one practices celibacy yoga. When that is perfected, one eliminates the sexually-charged energy. Then one embarks on purity-of-the-psyche, atma vishuddha yoga.

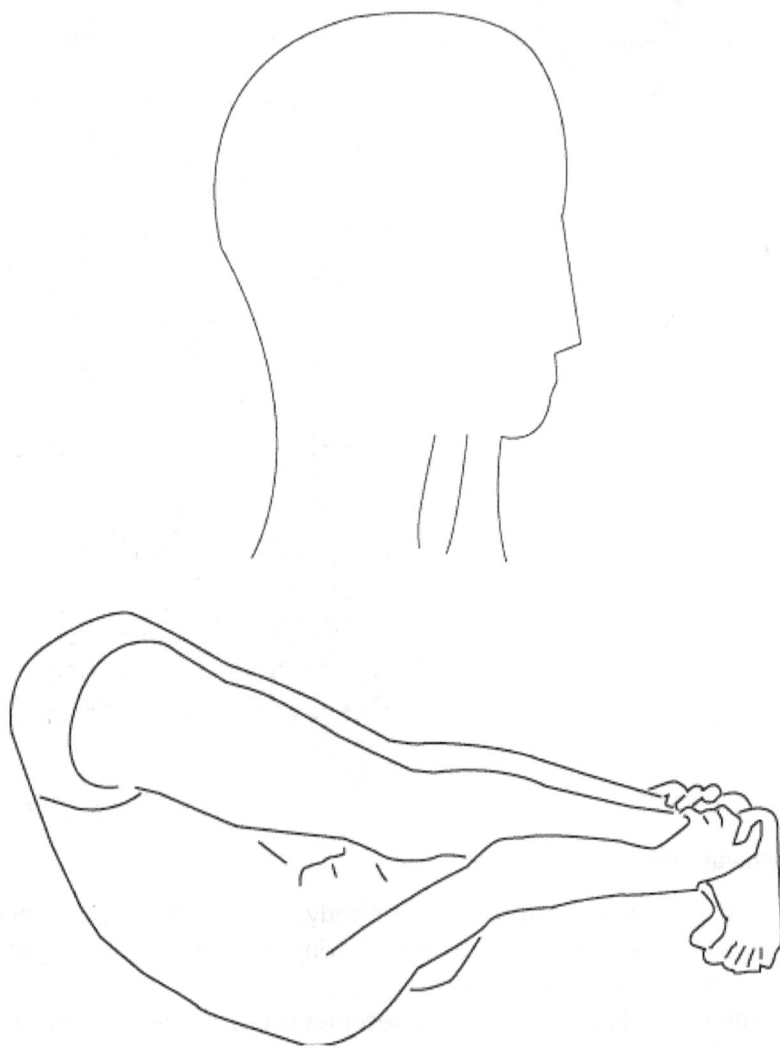

Mar 4, 2002
Yogesh was there while I did this posture. One should note that hatha yoga is important in these practices. One should not give up hatha yoga feeling that it is merely a physical exercise.

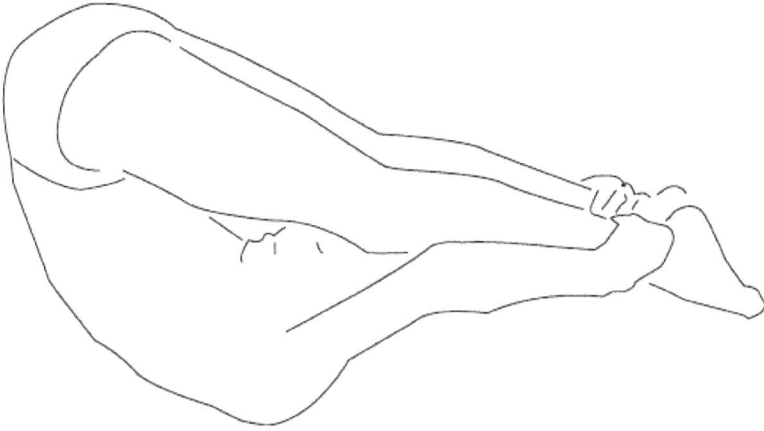

March 5, 2002

Yogeshwarananda

On this day, I took the intellect down to the base cavern, the lowest of the chakras in the kundalini system. That cavern seems like a large space, like a huge capsule-shaped metal tank. It is a chamber for converting the subtle material elements (tan matras) into feelings-energy.

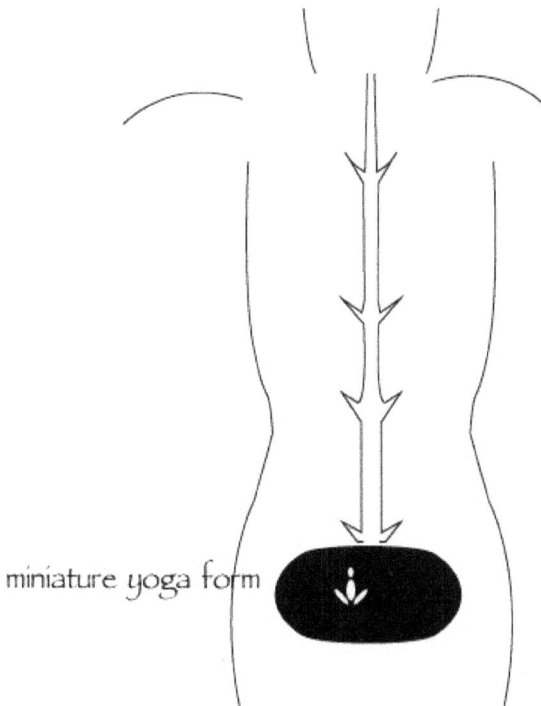

miniature yoga form

When one takes the intellect down into the base chamber, one may feel as if one entered a dark place, like inside a large metal tank which has no opening in which light cannot penetrate. However, one should not be scared. The intellect detects the subtle material elements there, particularly the subtle but heavier invisible energy from which solid matter is formed. In that place the intellect senses in all directions but it has a dimmer glow than the one it radiates when it is in the subtle head.

March 6, 2002

Yogeshwarananda

By his grace I was shown the brightness of the intellect as it is reflected on an astral material. It shun like sunshine reflected on glass. I realized that it was a reflected glare. It was a crystal clear brilliant light.

On this day I experienced the intellect in connection with the cosmic intellect which was overhead. That experience was not felt for very long. After a short time, the shrouding influence of the passionate energy enclosed the intellect and the supernatural perception ceased.

March 6, 2002

Yogeshwarananda

As I drove a car, I heard him speak in my brahmrandra. He said, "One should not subject the mind to excitement."

Krishna of Radha-Shyamasundara deities.

He said, "Forget the critics. Be successful as a yogi-devotee.

March 7, 2002

Yogeshwarananda

He said, "The noon session would accelerate the practice. Do not let go of it entirely."

Remark:

This was suggested since my employment made it impossible for me to do a noon session of exercises on most days. Yogeshwarananda was of the opinion that whatever little I could do, would accelerate progress."

March 8, 2002

Yogeshwarananda

He said, "The conceiving power is the same instrument that will be used for supernatural insight. Its material usage is inversely related to its usage as supernatural vision. It works by seeing, hearing and sensing in other ways. It converts those sensual impressions into energy markings for storage and reference. This causes the acquirement of more desires.

Remark:

This is an example of a detailed instruction given by Yogesh when he stayed in my brahmrandra. I saw a pad on the road as I drove a vehicle. The intellect formed a conception of that pad as being useful. It created an influence to induce my psyche to see the pad as a desired item. It wanted me to endorse an action for my body to pick up the pad. Yogesh observed that operation of my intellect as I looked at the pad. He made the remark to teach about intellect yoga.

March 9, 2002

Shiva

He showed that the nurturing subtle energy settle as milk in females and as white milky semen in males. This is before sexual overtones of enjoyment by organ contact are developed in the psyche. It occurs by proximity. It stops by the lack of the same proximity.

March 9, 2002

Yogeshwarananda

He gave a technique where there is a spike-shaped kundalini force under the intellect organ. Sometimes, this spike disappears and the intellect becomes connected with the cosmic intellect. This cannot be forced by the yogi. He must practice and put his psyche in a certain vibration, then he may experience the connection with the cosmic intellect.

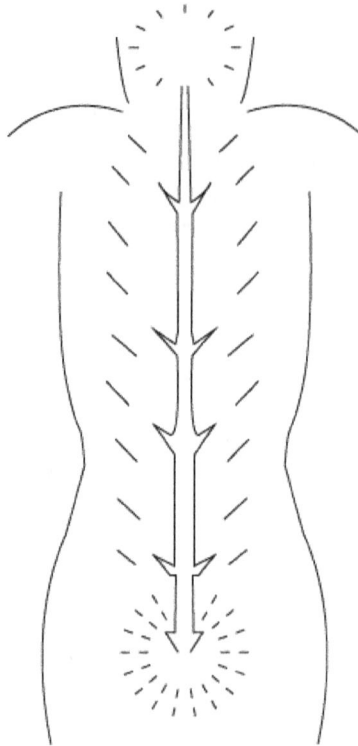

March 10, 2002

Yogeshwarananda

He showed a non-outgoing tratak.

Tratak is done by sitting in a dark room or even in a well-lit area, and staring off into nowhere. If the eyelids are open the eyes may burn or water after some time. If they do, one can close the lids for a time and then re-open them. If the practice of staring blankly is done with closed eyelids one can do tratak by feeling the optic power and feeling it pouring through the closed eyelids. Sometimes when doing this practice, one may find that the flow of energy through each eye vanishes, and just one pouring of energy comes through the area between the eyes.

Babaji, using Lahiri as his agent encouraged some yogis to popularize the brow chakra or the single flow of the optic power of the subtle body. The practice of focusing between the eyebrows is also mentioned in the Bhagavad Gita, which proves that it was standard in the time of Krishna.

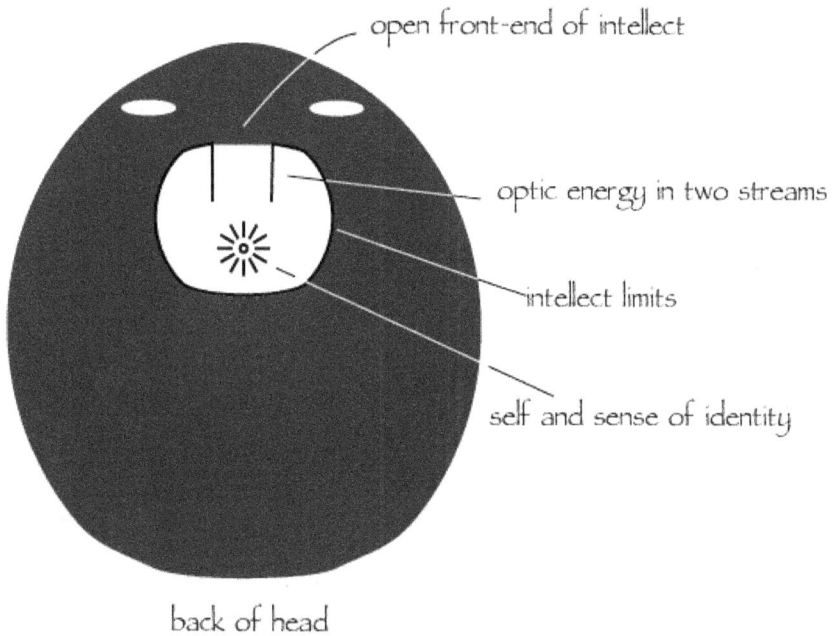

open front-end of intellect

optic energy in two streams

intellect limits

self and sense of identity

back of head

March 12, 2002

Yogeshwarananda / Shiva

On this day, by their combined grace, I moved my intellect in reference to the cosmic intellect. It did not last long but the experience gave some idea of how some great yogins exist in the chit akash, the sky of consciousness. I moved with the cosmic intellect to my right. Sometimes I was joined to the vast effulgence of it. Sometimes I was disconnected. The secret is prashanta which means to be free from anxieties. This means that the yogi abandons social and cultural responsibilities. He throws the social liabilities away.

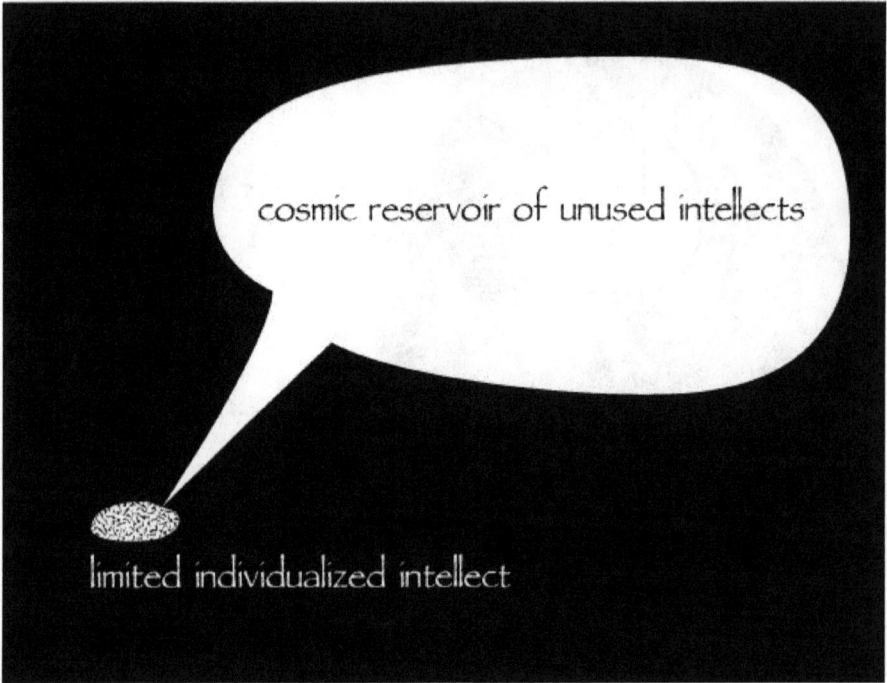

Part 6

Yogeshwarananda / Shiva

Under their influence, I realized that the activities of the intellect are powered by the intellect's absorption of the core-self's power. When the intellect and core are in connection, the core becomes attentive to the selections of the intellect. The core loses discrimination and adopts the ratings of the intellect.

The intellect's profile is always the same, which is to act to procure sensuality. This is because the intellect feels that its mission is to fulfill desires. However the desires are fed into the subtle form from the causal level in a very sneaky way, which is hard for the core-self to detect or even understand. The core is to an extent naive and relaxed by nature. It has a non-vigilant mood which it likes to· remain in. Thus the intellect usually takes the position as the director of the activities of the psyche.

One can just imagine the disadvantaged position, because at any time, one may discover the self in a dimension where it spends an entire life time or many life times, endorsing the operations of the intellect.

The above realization occurred because Yogesh came to my brahmrandra and found that I went into another dimension. Somehow I transferred into a parallel world. When he looked he saw that I was involved with a female in a sexual way. He beamed in some reformative energy to retrieve me. At the time, I became aware of him. I regained my conscience from this side of existence and got out of that parallel world.

Shiva was aware of the force that caused my subtle body to be transferred to that parallel place but he did nothing to stop the influence. I feel that he thought it was alright since he knew that Yogesh would observe and rescue me. Shiva must have desired that I learn a good lesson from the experience.

At the date of typing this remark, I still have not understood exactly the process of transferal to the parallel world. Perhaps in time, before I have to leave this body permanently, I may give an explanation. It is said that Brahma once blanked out the existence of some cowherd boys who were not in a spiritual category which was higher than Brahma's. They were still within his jurisdictional powers even though they were friends of Krishna. However it is not easy to know who or what force, causes one to slip into a parallel world. The danger is that one may slip into one at the time of departure from the body and one may be stuck there for thousands of years, just as we may be transmigrating in this earthly dimension in the same way.

Somehow when I slipped over into that world, I met a lady who was a girl friend of a fake monk in this world. She too slipped over somehow. In that world, she had a white-colored body, even though in this one, she uses a black one. The subtle body I used was so sexually-inclined that I found myself eating her thighs and sexual parts. In other words, that is the way of life in that parallel place. Things that we do here for perverted pleasures were normal occurrences here. Yogesh observed that association and rescued me.

There are many persons who take monk status in a disciplic succession which claims affiliation with Krishna. Many of these renunciants do no yoga. When they take monastic vows they get a mantra from the authority but it does nothing to protect them from female association. Subsequently they accept many women disciples just by as their predecessors did, even though strictly speaking a monk is not supposed to do that. If he has to direct females, he should appoint an advanced father to relate to them on his behalf. However the modern monks, especially the ones using Western bodies and the Indian ones who have many Western disciples, take women disciples. Most of them have sexual intercourses with these women in the astral world. Due to ignorance of their subtle activities, they consider themselves to be celibate.

The woman I was with in that parallel world, was introduced by one such monk who was aware of his sexual attraction to her. I discussed this with him. Hypocrite that he is, he still flashed himself on others, as a celibate authority.

March 14, 2002

Yogeshwarananda

He explained that some yogis, change their intellects. They cause theirs to re-enter into the cosmic reservoir of intellects. Then they take new intellects from the reservoir. When I questioned about the changes caused for such yogis, Yogesh explained that the impressions from the intellects transfer to the causal body continually. Thus even if a yogi changes his intellect, still his psyche formats in the same way since the new intellect absorbs the impressions from the causal form.

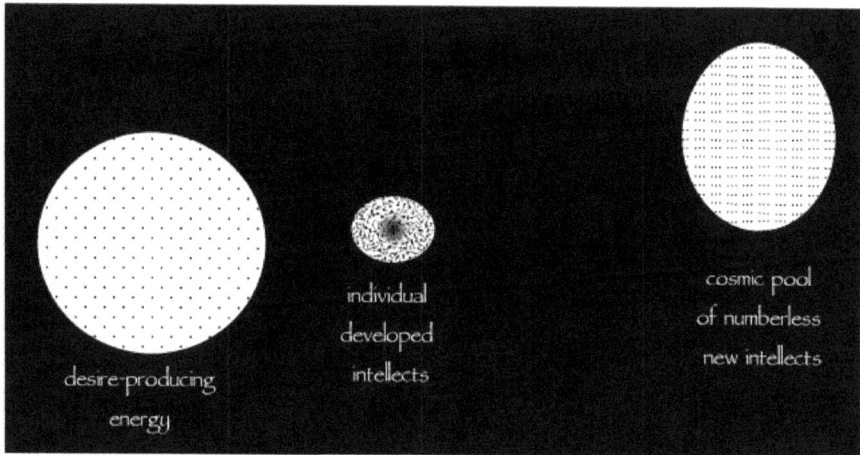

desire-producing
energy

individual
developed
intellects

cosmic pool
of numberless
new intellects

March 14. 2002

On this day I did a new posture. This was used during a session of hatha yoga with breath-infusion.

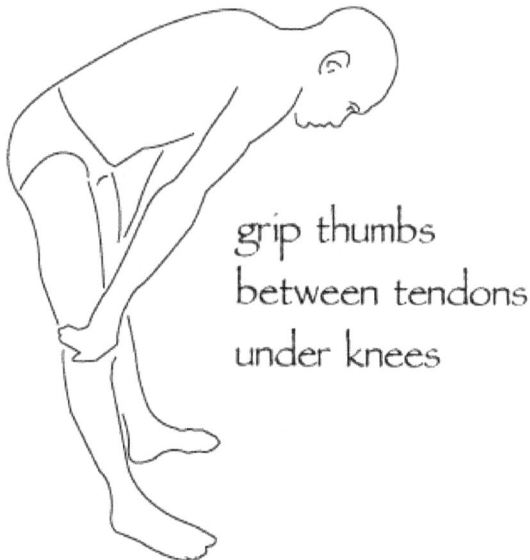

grip thumbs
between tendons
under knees

March 14, 2002

Yogeshwarananda / Shiva

Under their influence I entered the chit akash sky of consciousness through a hole by the right ear in the subtle body. It is a tratak hole.

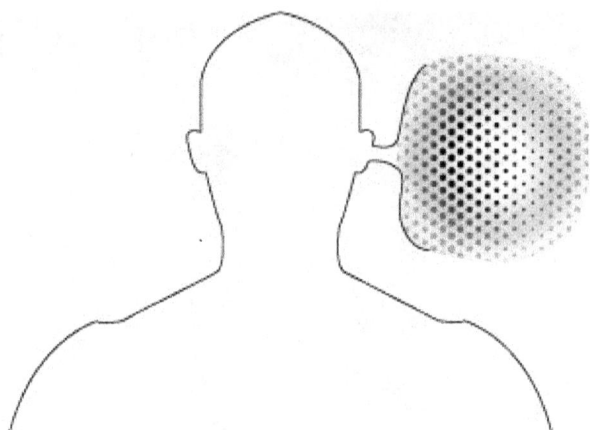

March 15, 2002

Babaji

He showed a brahmrandra eye focus. This is similar to the third eye focus which is done with two physical eyes turned up into the forehead.

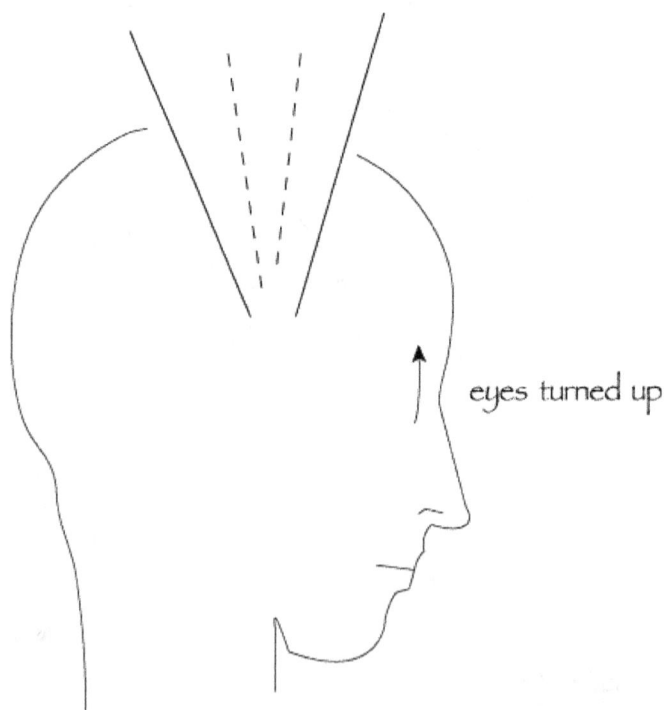

eyes turned up

March 22, 2002

Shiva

He instructed that I take this notation of a technique given by Babaji.

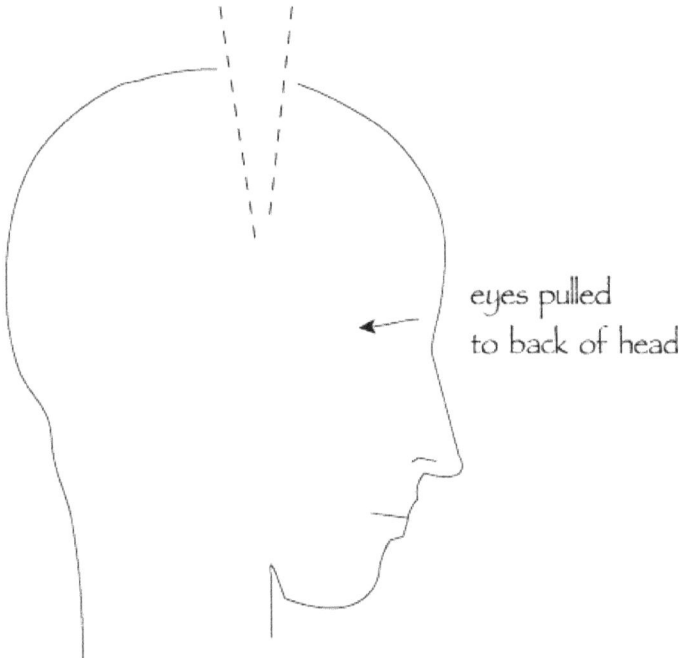

eyes pulled
to back of head

March 23, 2002

Yogeshwarananda

He said, "By taking water instead of air, you support the physical system and put yourself more out of touch with the subtle. Later it will be necessary to support the causal in preference to the subtle. One should know the nutrition of each."

Remark:

There are many half-wits who come to learn yoga. However not everyone can grasp it. Someone may think that he or she can learn yoga and become a great mystic like Babaji, but it is more than that. One should master the practice. Asking questions about the advanced states, will not cause one to be accelerated into it. Practice produces advancement but slowly. The practice must be on-going.

Sometimes a dull-witted person, a basic idiot, who was somewhat successful in cultural life, finds me. Then he wants me to explain the high end of yoga. Such people usually feel that they can reach the advanced stages in a jiffy, and still remain in touch with the cultural world they are so familiar with. But that is not possible. If one wants to shift over to the subtle plane, one can do so if one makes certain sacrifices. One cannot transfer in a half-hearted way. One cannot have both advantages. If we desire to master the subtle side, we should gradually learn how to forsake the gross level. Later if we advance, we may forsake even the subtle side to reach the causal plane. But somehow, the half-wits always ask me about the possibility of adhering to the worship of God on this side of existence and simultaneously reaching God on the other side. That is not possible. You can have one or the other according to how you aspire.

March 24, 2002

Yogeshwarananda

He said, "Sensual energy withdrawal is prompted by sincerity in leaving aside the foods offered by material nature. Some cannot do it."

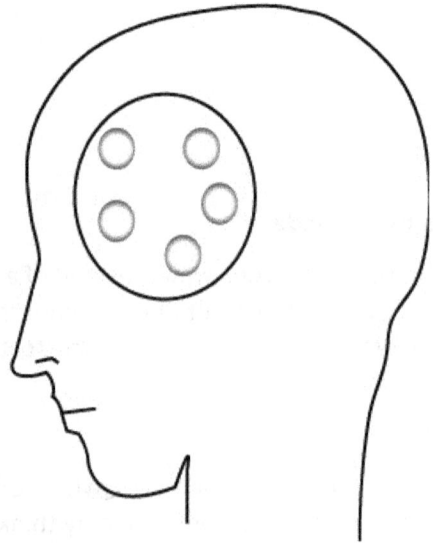

intellect suspends
its activities
orbs are immobilized

March 24, 2002

Babaji

He gave this technique:

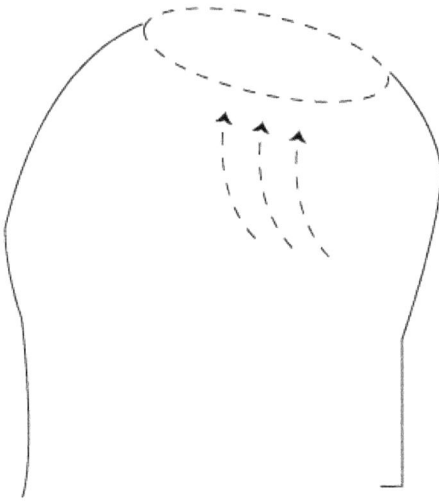

open head crown chakra

intellect focused upward

March 29, 2002·

Yogeshwarananda

He gave two important procedures

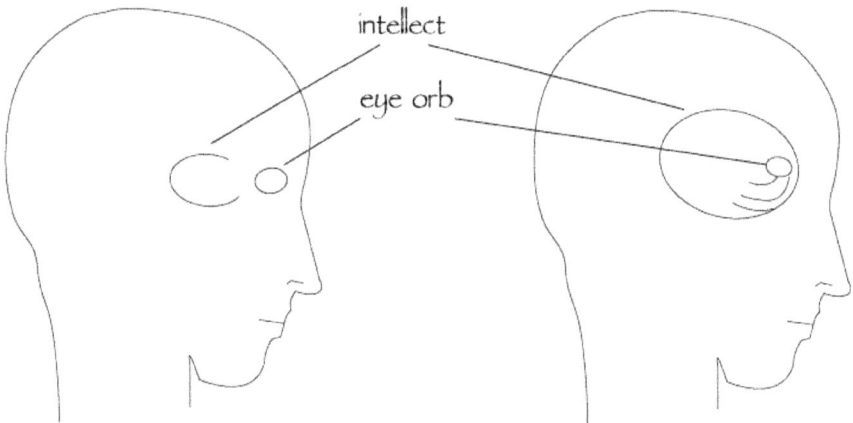

intellect

eye orb

March 31, 2002

Yogeshwarananda

He said," The stoppage of eye contact and related interest, brings a small result in the increase of inner vision. This is due to the cheapness of the value of mundane sensual interest withdrawal. However, any increment is an increase nevertheless. A small progression in yoga has significance. In any case, for success, one needs the small progressions. They accumulate."

April 6, 2002

Yogeshwarananda

He showed how the central orb in the intellect mechanism is interlocked with the vision orb or with any other orb like the hearing orb. This is done automatically. It produces an imagination, a sound concept or a symbol concept in the mind.

April 7, 2002

Yogeshwarananda / Yogi Bhajan

On this day Yogi Bhajan checked on a student, who visited to learn bhastrika breath-infusion. I learnt that method from Yogi Bhajan in 1971. Yogi Bhajan said this about the student, "I will help him to develop the practice."

Remark:

Sometimes a person runs around here and thee, looking for a teacher. All the while a teacher is present by his side in the astral world. Due to a lack of subtle perception, he does not understand that he is accompanied by a great yogin. Subtle perception is important.

Yogesh gave a brahmrandra development mudra hand gesture practice. In this the palms of the hands pull down the soles of the feet. On the subtle level the brahmrandra touches the big toes.

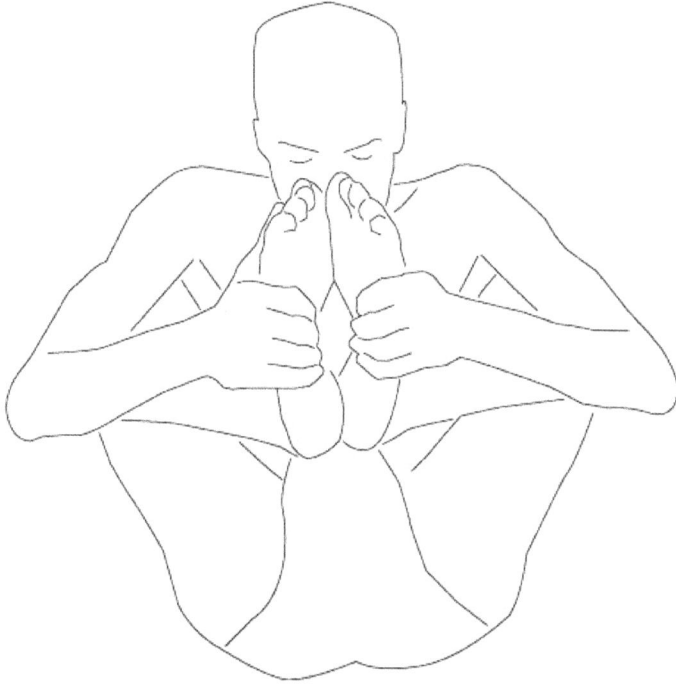

While I did this posture, Ma Durga inspired a yoni stand-up posture. This works on the lips of the female sexual organ for producing a celibate female body.

Sometimes I get such female techniques for either one of two reasons:
- for giving to female ascetics.
- for using on my own body for practice of self-tantric.

Self-tantric is the stage of practice where one does sexual kriyas without a partner. It is the most advanced stage of celibate practice.

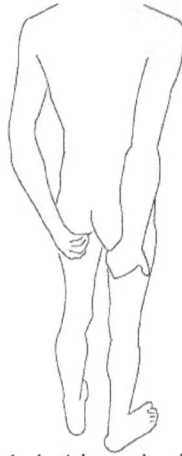

hands hold inside thighs

under buttocks

Yogesh gave a back-of-the-throat neck lock.

For this one applies the usual neck lock which is with the chin drawn back. One puts the hands on either side of the neck with the fingers pointing upwards.

rest hand

on side of neck and face

On this day, a friend met me in the astral world. He requested that I take a young woman for a wife. I rejected his plea because behind the young lady was a line of ancestors, begging for bodies. I already served some ancestors. Whatever little of my life is left, I should use for spiritual retrieval. In addition, the young lady, because she is in a developed country, is habituated to smoking marijuana and using contraceptives. What would I do with such a wife? O what a job it would be to reform such a lady and then to beget bodies for her ancestors? It would use up the rest of my time in this body.

April 9, 2002

Yogeshwarananda

He said, "Stop using the organ."

Remark:

In this case he spoke of the creativity organ in the intellect mechanism in the brain of the subtle body. It is comparable to the sexual organ which is so frequently used for enjoyment. If a yogi stops using the creativity capacity of the intellect, he develops supernatural perception to see objects in the sky of consciousness (chit akash). That is the secret. Unfortunately many of us are so addicted to the creative and visualization powers of the mind, that we cannot free ourselves from those habits. We are attached to this side of existence and to the imaginations which are enacted impulsively or deliberately in our minds, ideas which are in reference to what we experience in the mundane world and its corresponding subtle levels.

April 10, 2002

Shivananda

This yogi came to check my celibate practice, which is something he originally inspired me to take up. He said that the beads of sexual energy in my subtle form were in tact due to a consistent celibacy and due to avoidance of contact with sexual sight-objects

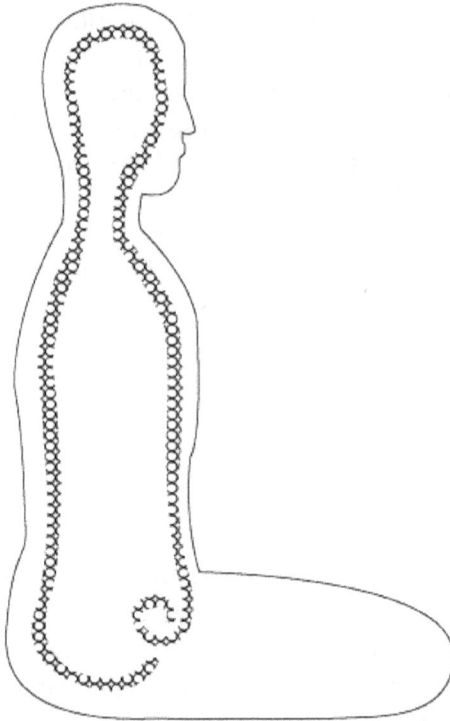

April 11, 2002

Yogeshwarananda

He said, "See! This is transcendence focus (dharana)."

Remark:

During a meditation there was a strong pull of concentration. It was firm and stable with no wavering. It was definite. It was a ray of energy before the brow chakra area. When somehow the sensual energies stop ranting and raving, visualizing and impressioning, then dharana, the 6th stage of yoga, can be practiced by a yogi.

Dharana comes about of its own accord after the yogi performed the correct austerities for a sufficient length of time.

April 13, 2002

Yogeshwarananda

He showed a tratak procedure. In this one uses a stubby focus out of the intellect's edge, instead of a long brow chakra focus. In tratak, one feels the sensing energy pouring out. Sometimes, it pours out for a short distance for an inch or less, and then it disappears, but it continues pouring out on and on for some time. This type of experience is a type of transcendence focus.

April 15, 2002

Yogesh showed how the inner perception of the intellect shifts out when one tries to see through the intellect. This is because by trying to see through it, when one has anxiety energies, one causes the intellect to defocus. It requires a removal of anxiety, a state which is called *shanti* in Sanskrit.

Even though by drugs or another means, one may assume subtle perception, one cannot force the intellect to see supernaturally. The vision into the sky of consciousness can be had by a steady consistent yoga practice, being loyal to the process.

March 17, 2002

Ma. Durga

This goddess inspired a woman's breasts energy technique.

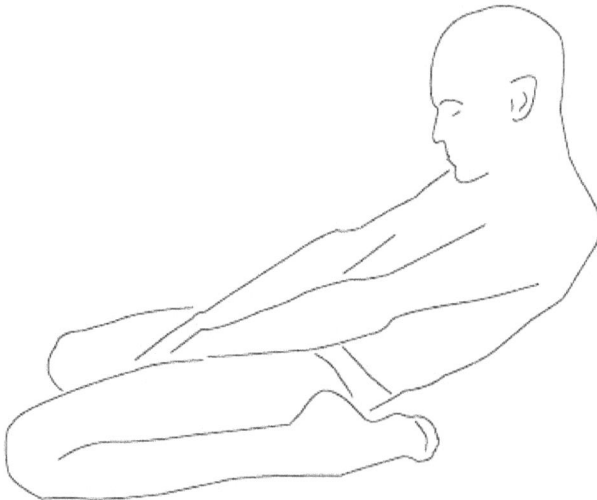

hands on inner thighs
breasts squeezed together

April 17, 2002

Yogeshwarananda

He showed that thoughts are loud like lightning claps heard on a stormy day. These thoughts produce loud sounds near the causal zone. It is a great disturbance. The samskaras or desire impressions, ruin spiritual peace and close spiritual vision.

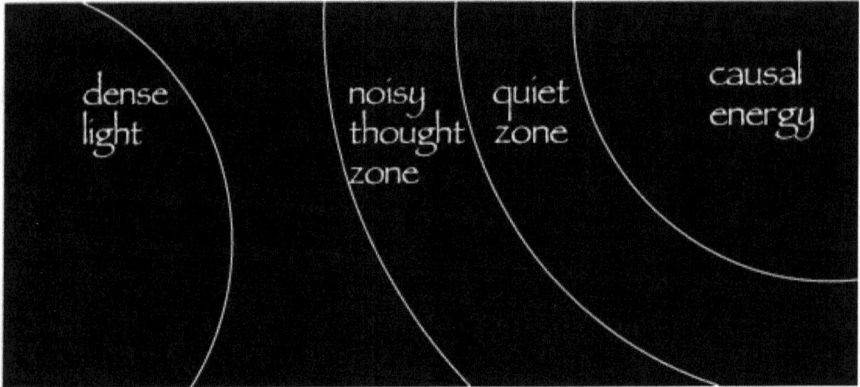

April 18, 2002

Ma Durga

She inspired an ovary/lower intestines pull up.

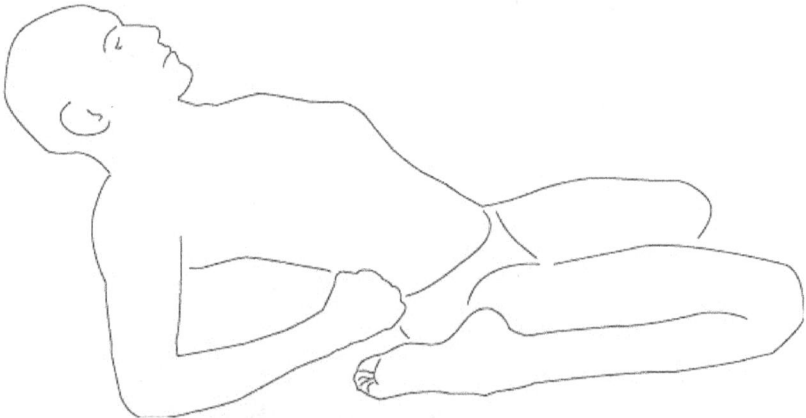

The goddess also gave this pump-down from the thigh-groin area. This is for females.

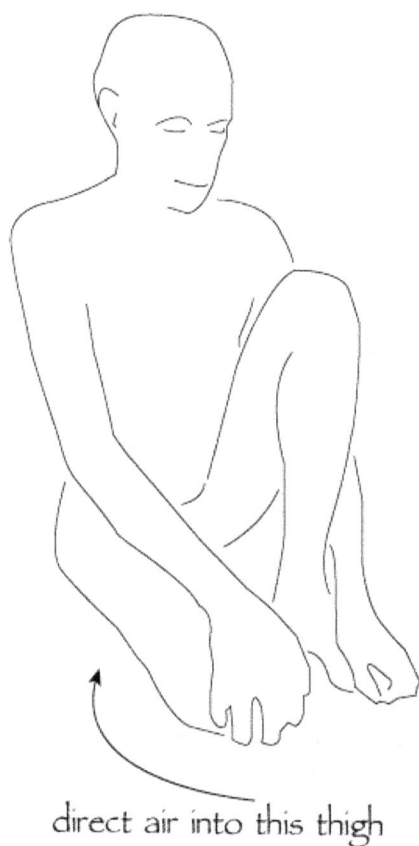

direct air into this thigh

Here is another one of Ma Durga's techniques for females. This one reformats the breasts.

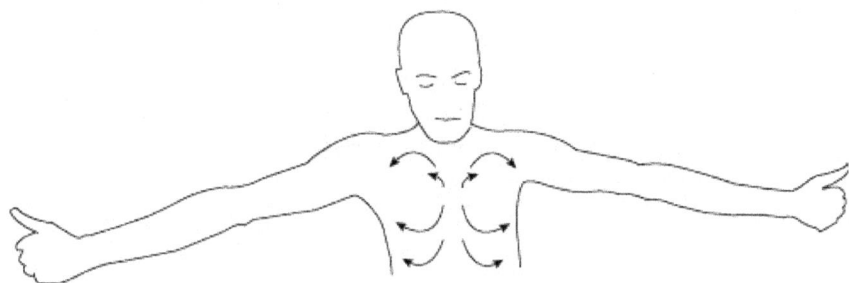

breath through breast/chest

These procedures given by Goddess Durga are not divulged in the yogic tradition of Shiva. These are taught in Ma Durga's lineage. From time to time, a yogi is shown these techniques but usually they are not practiced by males.

Gorakshnath knew these procedures but he did not teach them except to a few great disciples of his. Generally it is believed that these are a part of tantric yoga.

April 22, 2002

Yogeshwarananda

He showed how the sense of imagination is the subtle apparatus which is used by yogis for supernatural vision. This means that one will not get some other vision. Aspiring yogis must work to stop the imagination orb from focusing on this side of existence and from contemplating aspects having to do with this side. They will have to reform the imagination orb. They will not get some other type of vision. When the imagination is reformed, it opens as a supernatural light which penetrates mystic fog or a supernatural sight which sees through the clear sky of consciousness.

Yogesh on another occasion showed me a tratak practice where the energy is experienced as a space or as a channel, which draws in and goes out. When experiencing this, one does not focus strongly but lightly.

May 1, 2002

Yogeshwarananda

He observed seminal beads everywhere in the subtle body. This was an indication of the success of celibacy yoga, such that the sexual energy is distributed in the subtle form equally instead of being concentrated in the erogenous zones, the sex stimulating areas.

In the next stage of celibacy one removes this sexual charge. That occurs in the psyche purification or atma vishuddha yoga.

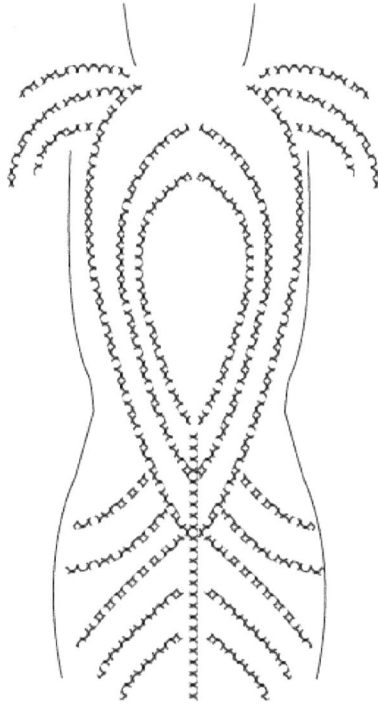

May 3, 2002

Yogeshwarananda

He asked, "Are they gone?"

Remark:

Because I has some visitors, he was not present in my brahmrandra for some days. Two persons came to learn breath-infusion and to talk about spiritual development.

Because I was preoccupied with these persons, Yogesh left. I knew that because I could not perceive him in my brahmrandra. However he returned.

He gave a groin-up clear-light technique:

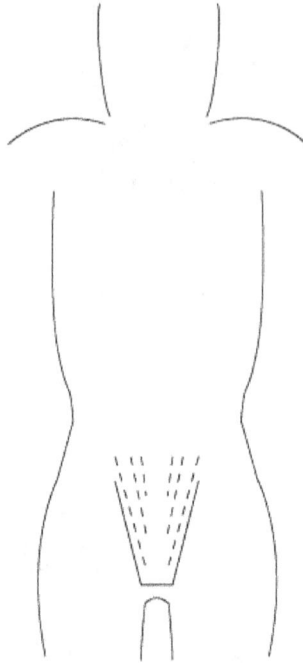

front of body

May 6, 2002

Yogeshwarananda

He gave a special stomach flex. By doing this one sees the needle-like nadis in the abdomen area.

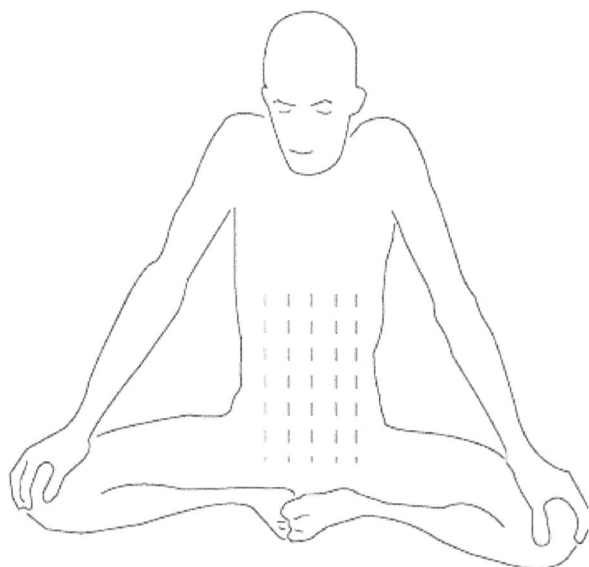

soles together

May 9, 2002

Ma Durga.

She gave a technique for women. This can be used even by pregnant women who are barred from certain postures which may strain the embryo area and cause premature contractions, thus endangering the embryo and the mother.

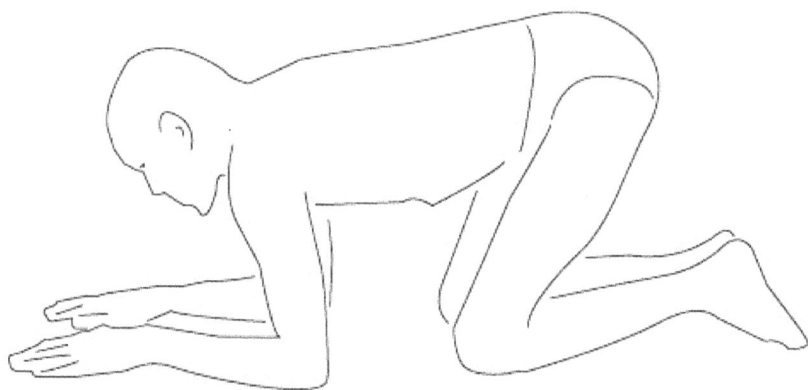

While I did that posture, Yogi Bhajan came. He said, "That is celibacy for all cells. That occurs when stretches are done which cause the cells to yield their hormones. That practice requires sincerity."

Yogesh had this to say, "Do pranavision. Visual vision is not always facilitated. Do not be attached to visual vision, since that would cause stagnation and neglect of other methods of progression. Always switch to pranavision when it develops. Get used to it."

I did this technique.

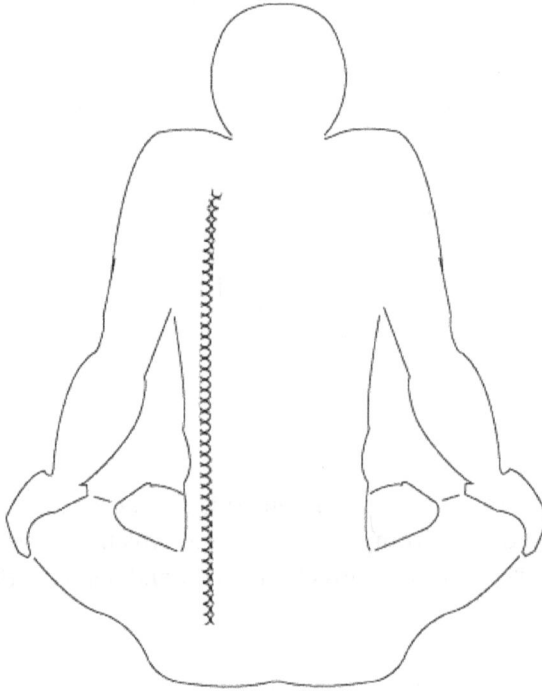

whirlwind transcendence force
left side of body

May 12, 2002

Yoga Ma as Sarasvati Ma

She reminded me of the story when Shankara explained to a debater that the analogy of the two birds sitting on the tree refers to the core-self (atma) and the intellect and not to the core-self and the supreme self (paramatma).

Shankara made a point that in the psyche, it is the intellect mechanism which hankers for attachment to objects and for the experiencing of mundane life. He claimed that actually the atma or core is detached. This is understood only when one reaches the high end of yoga practice and can become detached even from the intellect. With subtle vision, one sees the intellect as a separate subtle object and can determine what its operations are. At that point, one understands clearly what Shankara discussed.

Yogeshwarananda

He showed a technique in which the spine secretes a subtle fluid upwards.

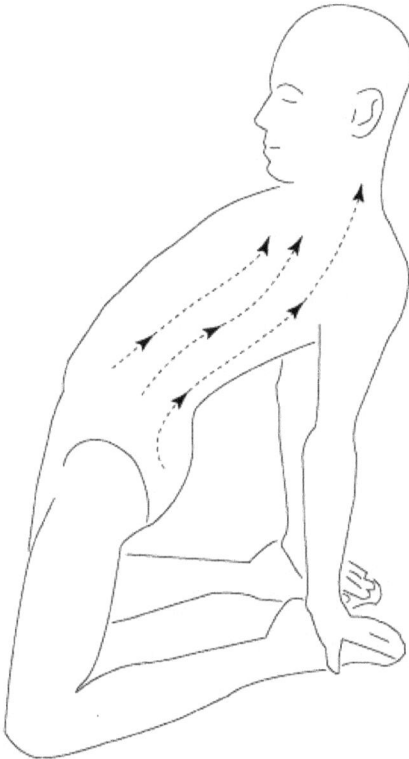

Ma Durga

She gave a balance posture for women. One does one side at a time.

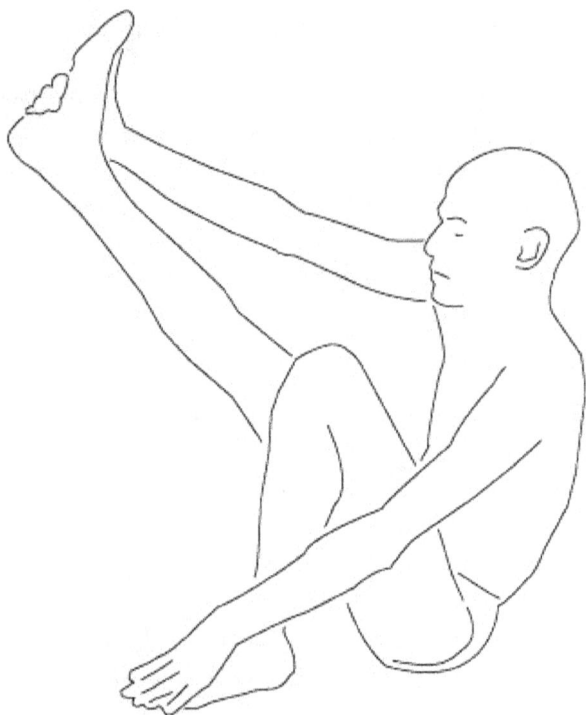

Yogesh explained that all images taken in by the mind disturb meditation at a later date. He said that it cannot be prevented except by sparing the mind the exposure to sense objects.

May 13, 2002

Ma Durga

She gave another female technique.

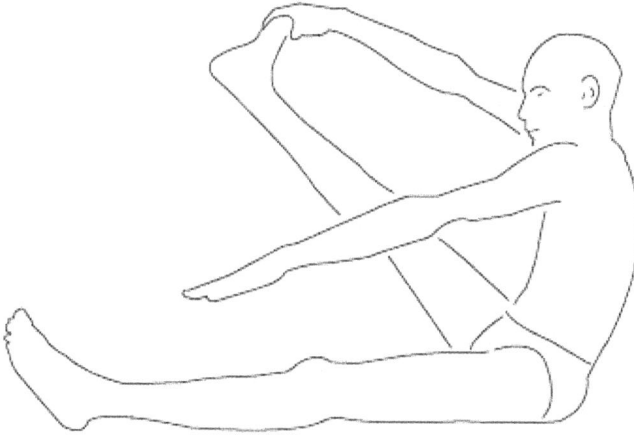

May 15, 2002

Yogeshwarananda

He said, "Make a notation for others."

Remark:

I had an idea not to take notes on something he explained. He objected. It was this. When one eats once a day, early in the morning, then late in the afternoon, the body cools down considerably. This is because the digestive heat (bhasvara agni) is not reinforced by more food intake. Thus a yogi who has diet under control must rest early in the evening or late in the afternoon, so that he does not exhaust himself.

Others who eat during the day or who even eat late in the afternoon or at night, do not have to take the precaution. Their bodies are heated by the continual intake of food.

When I first began to eat one main meal once per day, early in the morning, I lived in a cold climate. In the afternoon my body would cool down so much, that the cold weather would be a disturbance. I was forced to sleep with very warm clothing. Sometimes when the temperature dropped into the freezing zone, I would even have to wear gloves and thick socks for sleeping. Subsequently the children of my body would laugh. They ate in the late afternoon. Their bodies were heated by that food intake. They could not understand my behavior.

May 15, 2002

Yogeshwarananda

He said, "Use the down drawn-in tratak."

Remark:

This is an indrawn blank star gaze, whereby energy comes in. I was in a government office. Noticing that my intellect tried to get the eyes of my body to read every notice in the building, I asked Yogesh about that tendency. He was in my brahmrandra. He replied that to counteract the information-greedy intellect, one should do a draw-in tratak. That stops the intellect from seeking external information.

May 16, 2002

This is my notation. It is advice for beginners. Sugar intake causes tiredness. It gives a boost but after the next rest, one's psyche becomes reluctant to rise for exercises. One must fight its effects. It retards progress.

Sugar should be taken in very little quantities and in carbon hydrate foods which yield it into the body after being eaten. These foods do not give the pleasure of sweet taste, but they also do not have the disadvantage of direct sugar intake.

Association with persons who are addicted to sugar, does affect a yogi. If he forms a close friendship with someone who eats much sugar or who always likes very sweet foods, then he will more than likely assume the habit. It will then retard yoga progression.

May 16, 2002

Ma Durga

She gave a stomach ovary flex for females. Men can do this exercise but their knees should be not be spread out as much as shown,

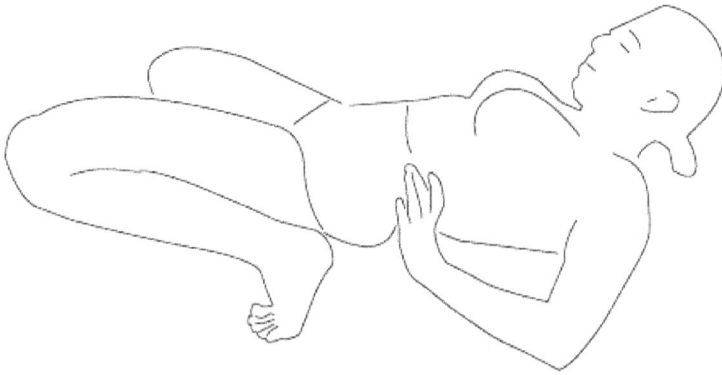

Ma Durga also gave this vagina air-pump-out. It is done on one side of the vagina and then on the other side. This is for female and male ascetics who have advanced in self-tantric practice.

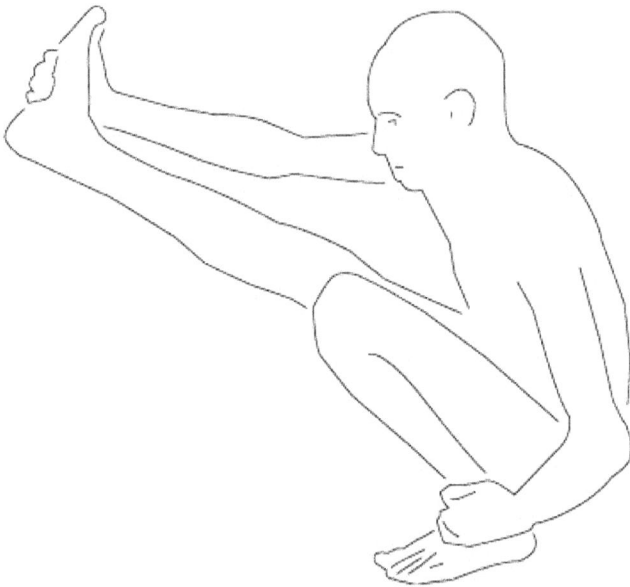

Self-tantric means that the ascetic works to subdue his or her sexuality without working with a partner. One needs special guidance and special support from advanced yogis. All the same if one takes to tantric practice and does so with a partner, he or she more than likely will be a failure, since the sexual energy is such that it hardly permits one to become free from it. Usually those who practice tantric with partners get lowered by the practice and ruin their spiritual development.

May 16, 2002

Yogeshwarananda

He explained, "The intellect acts as a puppet for the manifestation of compressed seed desires. The feelings-energy is like a blind man, being dependent on the intellect for information. The chitta eats the fulfillments which come into it. The incoming fulfillments take the form of impressions. In Sanskrit these are called samskaras which means impressions which entered the feelings-energy and paired off with seed desires. Some impressions cancel out certain seed desires, while others produce hybrid urges which come out of the feelings and motivate the intellect for further activities in the subtle and gross material world.

The core-self, the jiva, is apart from this but his proximity is required for the active exchange of this in-going and out-going energy.

May 17, 2002

Yogeshwarananda

He said, "Better to take seat in padmasana lotus posture to check it. Notice that there is no improvement in meditation, no deepness due to normal energy flow. There is a need for the flow of higher energy by asana posture and breath-infusion practice. Observe the kundalini spike at the back. That is active, arousing the chakras above it."

Remark:

This was said to me at midnight. Yogesh made the point that if one meditates without first doing asana postures and breath-infusion practice, the meditation will not be deep. This is due to ingestion of lower energies. If on the other hand one does the exercises first and takes in much new breath-energy, one's meditation will be more fruitful. However if one meditates immediately after resting the body, one will notice that the kundalini chakra gradually awakens all the chakras along the spine. This is noticed if one has pranavision.

May 18, 2002·

On this day I saw some nadi subtle tubes in the thigh and feet. This occurred in the posture below. In that position one does the down-draw breath-infusion while standing.

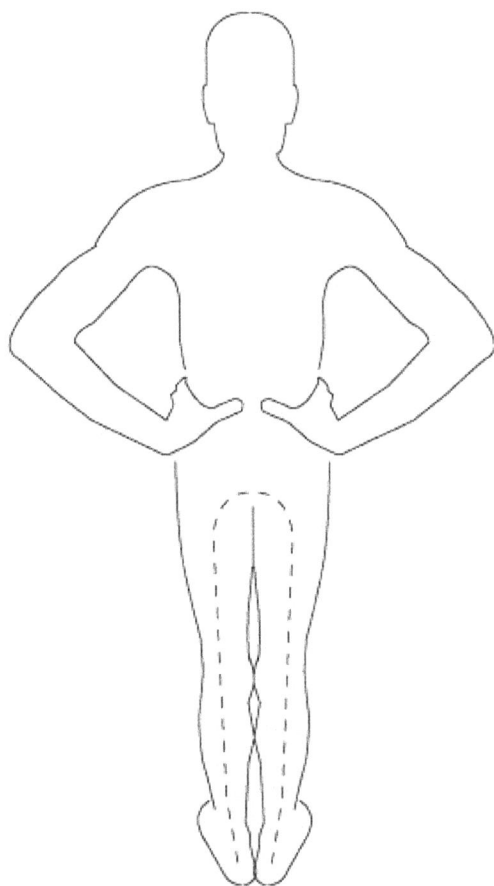

May 18, 2002

Yogeshwarananda

He gave an arm-pit technique.

May 18, 2002

A woman's technique

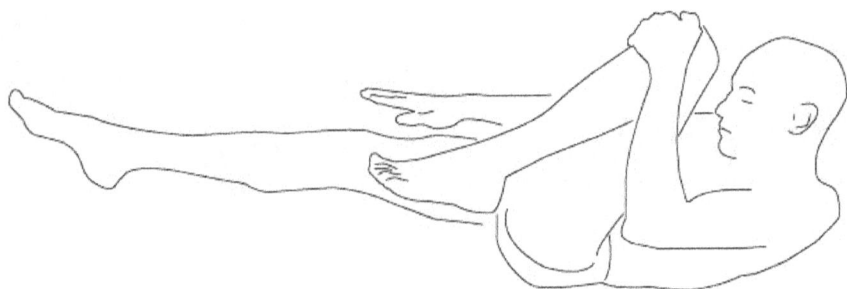

May 19, 2002

Yogeshwarananda

He gave a male/female touch point technique.

The two touch points are the esophagus ring and the vaginal mouth. This vaginal mouth has a sucking action in the subtle body. That can be seen during sexual intercourse or otherwise if one has mystic perception. This technique causes that sucking mouth to stop its needy actions for drawing in sexual fluids. As one does this technique one feels the esophagus ring with the hand and one looks down into the body through the mind, down the middle of the body to see the sucking mouth of the vagina.

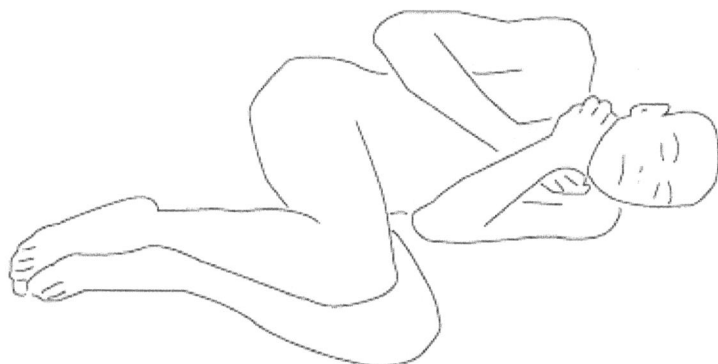

May 22, 2002

Yogeshwarananda

He gave this technique. This is done in lotus posture.

May 23, 2002

Yogeshwarananda

He instructed me to stop the intellect from pursuing any inquiries it may try to make into anything which is not technique-productive activity nor a mandatory cultural duty. This is a complete sensual interest withdrawal.

May 26, 2002

Vishnudevananda

Pulling the sex nerve high point.

He showed a posture to achieve this. The sex nerve in this case passes up the inner thigh. During sexual intercourse one can senses this nerve by the tingling sensation in the inner thigh.

fingers hold inner thighs

Yogeshwarananda

He showed how the intellect focuses. Usually there is an idea of something it is attached to, or of something that formed an impression. It focuses while expanding that view into other things, more conceptions. The atma or core-self sees this, while accepting and perceiving what the intellect projects in a vision form or in imagination. There are relevant verses in the second chapter of the Bhagavad Gita.

ध्यायतो विषयान्पुंसः

सङ्गस्तेषूपजायते ।

सङ्गात्संजायते कामः

कामात्क्रोधोऽभिजायते ॥ २.६२ ॥

dhyāyato viṣayānpuṁsaḥ
saṅgasteṣūpajāyate
saṅgātsaṁjāyate kāmaḥ
kāmātkrodho'bhijāyate (2.62)

dhyāyato = dhyāyataḥ — considering; viṣayān — sensual objects; puṁsaḥ — a person; saṅgas — attachment; teṣūpajāyate = teṣu — in them + upajāyate — is born, is created; saṅgāt — from attachment; saṁjāyate — is born; kāmaḥ — craving; kāmāt — from craving; krodho = krodhaḥ — anger; 'bhijāyate = abhijāyate — is derived

The act of considering sensual objects, creates in a person, an attachment to them. From attachment comes craving. From this craving anger is derived. (Bhagavad Gita 2.62)

क्रोधाद्भवति संमोहः
संमोहात्स्मृतिविभ्रमः ।
स्मृतिभ्रंशाद्बुद्धिनाशो
बुद्धिनाशात्प्रणश्यति
॥२.६३॥

krodhādbhavati saṁmohaḥ
saṁmohātsmṛtivibhramaḥ
smṛtibhraṁśādbuddhināśo
buddhināśātpraṇaśyati (2.63)

krodhād = krodhāt — from anger; bhavati — becomes (comes); saṁmohaḥ — delusion; saṁmohāt — from delusion; smṛti — conscience + vibhramaḥ — vanish; smṛtibhraṁśād = smṛtibhraṁśāt = smṛti — memory, judgement + bhraṁśāt — from fading away; buddhināśo = buddhināśaḥ = buddhi — discerning power + nāśaḥ — lose, affected; buddhināśāt = buddhi — discernment + nāśāt — from loss, from being affected; praṇaśyati — is ruined

From anger, comes delusion. From this delusion, the conscience vanishes. When he loses judgment, his discerning power fades away. Once the discernment is affected, he is ruined. (Bhagavad Gita 2.63)

Most of the contemplation done by the intellect is done non-willfully. This means that for most human beings, there is little originality for the core-self, since the core usually follows in abeyance behind the intellect.

May 28, 2002

Ma Durga with Yogesh observing. She gave a female technique practice. This is the vagina shark-mouth technique. It is done in the posture below.

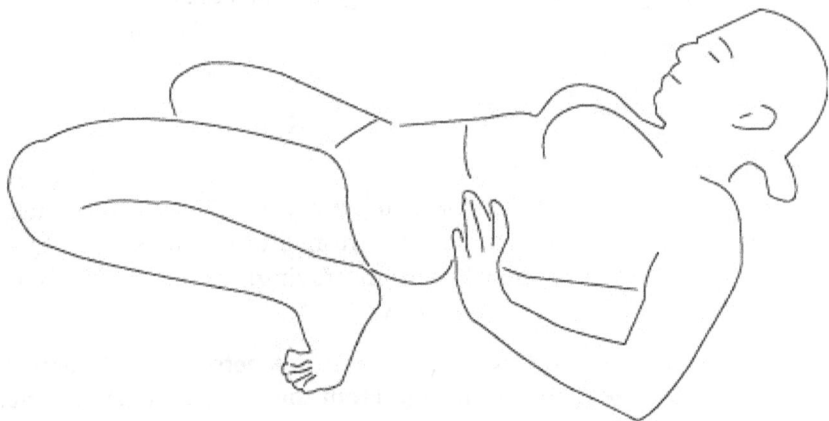

Remark:

A student who gets lessons from teachers, cannot always explain what he is given. Sometimes, a reader of these books, asks about further explanations. Whenever possible I will give these. In some cases, as in this technique, I cannot elaborate. Furthermore, I do not have a feminine body and the feminine profile was never natural to me. Thus I know little about these female techniques. I know however that they are practiced by the advanced students of Goddess Durga for female celibacy.

The female psychology is different. Certain exercises which are used by females have little value for the male ascetics. These female techniques inspired by Ma Durga are recorded for the benefit of female readers.

May 29, 2002

Here is another technique from Ma Durga.

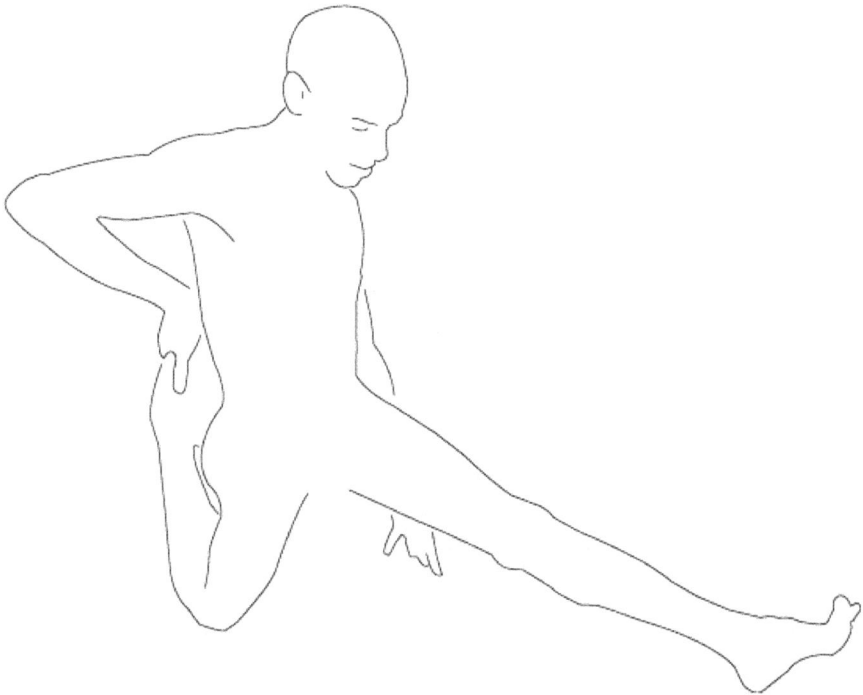

There is another such technique for female abdomen flexes with rapid breathing. The female abdomen exercises are important in a yogini's quest for celibacy. The female sexual apparatus is inside the body, as contrasted to the male organ which is outside. In a sense, females have an advantage. When they do abdomen flexes the sexual apparatus and reproductive glands are affected. Male reproductive glands and organs are outside the abdomen, which means they do not derive such benefits from the flexes.

abdomen pumps

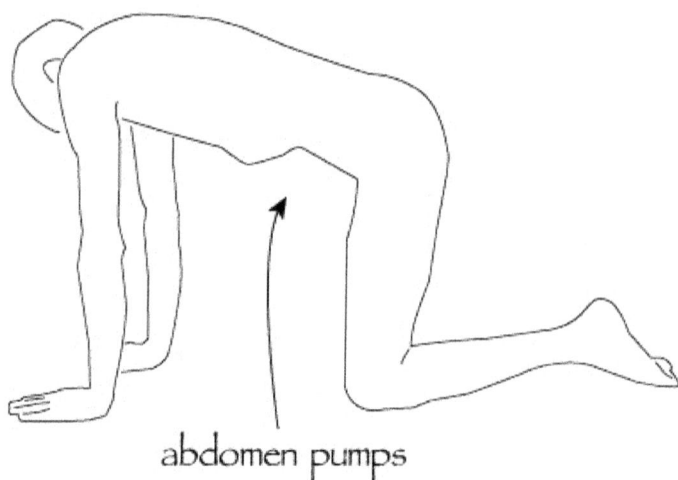

This is another of those female exercises. This is for spinal twist with rapid breathing.

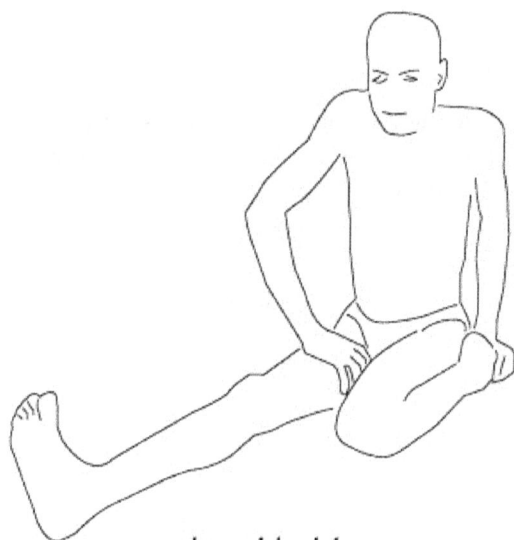

one hand holds toes

other hand holds inner thighs

do spinal twist

switch feet positions

repeat

May 29, 2002

Yogeshwarananda

He said, "Shankara's application of the pecking bird is relevant. Just as flowers exhibit colors which attract bees, the subtle energy flare of objects also causes this. In the intellect, see this white streak of energy that is the sutram or potent power which is the motivation for this."

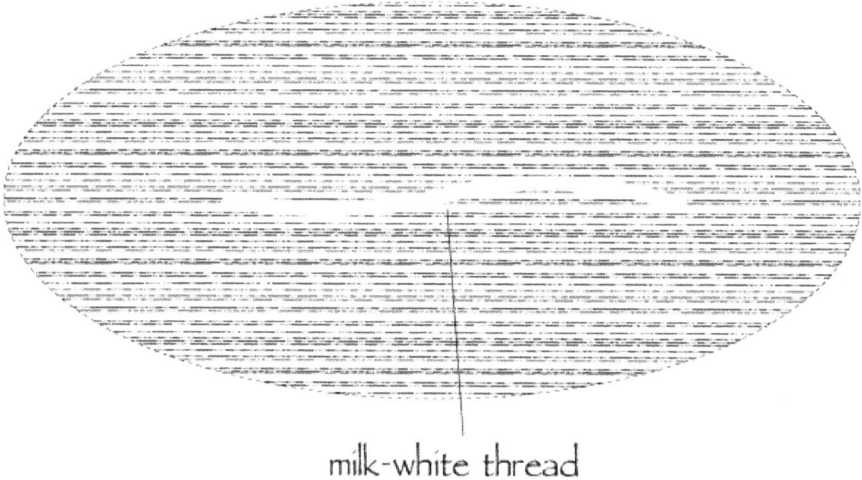

milk-white thread

Remark:

I asked Yogesh why the intellect pursues objects. He showed that on the day before, the intellect on its own accord, pursued a woman's breast. The woman passed where I was. She wore a low neck sweater and the top portion of her breasts, were exposed. Yogesh showed this in my memory files which he opened in the intellect. Shankara had rightly said that the fruit-picking bird in the analogy of the two birds in the Upanishads, is the intellect organ which impulsively acts to gain experiences in the subtle and gross material world.

Part 7

Hanuman

He showed a monkey-to-human technique. This was for reforming the monkey body I currently use.

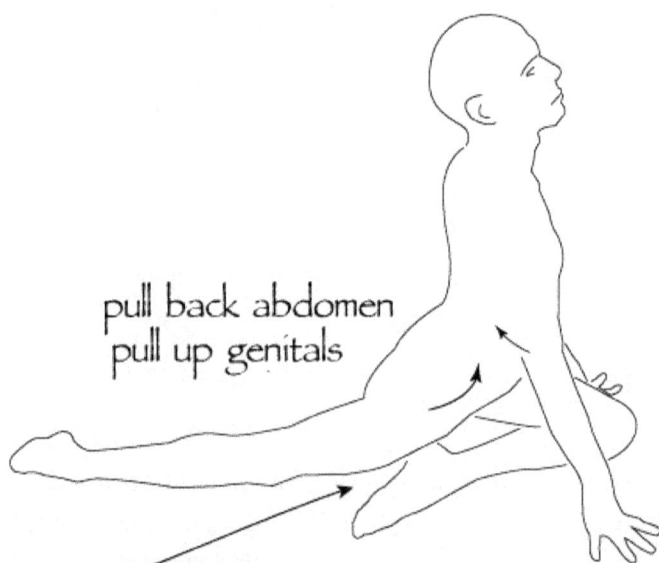

pull back abdomen
pull up genitals

heel under root of genital organ

do breath-infusion pulling from genitals

Babaji

He gave a bottom-of-the-brain to tongue technique.

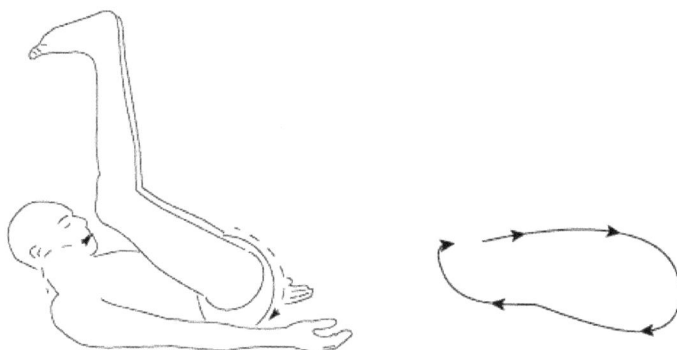

tongue stretched out
subtle fluid from subtle tongue
travels around body - enters back of head

May 30, 2002

Yogeshwarananda

He showed a balance of the nerves technique.

Such techniques are done to acquire a balancing of the right and left sides of the subtle body. When one tries to do meditation he may find that his inner energies pull to one side or the other. To balance this, some techniques are done, before meditating. It is not always important to balance the energies.

Sarasvati Ma

She gave an obeisance technique. This is done to one knee and then to the other. One says the mantra:
Om Sarasvatyai namah
Om Vasishtha Rishi Pitamaha namah

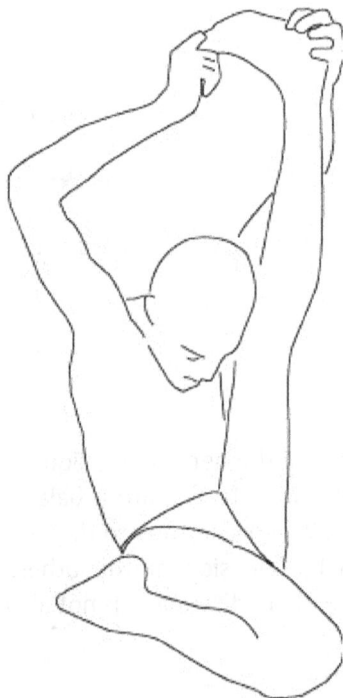

Remark:

Rarely in this yoga practice does one repeat such mantras daily. This yoga is not stagnant. It progresses daily. For instance, this particular mantra and the posture included is not used by me every day. The instruction was for me to use it on that specific day.

May 30, 2002

Babaji

He gave an intellect tratak procedure using a focused absorption process that he pioneered.

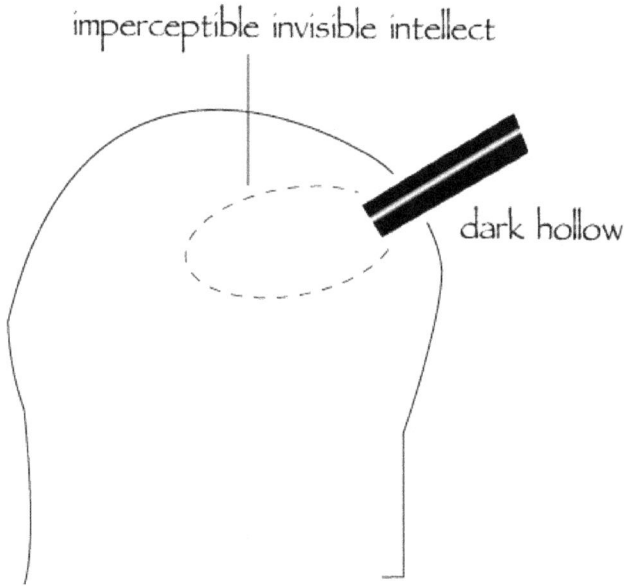

imperceptible invisible intellect

dark hollow

May 31, 2002

On this day I was in the subtle world when I was approached by a lady I knew in a spiritual community years ago. This is a married lady. While I was in that community, she took a liking to me but could not act on it because of moral constraints. However as in these cases, the subtle body keeps the impressions for future use. Yogesh, because he stayed in my brahmrandra, was aware of what I did when I met that lady in the astral world.

At the time, he said, "Any such suppressed desire will remain in the soil of subtle nature and grow slowly, while others that are tended to, grow quickly. Due to absorbing little attention, the slow-growing ones take a long time to come to maturity but they do manifest in time."

He added, "Beneath motherly affection is conjugal desire, which remains silent like a copper-eyed snake that waits for its opportunity. These so-called spiritual communities are traps for setting up future sexual affairs. The leaders or founders are the fools who unwittingly design such traps in the name of salvation or liberation."

Remark:

In that way, Yogesh uprooted my attachment to that lady. It is good therefore, to have a great yogin living in one's psyche, since he may save one from mishaps.

May 31, 2002

Babaji

He showed how some yogis offered their services to Skanda Kumara by doing a particular bow stretch.

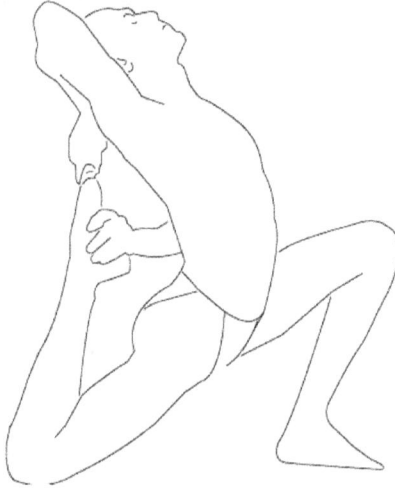

June 1, 2002

Babaji

He showed this intellect point-upwards technique.

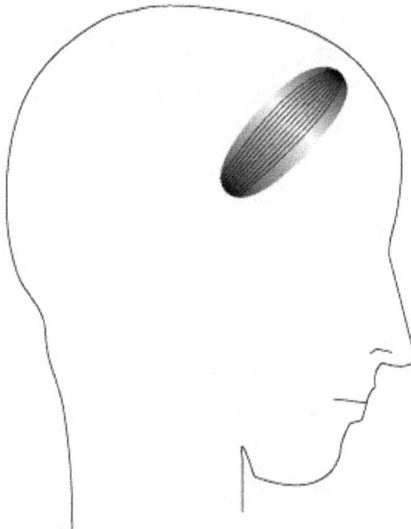

He showed a closed-eyelids tratak.

Remark:

Generally tratak means staring off into nowhere with the eye lids open. However special trataks are done with the physical eyelids closed. In this one, the yogi keeps them closed. This is because the physical vision has nothing to do with the subtle or supernatural perception. Gradually by practicing one develops the ability to sort between physical, subtle and supernatural vision.

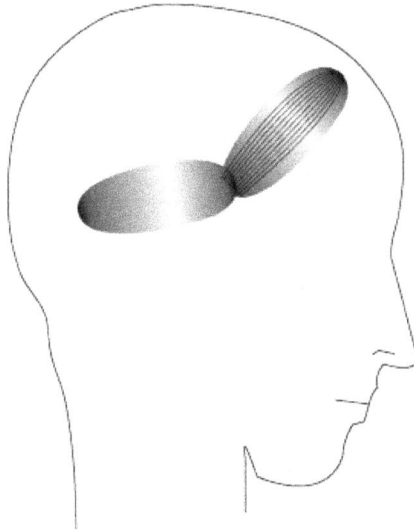

June 4, 2002

Yogeshwarananda

He instructed, "Train your individual feelings-energy (chitta) to be satisfied without gross fulfillment. That will rid it of the tendency to want feed-back from mundane excitements, allowing you to eventually exist on the causal plane without looking downward into gross manifestation."

Remark:

This is achieved by transferring to the feelings-compact energy and by remaining there in satisfaction as well as giving that energy a feedback of fulfillment from states of mind where there is no excitement coming in from the physical existence.

June 4, 2002

Babaji

He showed a technique. One closes the physical eyelids but opens the subtle vision underneath. This does not mean that the yogi actually sees into the subtle world. He may or may not. In either case, he will feel the subtle optic energy pouring out the subtle head. He uses the *Om* sound, as a turret, a turning tool, to turn the vision energy upwards. In this case the *Om* sound is not chanted by the yogi but is heard by him in the back of the head. This is the ghosha subtle naad sound which occurs in the back right/left side of the head.

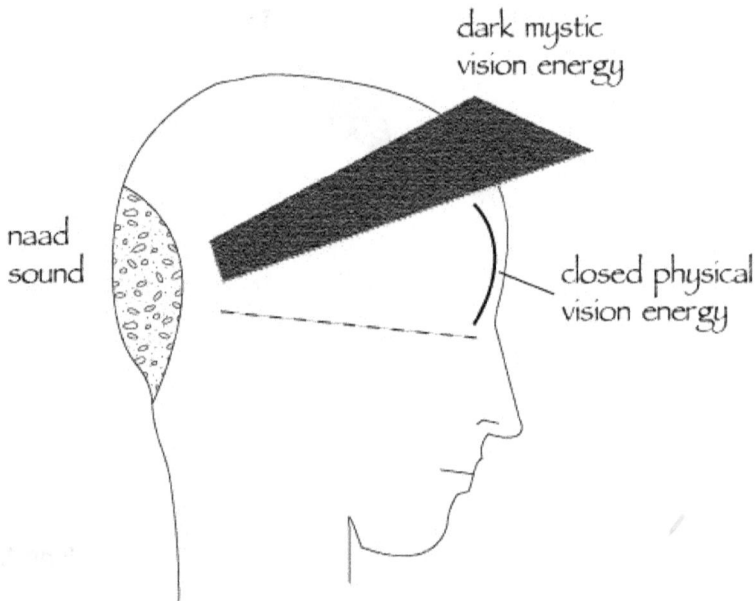

dark mystic vision energy

naad sound

closed physical vision energy

June 5, 2002

Babaji

He showed an ear sound turret-turning technique for turning the entire intellect upwards. This turns the intellect and its vision-power, instead of turning the vision power alone.

The ear sound used is usually heard in the vicinity of the right physical ear but it is actually in the subtle head. This is called the naad brahma sound. Some called it pranava. This is different to the sound *Om* which is chanted mentally or verbally.

June 5, 2002

Yogi Bhajan

He gave a back-of-the-neck cleansing technique.

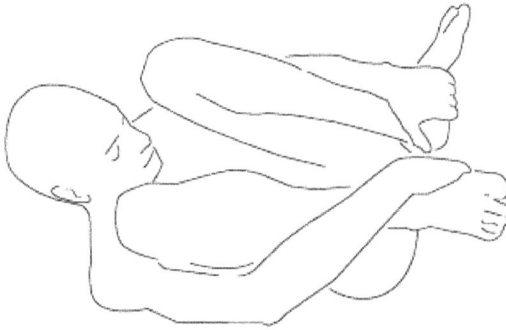

keep knees wide apart

grab insteps from inside

concentrate on neck

June 5, 2002

Yogi Bhajan

In the astral world at one of his intensive courses, he showed an easy rooster pose. He checked with some students who were at that astral place. He showed them some cleared nadis and cleared sections of my subtle form. He said that the clarity comes from a steady practice.

When this occurred, I realized that Yogi Bhajan did not recognize me. I then mentioned when I stayed at his ashram and told him that I was put in care of Brian and Prem Kaur, two of his supervising disciples, in Denver Colorado during the year of 1973. He remembered me. He said again that I was the guy with the odd turban. Then we had a good laugh.

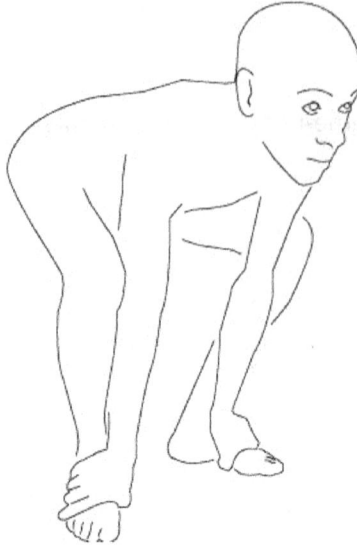

My relationship with Yogi Bhajan shows that a student of yoga, does not have to stay with the teacher at all times. In fact, if one has a little contact, one can advance, provided one sticks to the practice. One does not have to get close to a spiritual master or to be his favorite student or anything like that. It is the practice that matters.

Even though in the Mahabharata history, the tribesman Ekalavya was not a dear disciple of Drona, still as a practicing student, he mastered archery even to a degree that was greatly feared by Arjuna. As a result, Ekalavya thumb was removed by Drona's request, just to frustrate the principle of the superiority of practice. Practice is so superior that it outperforms a close association with a teacher. Please note this.

June 6, 2002

Babaji

He said, "Use that detail and others for focus. Use the memory to help."

Remark:

This was an up-turreted intellect focus on two lights which I saw the day before. These were either spiritual or supernatural lights, seen with either spiritual or supernatural vision. I was not sure which of the two it was. Babaji instructed that I meditate on the experience, keeping in mind that the two lights were still there even though I lost the view of them, due to closure of the spiritual and supernatural vision. He also told me to use the memory of the vision of Padmanabha Narayana who I saw spiritually years ago. In that way Babaji informed me that it was a spiritual vision.

June 8, 2002

Satyananda (Bihar School of Yoga)

He showed an inner body lock. This is a special lock that one does automatically once one gets the diet under yogic control.

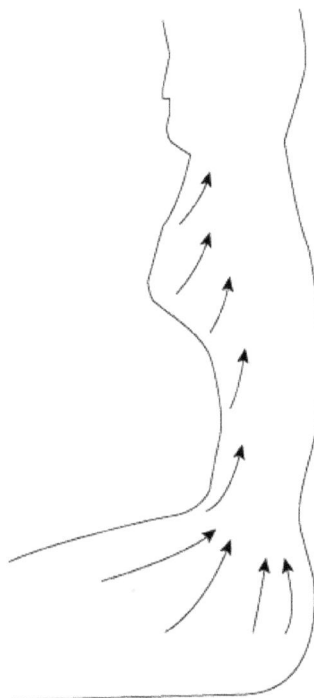

do this 12 hours after last meal

Yogeshwarananda

He gave an intellect centering on the brahmrandra with an *Om* sound. This is the inner *Om* sound which is heard in the back of the head. It may sound like a continuous *Eeeeee* sound.

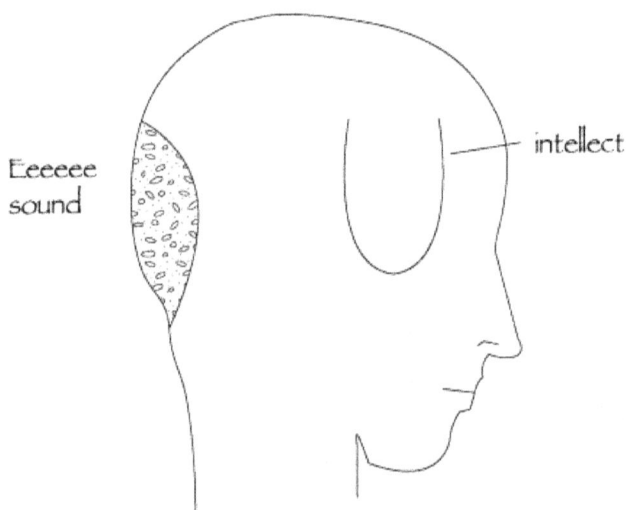

Eeeeee
sound

intellect

Yogi Harbhajan

He showed some toe flexes. When doing this exercise, the buttocks should not touch the heels.

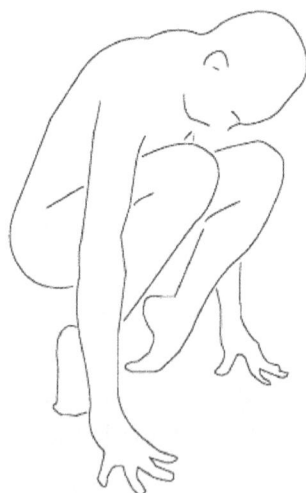

June 18, 2002

Yogeshwarananda

He gave the first technique of transcendence focus. This is done by listening to the high-pitched sound in the right side of the subtle head. Sometimes this sound appears to be outside of the head. Sometimes it seems to be inside but coming from another dimension. One hears it and then one focuses the vision power on it. During the focus one may drift. If one does, one should resume the focus while observing how one shifted.

June 20, 2002

Yogeshwarananda

He gave a technique for pulling into the sound zone on the right side of the subtle head. When doing this, if one cannot perceive the intellect as a distinct subtle object one may still pull it by pulling on the area where one usually analyses in the subtle brain. It is the same area where imagination occurs or where thinking calculations are made.

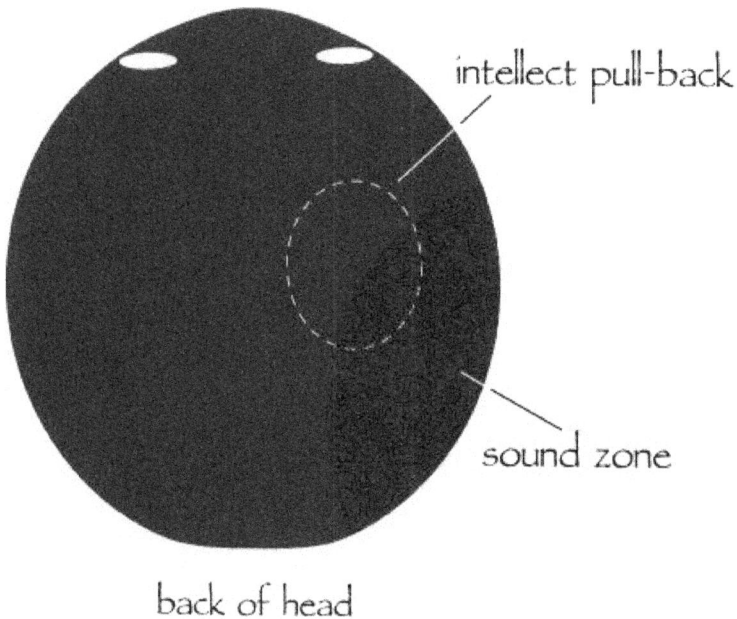

intellect pull-back

sound zone

back of head

Yogeshwarananda

This is a lumbar energization exercise. When done regularly the lumbar area of the subtle form develops a clear light.

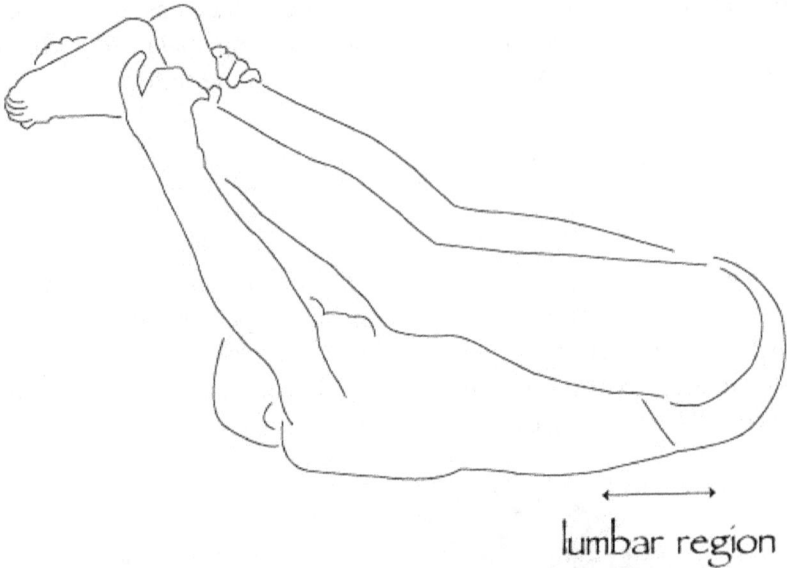

lumbar region

Yogi Harbhajan

This yogi visited me with some students. He used my subtle body to show some lights and the feelings-focus within it. He criticized their eating habits, saying that because they ate like hogs, their kundalini chakra raises and then drops to the base level repeatedly. He advised me to always do breath-infusion exercises on a mat.

Babaji

He gave the second technique for absorption focus. This was using a tratak hole with the ear sound in the right back side of the subtle head. The tratak hole occurred on its own. This particular one may never occur again.

Some are openings into other dimensions or parallel worlds. Some are·
openings into the chit akasha sky of consciousness,

Even though one may see or even experience a pull towards such holes,
one may not pass through another dimension. Fortunate are those who
escape into chit akasha.

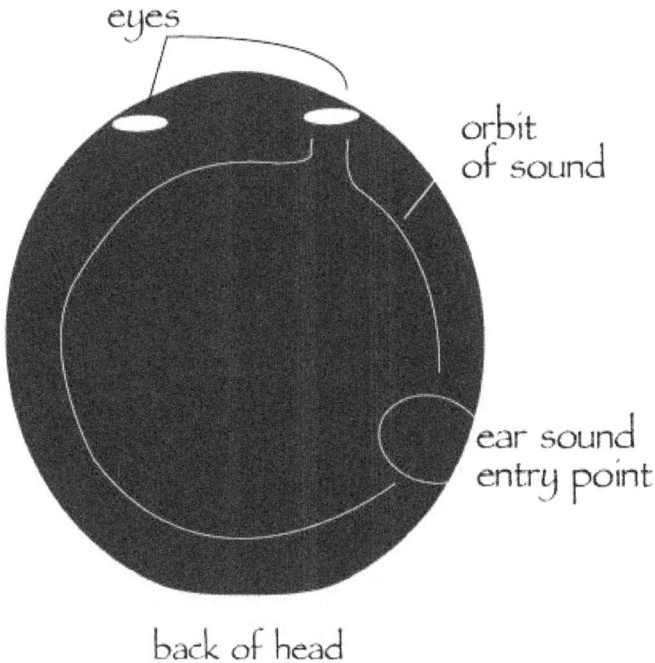

eyes

orbit
of sound

ear sound
entry point

back of head

He said, "Do the first technique which is always there. Do the second
technique after the first is established. If the second one is not there, wait for
it to manifest.

"In the meantime, pull the self back into the technique and keep the
intellect aligned according to the influence of higher energy, keeping it away
from thoughts and visualizations.

"When the second technique comes, use the first and second together.
If the second does not come merely stop when the allotted time for
meditation expires."

June 30, 2002

Agastya

He said, "Come. See this, the third technique."

July 1, 2002

Babaji

He instructed, "The focus is different to the brow chakra. Keep guard for the opening of the second technique. When it is manifested use a mild focus with tratak on the intellect. Use the sutram sound."

July 3, 2002

Yogeshwarananda

He said, "Successful sensual energy withdrawal is key-noted by effortlessly stopping the intellect from focusing on its desires. Then the absorption technique can be practiced consistently."

July 7, 2002

Yogeshwarananda

He said, "Absorb the impressions with less focus. If they have little impact, you will not have to share them with others."

Remark

This is a method for advanced sensual energy withdrawal. At that stage one controls the intellect and the sensual mechanism in such a way that one does not absorb strong impressions from the sense objects. Nothing sears the mind nor imprints on it deeply. One practices to stop the mind from allowing the sense objects to make deep impressions.

July 12, 2002

Yogeshwarananda.

He said, "Keep the focus separate from the opening of the eye vision. Relax the focus gradually. Point it where the eye opens."

Remark:

This is finding the distinction between the brow chakra vision and the intellect vision. Sometimes the intellect vision focuses through the brow chakra or it may focus down the optic nerves of the physical body for physical vision. One should find it by itself without its adjuncts.

July 14, 2002

Yogeshwarananda

Somehow he sent a female yogini who had a buxom form. Her subtle form first entered mine to get the feel of the exercises I did. Then it separated from my form. Then she did whatever I did. On this day, I did a female technique on the back of my body and another one in the rooster pose.

breathe air through breasts and vagina

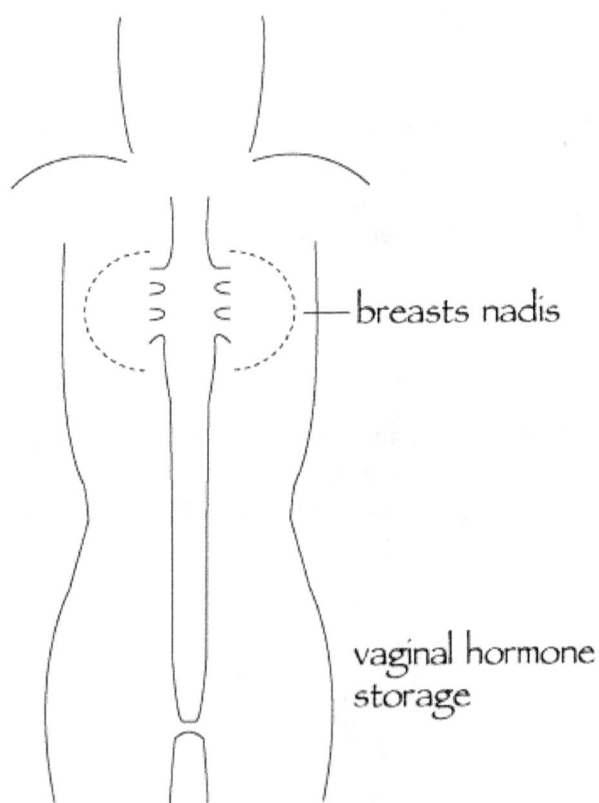

breasts nadis

vaginal hormone
storage

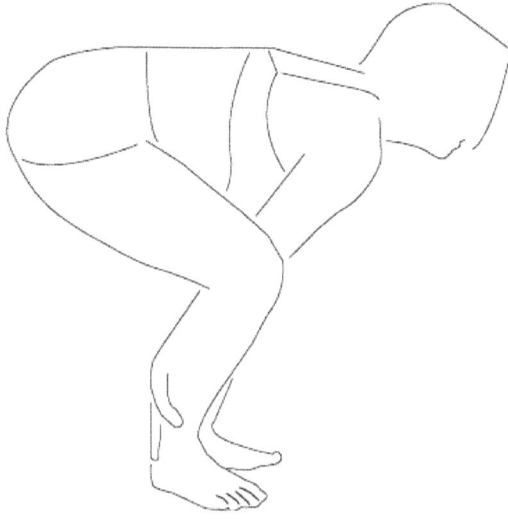

July 13, 2002

Swaminarayana

This divine person is considered to be the Complete Personality of Godhead by many Gujaratis. I was meeting him in his sunlight body. We discussed the ways of opening the subtle senses. In that discussion he gave three important practices:

- sound sutram
- anila sense of touch in the dark intellect
- development of vision from the open-forehead tratak by contemplation through holding oneself there and staying there like a police guard.

Remark:

This instruction was relayed to me to give to a devotee of Swaminarayana. However I did not send it to him because his life-style was antagonistic to these practices. He is not in a position to do this. This is a preparation for the first technique in transcendence absorption focus, just before one progresses to the second technique.

The sound sutram is a high-pitched sound that is heard on the right/left side of the subtle head, near the right/left subtle ear. This is a continuous ringing sound, which is very similar to a continuous peel of a bell in the tone of Eeeeee. This is regarded as the real *Om* sound which does not have to be chanted by the yogi. He listens to it only. He becomes absorbed in it. This sound comes from the supernatural sky which is part of the chit akash, the sky of consciousness. This is a mercy facility for beginners, who are supernaturally blind. By listening to this sound, one can develop supernatural vision.

Sant Kirpal Singh used to stress this sutram sound which is called naad brahma. He used to initiate his disciples into the hearing of it.

The anila sense of touch in the dark intellect.

Swaminarayana mentioned this because many of his modern followers have an intellect that is dark. This is due to their absorption with materialistic living, and their lack of yoga practice. These people feel that merely by chanting the Swaminarayana great prayer (mahamantra) repeatedly they will attain perfection. However despite their belief their intellect remains dark. To do higher yoga, contemplative focus, one must have an intellect that is insightful.

Swaminarayana however, gave a procedure which one can practice even with a dark intellect. One can do this by focusing on the sense of touch in the intellect. Even though there may not be perceptible lights in the subtle head, still there always is the sense of touch, the feelings there. One should focus on that.

Development of vision from the open-forehead tratak by contemplation while holding and guarding that place.

This is a mystic practice which one can do if one has patience and faith. It is done in this way.

One closes the eyelids and remains in a dark place,

One then feels energy in the forehead area. After sometime one will feel as if that area has no closure to it, as if it is open, and as if energy comes into it and goes out of it. Sometimes it appears as if the energy remains there without coming in or going out. One holds the attention there and remains there just as a policeman who is assigned guard duty.

July 15, 2002

Yogeshwarananda

He discussed an advanced sensual energy withdrawal. He said, "When too much information is absorbed, one desires to express it to others. Decrease the intake force of the senses."

July 24, 2002

Yogeshwarananda

He advised that I increase the time of morning meditation. I would have to change my life style so that I do not have to spend so much time working for an income.

July 13, 2002

Yogeshwarananda

He instructed, "Since they cause deep imprints and also cause the need for sharing the unwanted information, stop strong mental notations. This is part of developing paravairagya, an acute degree of dispassion."

August 4, 2002

Gorakshnath

He gave two techniques

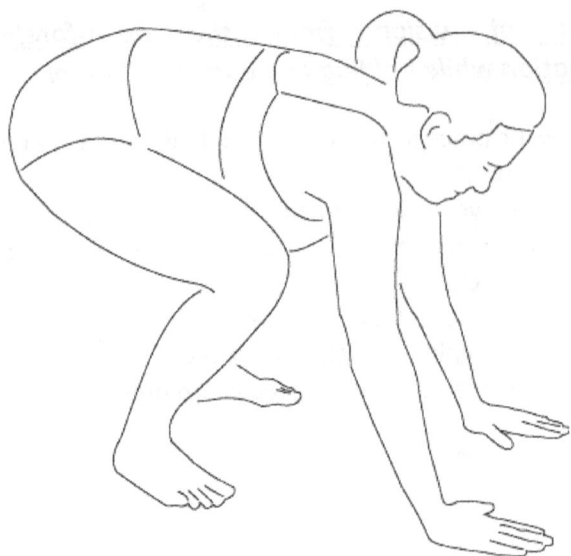

August 8, 2002

Yogeshwarananda

He requested, "Do this instead. Help me finish these practices."

Remark:

Sometimes Yogesh used my body to complete yoga austerities which he was unable to finish while he had a gross form.

He had me lean back on a head sound in the right back corner, and go up like a spike in the center back, near it. I had a flash of white-blueish light from the cosmic sense-of-identity which shone to my right at an angle. These are mystic practices which he wanted me to execute so that he could make certain observations.

Later, some months later, Yogesh said that since I was so committed to writing these yoga journals, I would relieve him of the duties to explain the details of mystic yoga. He felt that my explanations would complete some tasks which he was unable to finish because his material body was terminally ill.

September 9, 2002

Yogeshwarananda

Strangely, he showed a woman's technique. In this posture a woman sits between the heels with her fingers spread over her breasts. She does breath-infusion while pulling the milk system hormones up to the neck. After she draws that up, she pulls it further into the head.

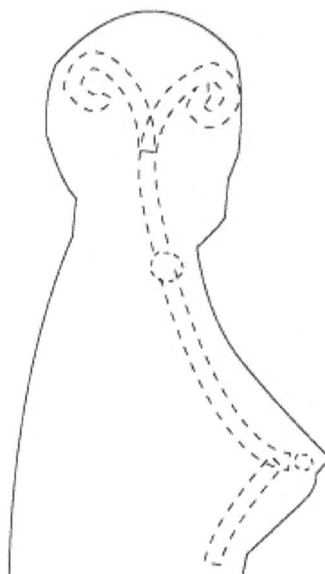

Here is another woman's technique, which he gave. This is a vaginal cleansing posture.

Here is another. This is a vaginal pulp and slime draw-out.

Here is another. This is a breast pump-out. This one is done after the body is fully energized by breath-infusion.

Shiva / Yogeshwarananda

They inspired a subtle energy infusion downward.

This is air infused through the spine from an opening in the top of the neck. The energy goes down to the base of the spine into a red black ball of subtle fire.

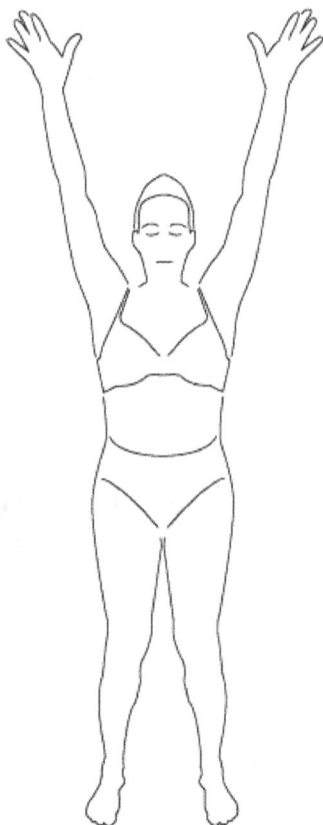

September 13, 2002

Shiva

He inspired a top lung breath. This is done sitting between the legs.

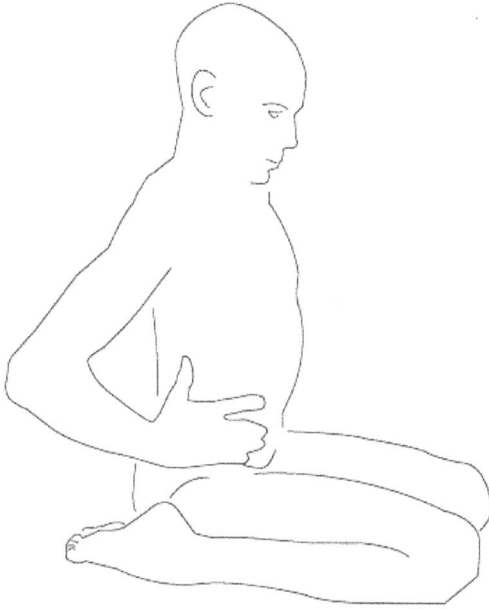

September 13, 2002

Shiva

He inspired a neck slit.

This is done while standing, with the arms hanging down like an ape's. The head is dropped like an ape's too. One does breath-infusion pumping air into the base of the spine. If one does it properly, one will perceive a red-black ball or a clear fire force at the base. After a time, the energy will accumulate. It will move up the back of the body and break out at a slit in the neck.

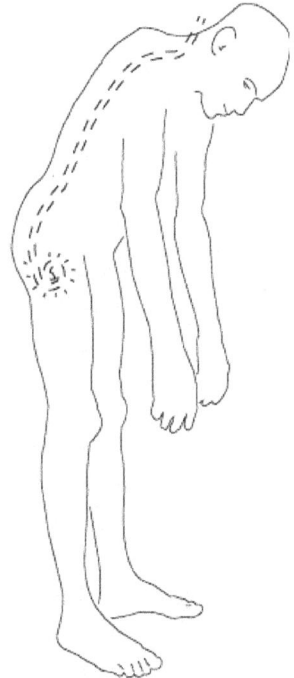

September 14, 2002

Yogeshwarananda

He explained, "The focusing power is arrested by impressions of objects taken in during waking hours. It holds these for development in the subtle energy reserves.

Then it expresses these later, thus obstructing desired concentration practice.

"Whatever is absorbed must later be released as a distraction focus. Due to holding the impressions, the focusing organ cannot release itself to do transcendental absorption."

Remark:

This is some information on why a yogi fails at the 6th stage of yoga, which is deliberate transcendence focus.

September 28, 2002

Yogeshwarananda

He showed a subtle body bend-over. This is done with the subtle form while the gross body is in lotus posture.

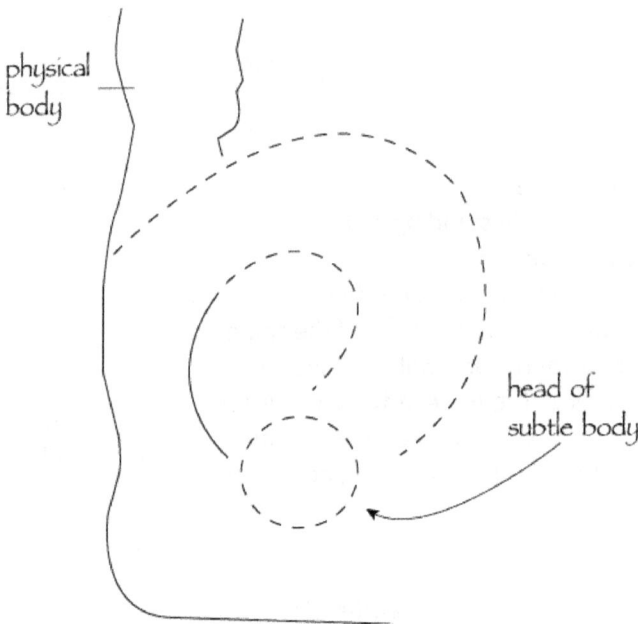

physical body

head of subtle body

September 20, 2002

Yogesh suggest that one should always stand before assuming the rooster pose and its variations. This means that if one is in another position, besides standing, one should first stand before assuming any of those postures.

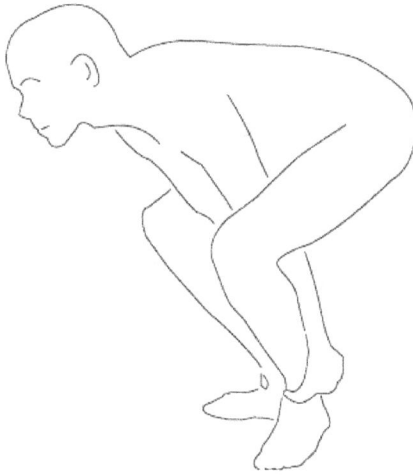

September 30, 2002

Babaji / Yogeshwarananda

They inspired a tratak / sound alternate meditation. In this process one switches back and forth, between focusing on the sound on the right side of the subtle head, and the tratak procedure of lifting the poured-out visual energy into the brow chakra.

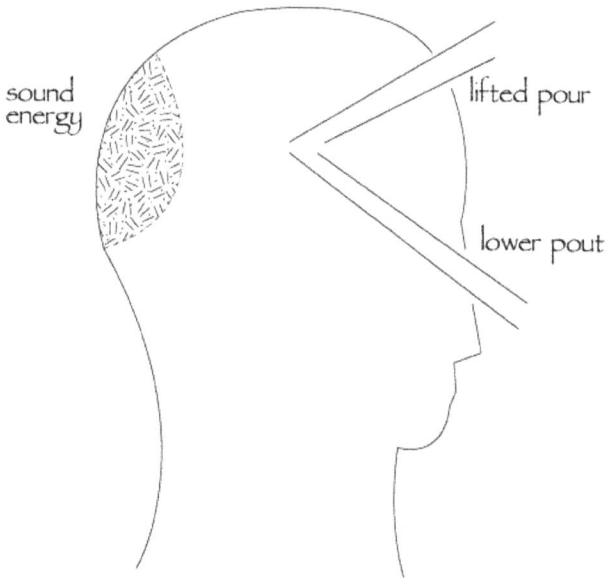

sound energy

lifted pour

lower pout

October 2, 2002

Yogeshwarananda

He said, "The subtle energy reserve causes a forceful intake of sensual impressions. These deter the insightful intellect and cause renewed endeavor for reporting events. It stimulates further imaginations which are the schematics for impression sceneries which will be produced in the future, thus curtailing yoga practice.

October 9, 2002

Shiva

He gave a rooster pose for women. This is done after intense breath-infusion.

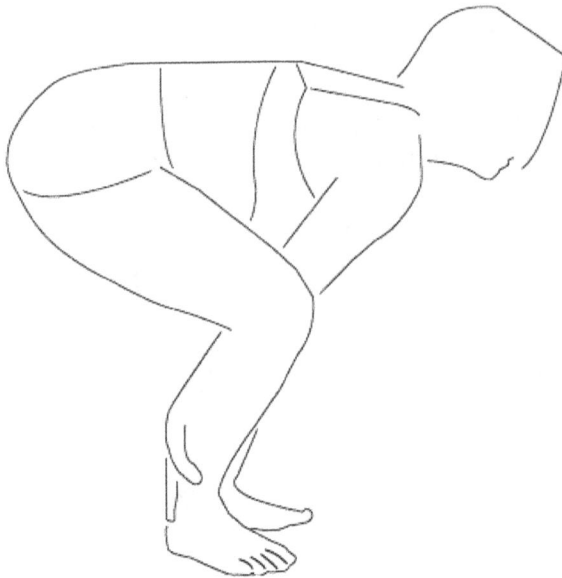

Here is another posture for women to draw blood out of the buttocks area. This is done from a standing position.

He gave this other posture for the subtle body. This is to be done by males or females who are preparing for absorptions. It is done by yogis who can distinguish between the gross and subtle bodies.

This is done while the gross body stands, or while it is in lotus, or while it is on the knees.

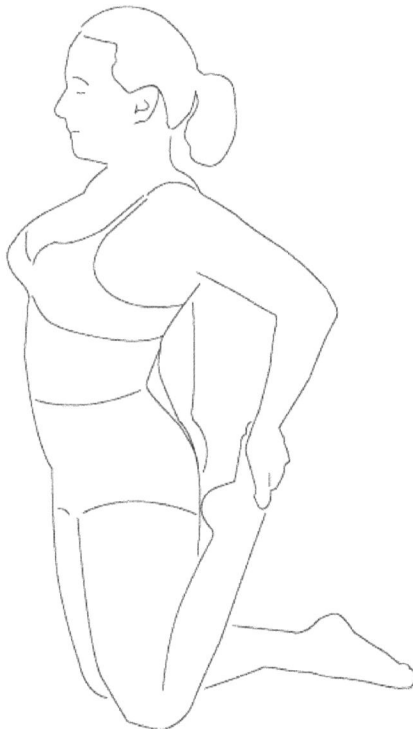

While doing the above posture in the subtle body, the foot which is lifted near the buttocks should be twirled to the front of the body. The subtle body is quite flexible and can do this.

Shiva

He gave a subtle body pose. This one is done while the gross body remains in the same posture or in any other posture.

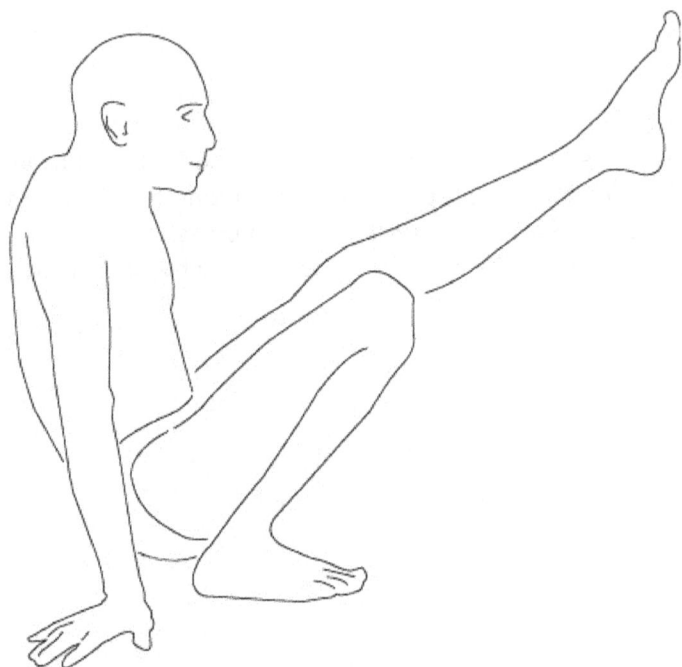

Part 8

Yogeshwarananda

He gave a testes-tubes stretching exercise.

This is done by assuming the lotus posture and going forward to stretch up and down. When this is done carefully with attention, one stretches some of the tubes which lead out of the body into the testes.

This exercise does wonders for making it easy to sit in lotus posture for long periods.

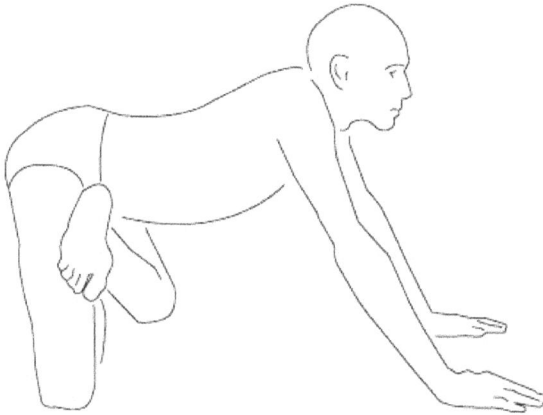

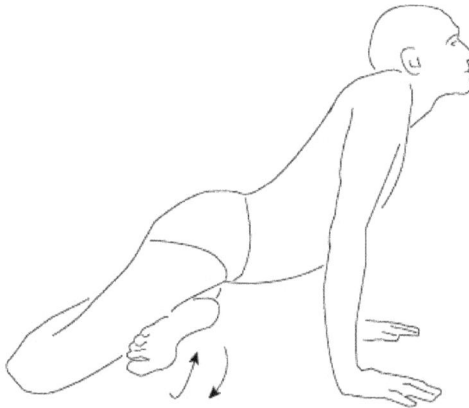

move body up and down

Mahayogini Mataji

This is the sister of Babaji, one of the few females to become a siddha. She gave this female procedure. She did not explain its function. In that pose, the female sits in easy posture. She keeps one foot in easy pose and puts the other foot on the side of the buttocks. One hand is on the inside knee of the foot in easy pose. The other hand is on top of the knee of the other foot.

She gave another technique for women. In this one, the woman stands with one hand on the hip. The other hand grasps the inner thigh near the sexual organ and pulls up a little. The knee is projected.

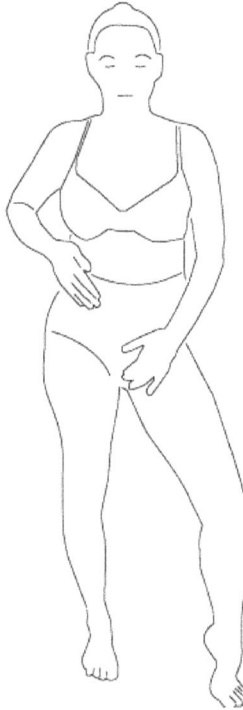

October 15, 2002

On this day, in relation to some techniques given by Babaji and Yogesh, I realized that one is drawn away from the high pitched supernatural *Eeeeee* sound by thoughts and ideas. The subtle sensing mechanism of the subtle body works in that way. One should keep a distance from the disturbing sensuality and from people who are under its control. One should not let their ideas penetrate the psyche. This is necessary to master the 6th stage of yoga practice, that of dharana deliberate linking of the attention to a higher concentration force, person or environment.

Shiva

He said, "So long as there are thoughts, the intellect light cannot be seen. Patanjali is correct."

Babaji / Yogeshwarananda

Under their influence, I was instructed to find the open space passage of the visual orb, and to use the high pitched *Eeeeee* supernatural sound as an anchor point. I was to put the attention into the orb and try to lift it with the ahankara sense-of-initiative ray.

Yogesh informed me that the lotus swing-forward posture (page 233) causes sexual energies to be released from the groin area. It also stretches tubes which are connected to the sexual apparatus. It makes it easy to sit in lotus for long periods. For women it stimulates their feelings-energy reserve in such a way as to cause their psyches to flush the need to have embryos.

This action in females is important in the quest for spiritual perception. Many celestial women do not have the pregnancy mechanism in their subtle bodies. That capacity is present in lower feminine forms.

October 29, 2002

Mahayogini Mataji

She gave a woman kanda bulb clearance.

The kanda is a small bulb-like gland for holding concentrated sexual fluids in the subtle body. In advanced celibacy yoga, this kanda is eliminated. In this posture, the female sits between the heels. The knees are spread out while doing this. The body is curved back. The head is tilted back a bit. Each hand grabs the inside bulge of the flesh which protrudes on the inside behind the knees. This is held by the fingers. One uses breath-infusion rapid breathing or a slower deep down-draw breath, to pull the fluid up and out of the kanda.

November 6, 2002

Yogeshwarananda

He gave a technique for the subtle body. These exercises prepare the yogi to transfer consciousness from the physical form. It develops pranavision first. Later, after much practice, it develops supernatural sight.

For this practice, one squats and pushes down the fingers. One leans over to contemplate the energy reserves. One does the rapid breathing and when the system is charged, one interlocks the fingers and moves them back and forth, until the itching sensations in them stops. Then one pushes the fingers down again and does rapid breathing for at least two sessions. In some instances, one should keep doing this repeatedly, until one is satisfied that all the carbon dioxide is removed from the hands. One can tell this by the lack of itching when the fingers are interlocked and moved back and forth and by the charged energy feelings.

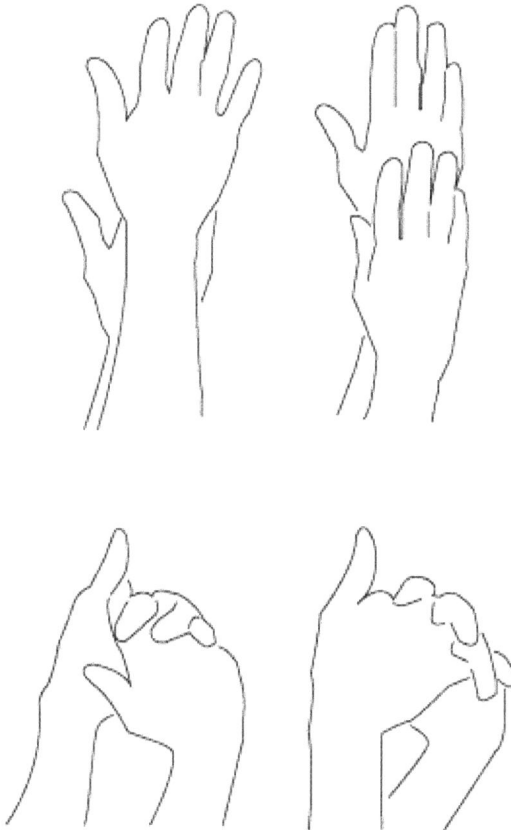

The astral body does some unique movements during such exercises. One should observe that. One should keep the eyes closed so as not to be distracted by physical light or objects.

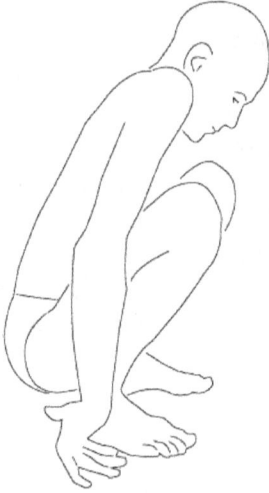

physical body   subtle body

November 7, 2002

Shiva

He instructed, "Make the two hollows into one hollow vision-energy."

Remark:

This was an instruction in tratak practice, where one mystic action brings the two-fold vision-energy together. This energy usually pours out of the subtle body at the eye sockets. Sometimes it remains still without pouring out. It is a form of liquid light.

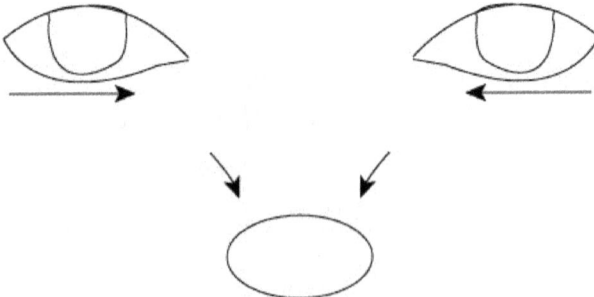

November 8, 2002

Yogeshwarananda

He said, "The imagination faculty is supersensitive. Use tratak to tame it. Curb its attraction to excitements. Make it habituated to blankness on the mundane sensual side.

Remark:

This type of blankness is not a depression. It is a satisfaction in not pursuing the sense objects and not dwelling on sensual excitements on this side of existence.

November 10, 2002

On this day during meditation, I found myself in a concentrated energy capsule surrounded by mental darkness. I did not have a technique for escaping from this. After some time the capsule disappeared and I found myself back in the head of the subtle form.

Remark:

Such experiences are called jada absorption, meaning that they are trance states in which one has no mystic perception. This happens periodically in yoga practice.

November 12, 2002

Yogananda

He showed a midway stomach flex. He said it was shown to him by a great yogin when he was in his last physical body.

November 13, 2002

Yogananda

He showed a preliminary alternate breathing. It is done in lotus after a session of breath-infusion.

The method is as follows:

Inhale fully by pulling in hard. Hold the breath in for a short time. As soon as you feel that it is absorbed by the lungs, exhale fully. This absorption takes about 3 to 4 seconds. One must keep the eyelids closed, one concentrates to feel how the lungs absorb the air.

After exhaling fully, one should hold the air out and feel how the lung cells used the absorbed air which was absorbed just before one exhaled.

The idea is to concentrate on how the air is distributed through the lung cells into the body. One trains the mind to track the path of absorbed air. This leads to pranavision and nadi vision, the sight of the tubes in the subtle body.

November 15, 2002

Yogeshwarananda

He showed the stilled quieted imagination orb. It has an elongated egg-shape. It did not move as fast as the speed of light as it usually is. Instead it was a still non-moving object. It was in a buttery solution. This orb picks up impressions to form ideas on its surface. When the ideas sink into it that causes various impulsive ideas and images which are called associative thinking. Patanjali laid down the rule that for success of yoga, one has to put an end to this.

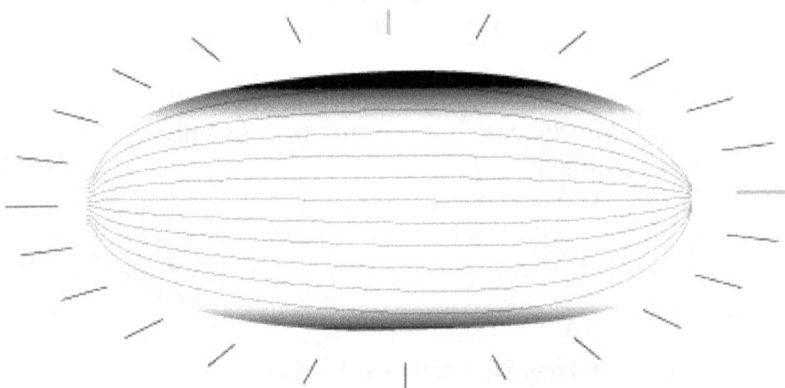

November 17, 2002

Shiva

He advised that I contemplate the distribution of air and reserve energy during
- inhaled air, which is held in while the lungs do not exhale.
- passive lung action, after exhaling when the lungs are not allowed to inhale.

In this exercise one should inhale for a short duration, during which one should mentally say,

Om pranavayave namah.

Then one should exhale and hold the breath out while being attentive to perceive how the lung absorption system operates.

Yogeshwarananda

He gave a brow chakra stimulation exercise. For this one squeezes the eyelids down on the eyes. Periodically one swings the neck and head from side to side. One repeats this over and over. One should do some breath-infusion from time to time. The eyelids should be kept closed.

Ma Durga

She gave a pregnancy stomach-flex for releasing womb-greed. This is mostly for females. Males may practice this to remove their fondness for children and their need to be a father figure. It may be considered that fondness for children should not be eliminated and that the father figure tendency promotes righteous life in human society. In so far as an advanced yogi wants to be liberated from material existence, he must abandon these tendencies, otherwise he will keep coming back into this dimension, where infant bodies are required. One should consider that what we call children is a great illusion since it consists of an adult stuffed into a child's body.

For that matter what is really liked about children is the fact that their adult propensities were suspended by action of material nature. In other words, we appreciate that handicap of those adults who become our children. They are not children. This is proven as soon as material nature removes the suspension by allowing them sexual expressions in adult bodies.

November 26, 2002

Yogeshwarananda

He gave an elementary alternate breathing practice. This is for developing sensitivity to the movement of charged reserved energy in the subtle body.

do this

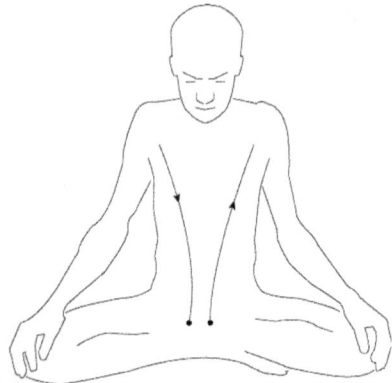

then this

The two dots in each figure are ending stubs for each nadi passage. Inhaled breath jumps from one dot to another by electrostatic charge.

November 27, 2002

Rama Bharati

He poured some of his practicing energy into my brahmrandra crown chakra and said it was easier to reach the chit akash by using charged subtle energy focus during breath retention.

November 28, 2002

Yogeshwarananda

He explained that feelings-vision is seeing through feelings. Subtle vision is seeing through the brow chakra or the two subtle eyes. Supernatural vision is seeing through the imagination orb.

December 6, 2002

Yogeshwarananda

He instructed that one should concentrate upon mula prakriti, which is the source of the multiple impressions, forms and fulfillments. He thought it was a waste of time to focus on anything in the external world.

December 6, 2002

Durga Ma

She showed a suck-up technique for purifying the kanda in the female psyche. This is located in the same area as it is in a male subtle body, except that for a female that is the space in the vaginal passage where heat and viscous fluids occur. One does breath-infusion and down-draw hard pulling breaths.

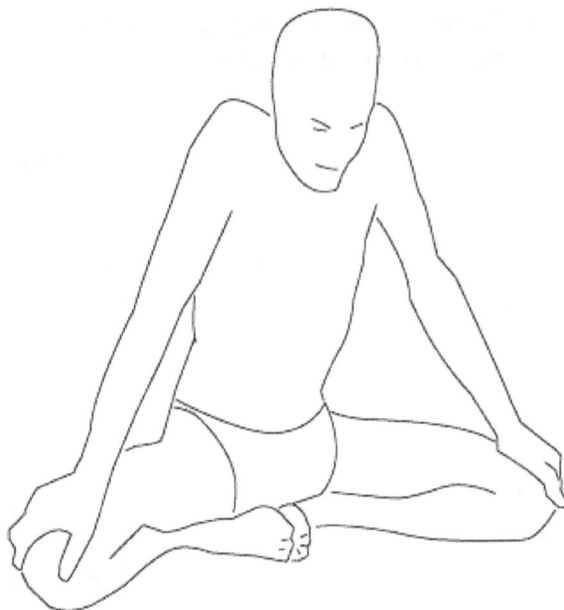

December 15, 2002

Rama Bharati

In the astral world, he gave the author the sannyasa order under two names:

- Swami Vigneshwarananda Bharati
- Swami Krishna Madhvacarya Bharati

He explained that Vigneshwarananda means that I should remove obstacles to technique yoga practice. Krishna meant that I was using a black (krishna) colored body and is a Krishna devotee. He gave a bamboo rod, placing it in my right hand. It then turned into a Shiva trident, a trishula. Then he said that the mantra was Shivoham. He said that I was now in the Shankara order of sannyasis.

He then pointed to the rod. He said, "When I am not present that should be carried in your right hand. When I am present I will usually stand to your right and then the rod should be in your left hand.

I switched it to my left hand.

December 17, 2002

Rama Bharati

He said, "Late eating means late sleeping, either by late sleeping or by forced early rising with a reluctant conniving lifeforce. When there is late eating the life force feels responsible to process the food and to concentrate on digestion. It wants the body to recline and rest while it processes food. It withdraws itself from the waking centers in the brain, thereby causing drowsiness, relaxation and sleep with a reluctance to rise and be active.

December 22, 2002

A subtle body, tongue-stretching exercise. In this the subtle tongue is stretched around the body until it reaches the top of the head.

December 23, 2002

Yogananda

He showed an alternate breathing technique which is done after breath-infusion

in-breath energy path

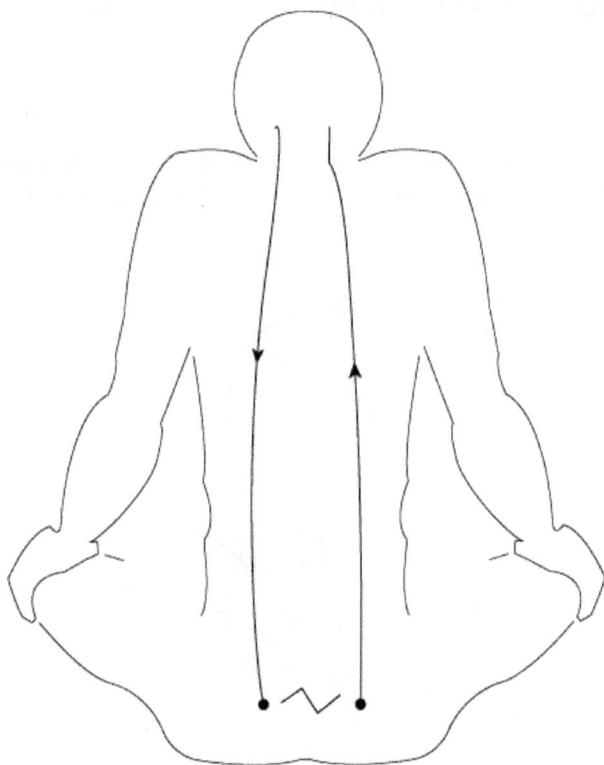

this in-breath travels down the left side
then it holds a polarity charge
at the bottom of the left subtle tube
then it bridges
to the bottom of the right subtle tube
like an electric charge
arcing from one wire to another

out-breath energy path

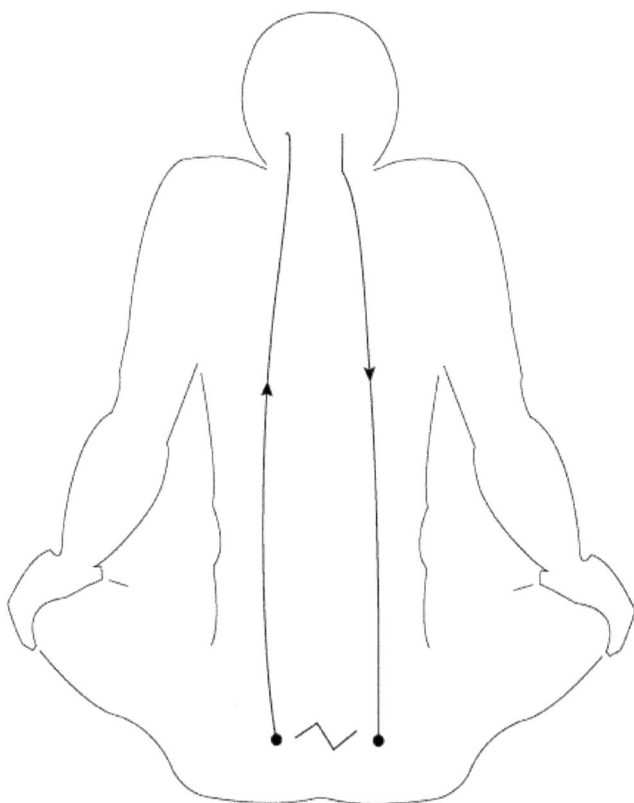

the charge energy movement during
the out-breath travels
opposite to the in-breath flow
in this case, the energy
moves out of the right nostril
but the charge appears
to move down the right side
it jumps over when the out-breath stops
it travels upward

Breath-infusion is a very technical science, known in detail to only a few yogis. Thus is because it cannot be understood by theory. One should practice. In addition one must bring the subtle body to a certain level of purification before one can practice breath-infusion in earnest.

Yogananda made an additional comment. He said, "After doing alternate breathing sufficiently, the imagination has to be tracked and confronted. Anytime it acts one should go to its location which is the location of the ideas and images. One should hold it still at that mental place."

December 27, 2002

Yogananda / Yogeshwarananda

Notes and diagrams for alternate breathing

left nostril air intake

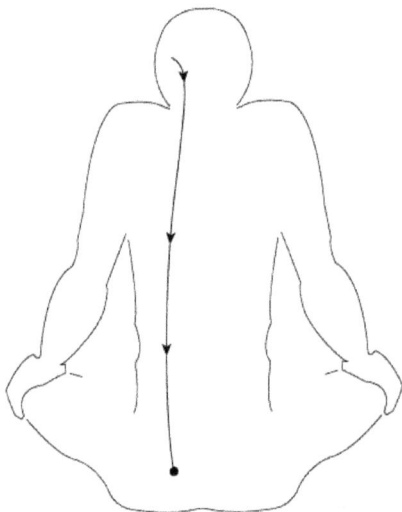

charged energy movement
with air held in

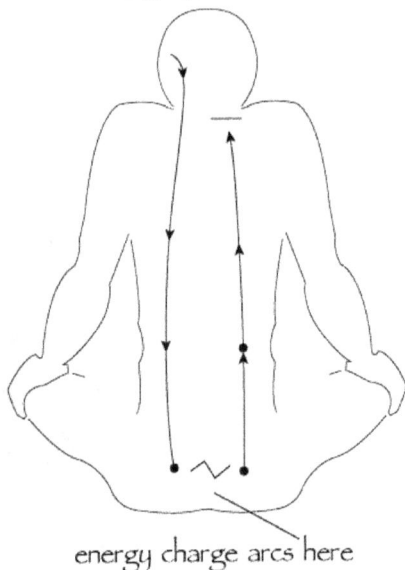

energy charge arcs here

right nostril exhale   charged energy movement
                                              with air held out

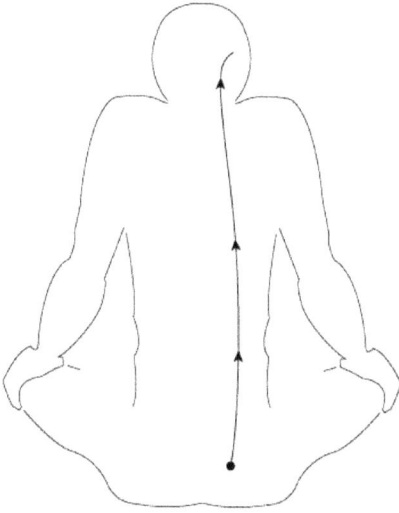

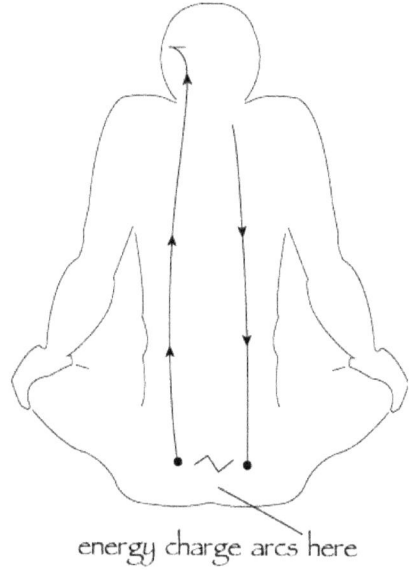

energy charge arcs here

December 28, 2002

Shiva / Yogeshwarananda

Here are instructions for alternate breathing:

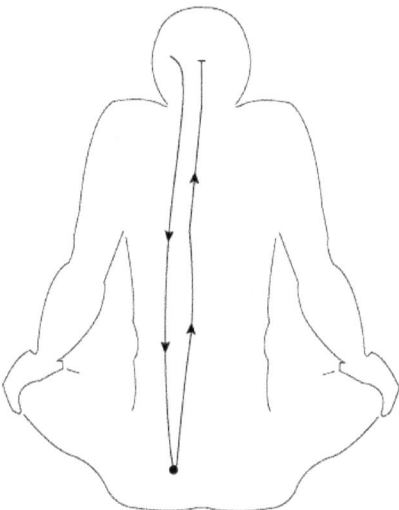

left in-breath   right out-breath

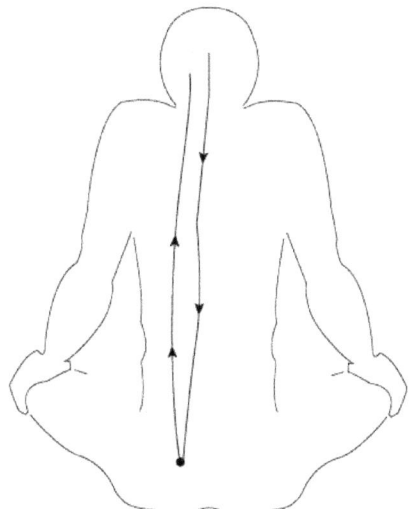

right in-breath   left out-breath

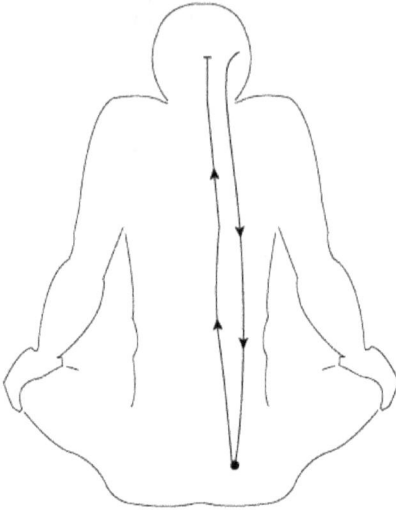

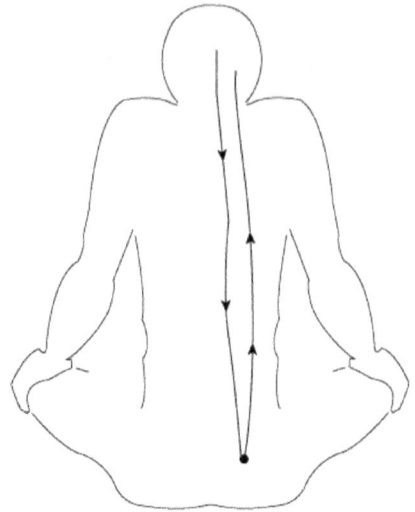

breathe in through left side and out through right side 6 times,
then breath in though right side and out through left side 6 times

The yogi should know that there is a supernatural person who supervises the transmission of energy through the subtle air. That person works in conjunction with the supernatural person who supervises the movement of physical air. Together they are called Pranavayu.

On this day, Shiva wanted to state that Shivoham means:

- I am auspicious.
- I am liberated from social responsibilities which are the tridents which I threw in a corner.

Shivoham was given to me by Rama Bharati as my sannyasa mantra. Now Shiva told me its meaning. Some ascetics say that Shivoham means I am Shiva or I have become Shiva or I am one with Shiva. But Shiva gave a different meaning.

December 30, 2002

Yogananda (in the presence of Yogeshwarananda)

He gave this procedure for breath-infusion. This is done one side at a time with in and out breath on one side only. The infused energy does not jump to the other side. One breathes in the left side and then breathes out the same left side. Then one breathes in the right side and breathes out the same right side. One applies the chin-neck lock and the abdomen lock.

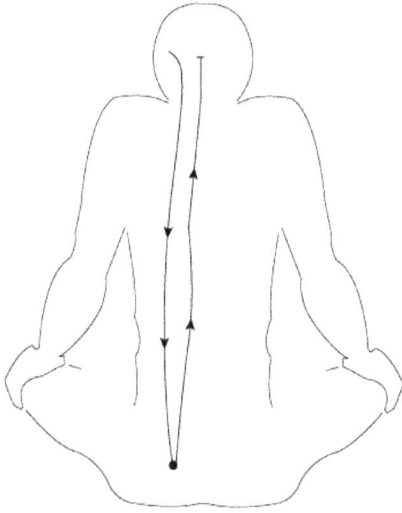

left in-breath path

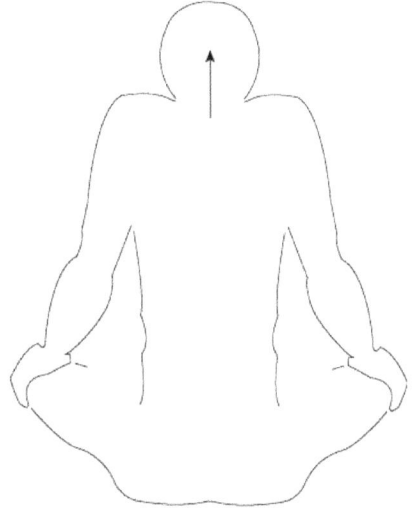

left side out-breath energy charge

December 30, 2002

Yogeshwarananda

He explained that breath-infusion frees the psyche from thought bombardment and thought formation. It causes the imagination orb to turn into supernatural vision

December 31, 2002

Yogananda

He gave this breath-infusion process.

In this one absorbs on the left side and then emits it from the right side. Then one absorbs on the right side and emits from the left side in turn. One takes in the air and then holds it while one senses the infused energy charge. That polarized energy does not arc to the other side but one directs it to go up the alternate side. In this case the air is sent down one side and held there mentally, not allowing it bridge to the other side. It then diffuses at the bottom. Thereafter one expels the air through the other side. It ascends creating a turbulent cloud as in the diagram.

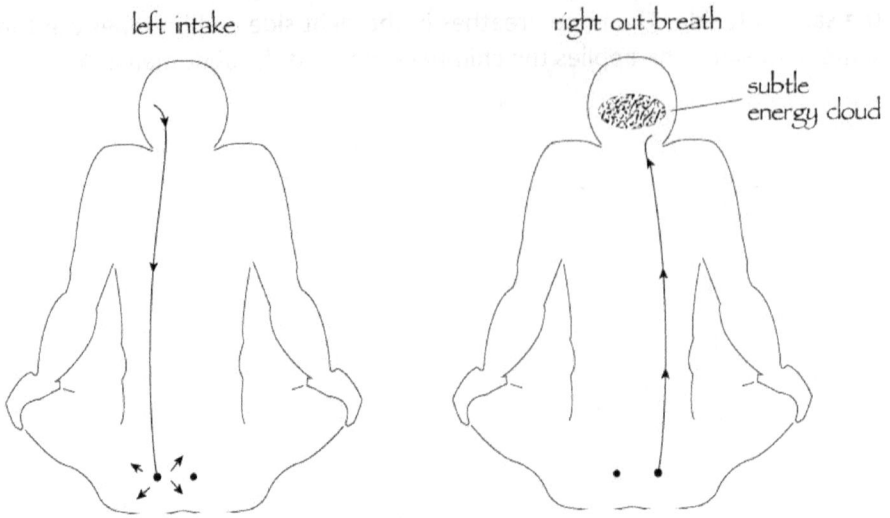

left intake   right out-breath

                                                    subtle
                                                    energy cloud

January 3, 2002

Muktananda

Under his influence I did alternate breathing with three counts. In this one inhales on the left side, then exhales on that same side, then inhales again on that side, but exhales on the right side. One then alternates by inhaling on the right side, exhaling on that same right side and then inhaling again on that right side and exhaling on the left side finally. One then repeats the procedure. The three counts mean that for the duration of inhaling, holding the breath, and then exhaling and holding the breath out, one maintains an even count of three. To make the count some yogis hold the wrist to sense the heart beat pulse and uses that for the counts. Others say mentally, *Om* one, *Om* two, *Om* three. Or they may use another mantra.

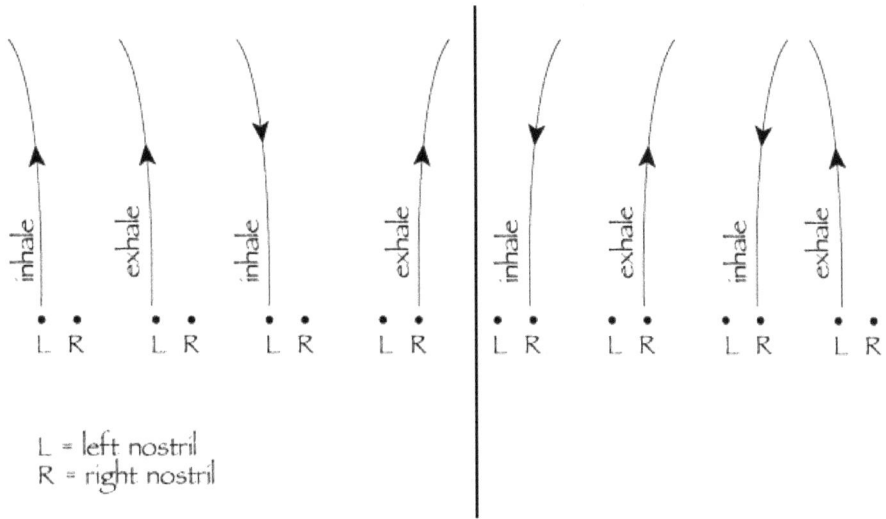

L = left nostril
R = right nostril

One should note that haphazard counting during breath-infusion is natural. This is no cause for alarm. The intellect may lose track of a count or the feelings-energy may throw the intellect out of focus. If one loses count, one should begin again without worrying about the loss. One may have to do this repeatedly.

Arjuna did ask Krishna about the haphazardness of the mind. Krishna said that it could be adjusted by repeated discipline. One must remember this instruction from the God.

Breath-infusion frees the psyche from impulsive thoughts and makes the intellect pay attention to the energies in the psyche. Breath-infusion is the technique for psyche purification.

January 1, 2002

Muktananda

He said, "Because the imagination orb has sexual interest as its priority for fulfillments, the energy from the sexual pleasure nerve should be directly linked to the orb. Feed it on the inside only. I struggled terribly with kundalini chakra, especially with the sex kanda."

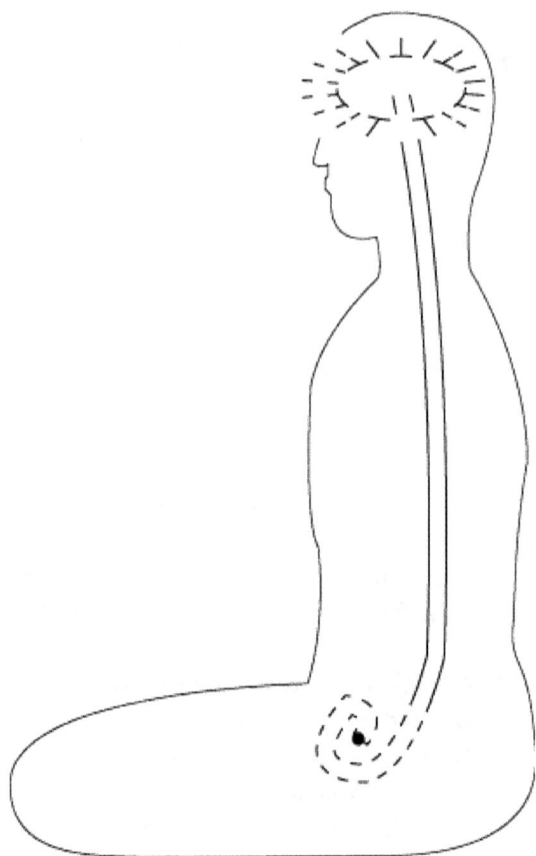

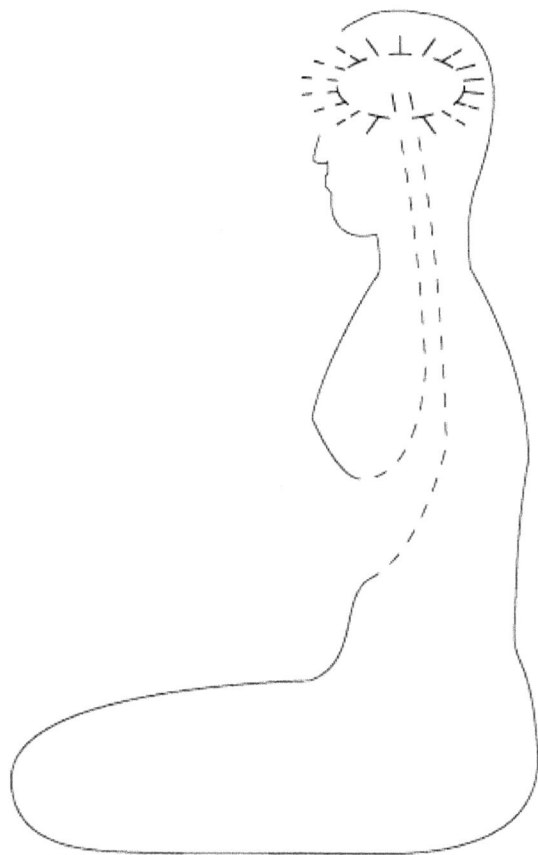

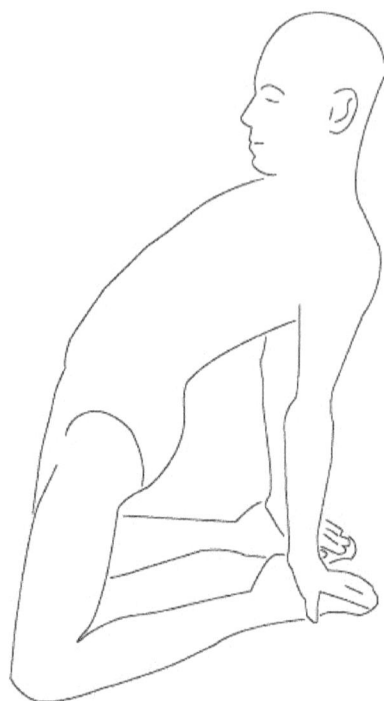

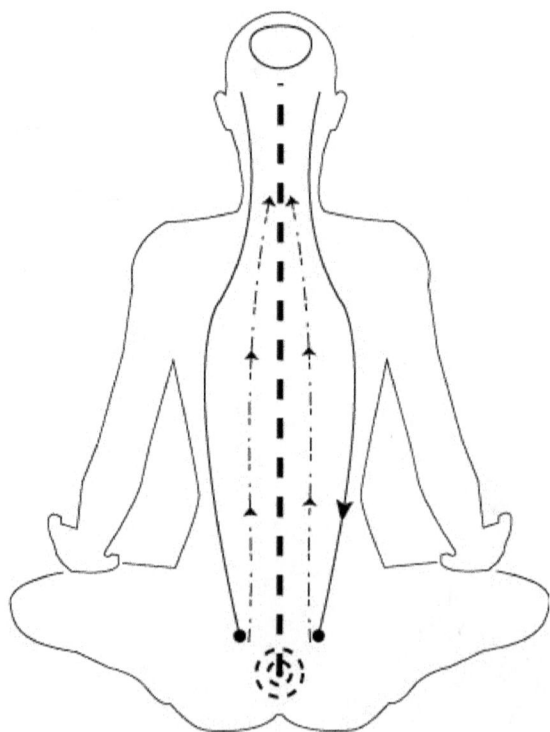

January 3, 2003

Muktananda

He taught subtle body stretches. These are done while doing alternate breathing in lotus posture, after one surcharged the psyche with fresh energy and caused the intellect to reduce its impulsive thinking and visualization behavior.

The actions of the subtle body are made while the gross form remains in lotus posture. While holding the breath in, one stretches the subtle spine, so that the subtle head reaches back to the tail bone, thus touching the crown chakra to the base.

When one can do it with confidence, one does a self-tantric practice, whereby the mouth of the subtle body grips the sex pleasure nerve in the lower pubic area. This is the clitoris in the females and the circular muscle at the base of the penis in males. When this is done the energy stored in the subtle kanda bulb is released and the circular path of energy from the base chakra to the top of the head, is completed. This energy is a manifestation of the kundalini chakra. This should be realized by mystic experience.

January 4, 2003

Muktananda

He gave a breath-infusion method. In this one does each side four times in turn. When doing certain breath-infusions, the yogi should have time to spare for the practice. Bhastrika can be done in a limited time and in a hurry but alternate breathing and others types of time-consuming slow-breathing techniques require great patience and concentration. This means that one should have a lifestyle that permits spare time for practice. One must be isolated. One's diet must be controlled.

in left side   out right side   in right side   out left side

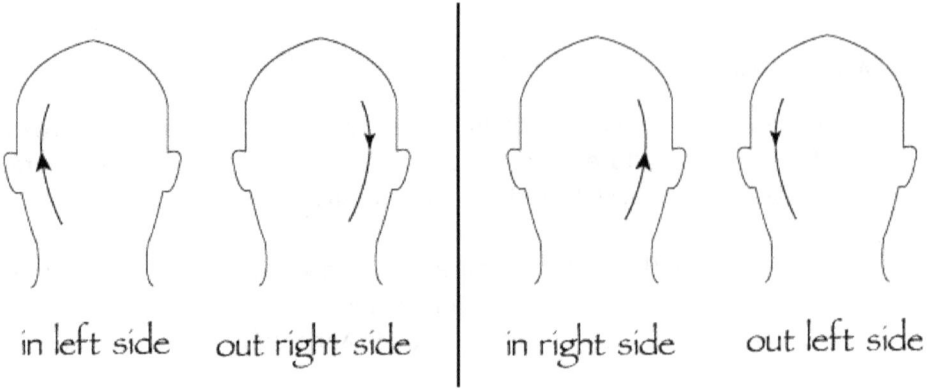

January 4, 2003

On this day. Bhaktivedanta Swami came with a disciple of his. This disciple had recently used a Guyanese body. That form deteriorated and died when it was in its forties. They spoke when the disciple, a father of children, said that he still was disinclined to yoga practice, even though he passed away from the physical form. Then Muktananda suddenly appeared in that astral place where we were associating. He said to the disciple, "Yes, and the evidence is that your chanting did not work. You did not get the results intended. You have not gone back to Godhead as Swami promised. You simply did not get results even when your body was alive"

Pointing to Bhaktivedanta, Muktananda said, "He branded everyone but himself as bogus spiritual leaders and as impersonalists. No one but him was Krishna conscious to his view."

Bhaktivedanta spoke up. He said, "That was our system because we were trained to do that. I should not be blamed. They told me to repeat that."

After this they went away.

Remark

This all started with the remark of the deceased disciple of Bhaktivedanta. He was brought to me by Bhaktivedanta because he found the Swami in an astral dimension and complained that he followed the Swami's instructions and still did not go back to Godhead, as the Swami promised for those who followed strictly. The Swami brought him to me for a discussion. However Muktananda arrived there at the same time. Seeing us, Muktananda said what he said and went away.

That disciple and others like himself failed to take note of certain verses in the Bhagavad Gita. They placed complete trust in Bhaktivedanta Swami. As such they did not closely check his Sanskrit translations. Regarding the disciple's observation that his essential consciousness with its tendencies, biases and limitations, did not change at the time of death, there is a verse in the Bhagavad Gita that supports his realization.

यं यं वापि स्मरन्भावं
त्यजत्यन्ते कलेवरम् ।
तं तमेवैति कौन्तेय
सदा तद्भावभावितः ॥ ८.६ ॥

yaṁ yaṁ vāpi smaranbhāvaṁ
tyajatyante kalevaram
taṁ tamevaiti kaunteya
sadā tadbhāvabhāvitaḥ (8.6)

yaṁ yam - whatever; vāpi = va — or + api — also; moreover; smaran — recalling; bhāvam — texture of existence; tyajaty = tyajati — abandons; ante — in the end; kalevaram - the body; taṁtam - that that; evaiti = eva - indeed + eti — is projected; kaunteya - O son of Kuntī; sadā - always; tad — that + bhāva — status of life + bhāvitaḥ — being transformed

Moreover, whatever texture of existence is recalled when a person abandons his body in the end, to that same type of life, he is projected, O son of Kuntī, always being transformed into that status of life. (Bhagavad Gita 8.6)

January 6, 2003

Yogeshwarananda

He said, "Use paravairagya. That body cannot do it there. It has to feed into it as a tendency for cultivation of practice on the other side. This is why I scrapped that body. Even if done, it reverts back to its natural way, as soon as the effects of the endeavor wears off. One has to continually bring over the discrimination, like supplying fuel to a lamp."

Remark:

My subtle body slipped over into a parallel world. It was socially-involved there, completely forgetting its role on this physical side. Yogesh explained that he got rid of his subtle form because of its tendency to revert back to its natural way of acting indiscriminately.

Muktananda

He said, "Even a small release of kundalini energy anywhere in the psyche is great. Others only get a release in sexual intercourse. Appreciate the little releases. Practice more."

This was said when I had a hip kundalini release.

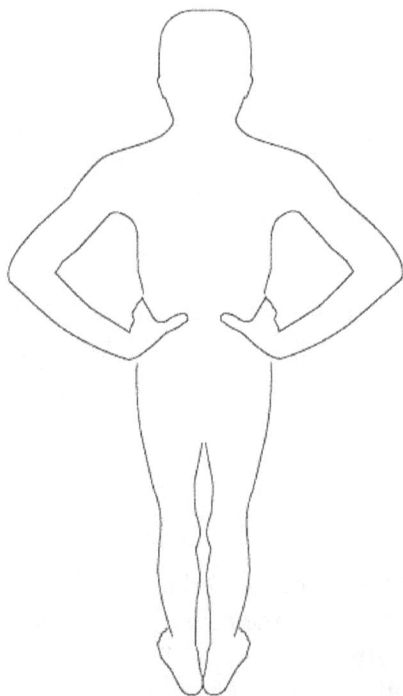

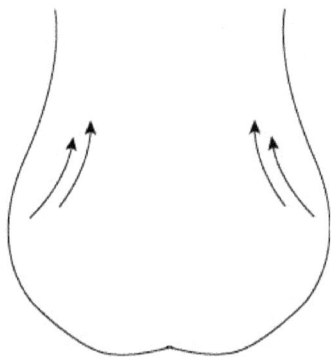

do breath-infusion

hands on hips

thumbs on spine

Index

intellect, continued,
   still-stun, 16, 18
   suspension, 18
   telescoping, 38
   vision, 102

J

jada absorption, 239
Jambavan, 145
Jarasandha, 76
jiva, 192
jnana chakshu, 33
jokes, 122

K

Kailashpati, Shiva, 59
Kali, 53, 54, 132
Kamarupa, 156
kanda, 28, 97, 236, 243
Kansas City, 103
kill body, 45
Kingdom of God, 38
Kirpal Singh, 220
Krishna,
   devotee, 244
   Sadashiva, 79
   Balarama, 37
Krishna Madhvacarya, 244
kundalini,
   absent, 19
   arousal, 31, 125
   battery, 130
   ever active, 154
   fire, 44
   food related, 112
   light, 86
   middle, 146
   origin, 143
   sex expression, 130
   sex pleasure, 77
   unimportant, 44

L

lalata chakra, 8
liabilities, 105
lifeforce, ever active, 154
light of knowledge, 33

light, liquid, 238
lightning claps, 180
limited being, 18
lingam, 47
liquid light, 238
liquor, 144
locks, detailed, 42
Los Angeles, 122
lotus posture deity, 145
lumbar energization, 214
lung lock, 42
lung/causal cove, 137
luxurious conditions, 122

M

Ma Sarasvati, 46
Ma Uma, 131
Madhvacarya, 244
Magadha, 76
Mahabharata, 79
Mahadeva, 30
mat, 102, 105
mauna, 26
meditation, early, 8
memory,
   core-self compared, 91
   Patanjali's advice, 109
   power, 136
   revealing, 51
   sex organ, 141
mergence, 17
middle finger clearance, 23
middle kundalini, 146
milk 163
milk procedure, 223
mind sweeps, 125
mind-intellect-lifeforce, 34
mischievousness, 115
Missouri, 103
molar teeth, 44
monkey body, 132, 145
monkey-to-human, 202
moon-dish cosmic energy, 148
moons, 37
motherly affection, 205
Muktananda, Bhaktivedanta, 258

About the Author

Michael Beloved (Yogi *Madhvāchārya*) took his current body in 1951 in Guyana. In 1965, while living in Trinidad, he instinctively began doing yoga postures and tried to make sense of the supernatural side of life.

Later in 1970, in the Philippines, he approached a Martial Arts Master named Arthur Beverford. He explained to the teacher that he was seeking a yoga instructor. Mr. Beverford identified himself as an advanced disciple of *Śrī* Rishi Singh Gherwal, an Ashtanga Yoga master.

Beverford taught the traditional Ashtanga Yoga with stress on postures, attentive breathing and brow chakra centering meditation. In 1972, Michael entered the Denver, Colorado Ashram of *kundalini* yoga Master *Śrī* Harbhajan Singh. There he took instruction in bhastrika pranayama and its application to yoga postures. He was supervised mostly by Yogi Bhajan's disciple named Prem Kaur.

In 1979 Michael formally entered the discipic succession of the Brahmā - Madhava-Gaudiya Sampradaya through *Swāmī* Kirtanananda, who was a prominent sannyasi disciple of the Great Vaishnava Authority *Śrī Swāmī* Bhaktivedanta Prabhupada, the exponent of devotion to Sri Krishna.

However, yoga has a mystic side to it, thus Michael took training and teaching empowerment from several spiritual masters of different aspects of spiritual development. This is consistent with *Śrī* Krishna's advice to Arjuna in the *Bhagavad Gītā*:

Most of the instructions Michael received were given in the astral world. On that side of existence, his most prominent teachers were *Śrī Swāmī* Shivananda of Rishikesh, Yogiraj *Swāmī* Vishnudevananda, *Śrī Bābāji Mahasaya* - the master of the masters of *Kriyā* Yoga, *Śrīla* Yogeshwarananda of Gangotri - the master of the masters of *Rāj* Yoga (spiritual clarity), and Siddha *Swāmī* Nityananda the Brahmā Yoga authority.

The course for kundalini yoga using pranayama breath-infusion was detailed by Michael in the book *Kundalini Hatha Yoga Pradipika*. This current book was composed from meditation and breath-infusion notes which were originally shared in staple bound booklets as Yoga Journals.

Michael's preliminary books relating to this topic are *Meditation Pictorial*, *Meditation Expertise*, and *Meditation ~ Sense Faculty* (co-author). Every technique (kriya) mentioned was tested by him during pranayama breath-infusion and samyama deep meditation practice.

This is a result of over forty years of meditation practice with astute subtle observations intending to share the methods and experiences. The information is published freely with no intention of forming an institution or hogtying anyone as a disciple.

Publications

English Series

Bhagavad Gita English

Anu Gita English

Markandeya Samasya English

Yoga Sutras English

Hatha Yoga Pradipika English

Uddhava Gita English

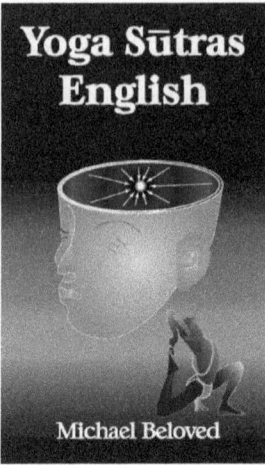

Yoga Sūtras English

Michael Beloved

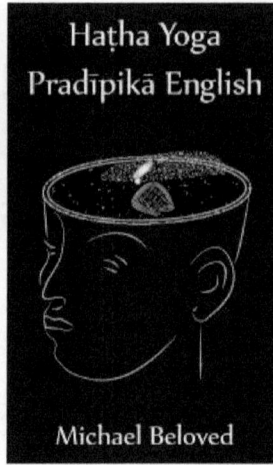

Haṭha Yoga Pradīpikā English

Michael Beloved

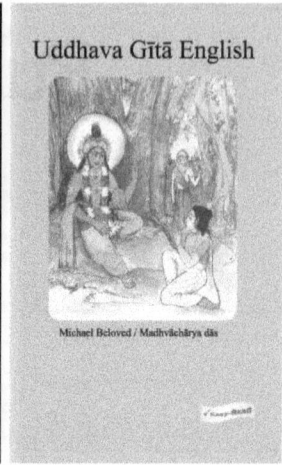

Uddhava Gītā English

Michael Beloved / Madhvāchārya dās

These are in 21ˢᵗ Century English, very precise and exacting. Many Sanskrit words which were considered untranslatable into a Western language are rendered in precise, expressive and modern English.

Three of these books are instructions from Krishna. **In Bhagavad Gita English** *and* **Anu Gita English**, *the instructions were for Arjuna. In the* **Uddhava Gita English,** *it was for Uddhava. Bhagavad Gita and Anu Gita are extracted from the Mahabharata. Uddhava Gita was extracted from the 11ᵗʰ Canto of the Srimad Bhagavatam (Bhagavata Purana). One of these books, the* **Markandeya Samasya English** *is about Krishna, as described by Yogi Markandeya, who survived the cosmic collapse and reached a divine child in whose transcendental body, the collapsed world was existing.*

Two of this series are the syllabus about yoga practice. The Yoga Sutras of Patanjali is elaboration about ashtanga yoga. Hatha Yoga Pradipika English, is the detailed information about asana postures, pranayama breath- infusion, energy compression, naad sound resonance and advanced meditation. The Sanskrit author is Swatmarama Mahayogin.

My suggestion is that you read **Bhagavad Gita English**, *the* **Anu Gita English,** *the* **Markandeya Samasya English,** *the* **Yoga Sutras English,** *the* **Hatha Yoga Pradipika** *and lastly the* **Uddhava Gita English**, *which is complicated and detailed.*

For each of these books we have at least one commentary, which is published separately. Thus your particular interest can be researched further in the commentaries.

The smallest of these commentaries and perhaps the simplest is the one for the Anu Gita. We published its commentary as the <u>Anu Gita Explained</u>. *The*

Bhagavad Gita explanations were published in three distinct targeted commentaries. The first is Bhagavad Gita Explained, which sheds lights on how people in the time of Krishna and Arjuna regarded the information and applied it. Bhagavad Gita is an exposition of the application of yoga practice to cultural activities, which is known in the Sanskrit language as karma yoga.

Interestingly, Bhagavad Gita was spoken on a battlefield just before one of the greatest battles in the ancient world. A warrior, Arjuna, lost his wits and had no idea that he could apply his training in yoga to political dealings. Krishna, his charioteer, lectured on the spur of the moment to give Arjuna the skill of using yoga proficiency in cultural dealings including how to deal with corrupt officials on a battlefield.

The second Gita commentary is the Kriya Yoga Bhagavad Gita. This clears the air about Krishna's information on the science of kriya yoga, showing that its techniques are clearly described for anyone who takes the time to read Bhagavad Gita. Kriya yoga concerns the battlefield which is the psyche of the living being. The internal war and the mental and emotional forces which are hostile to self-realization are dealt with in the kriya yoga practice.

The third commentary is the Brahma Yoga Bhagavad Gita. This shows what Krishna had to say outright and what he hinted about which concerns the brahma yoga practice, a mystic process for those who mastered kriya yoga.

*There is one commentary for the **Markandeya Samasya English**. The title of that publication is Krishna Cosmic Body.*

There are two commentaries to the Yoga Sutras. One is the Yoga Sutras of Patanjali and the other is the Meditation Expertise. These give detailed explanations of ashtanga Yoga.

The commentary of Hatha Yoga Pradipika is titled Kundalini Hatha Yoga Pradipika.

For the Uddhava Gita, we published the Uddhava Gita Explained. This is a large book and requires concentration and study for integration of the information. Of the books which deal with transcendental topics, my opinion is that the discourse between Krishna and Uddhava has the complete information about the realities in existence. This book is the one which removes massive existential ignorance.

Meditation Series

Meditation Pictorial

Meditation Expertise

Core-Self Discovery

Meditation Sense Faculty

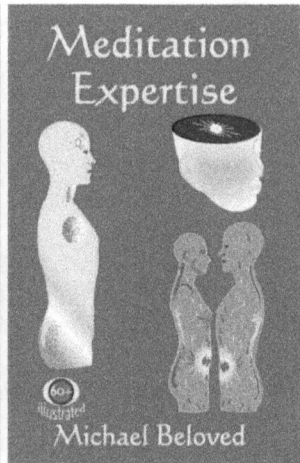

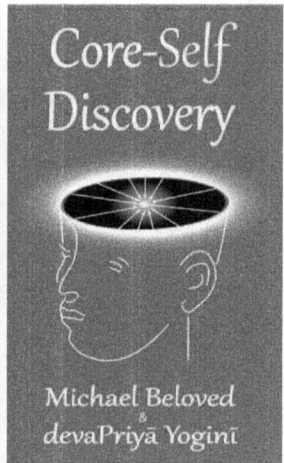

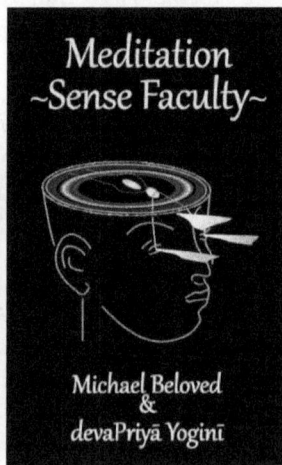

The specialty of these books is the mind diagrams which profusely illustrate what is written. This shows exactly what one has to do mentally to develop and then sustain a meditation practice.

*In the **Meditation Pictorial**, one is shown how to develop psychic insight, a feature without which meditation is imagination and visualization, without any mystic experience per se.*

*In the **Meditation Expertise**, one is shown how to corral one's practice to bring it in line with the classic syllabus of yoga which Patanjali lays out as the ashtanga yoga eight-staged practice.*

*In **Core-Self Discovery**, (co-authored with* devaPriya Yogini*) one is taken though the course of pratyahar sensual energy withdrawal which is the 5th stage of yoga in the Patanjali ashtanga eight-process complete system of yoga practice. These events lead to the discovery of a core-self which is surrounded by psychic organs in the head of the subtle body. This product has a DVD component.*

***Meditation ~ Sense Faculty** (co-authored with* devaPriya Yogini*) is a detailed tutorial with profuse diagrams showing what actions to take in the subtle body to investigate the senses faculties. The meditator must first establish the location and function of the observing self. That self must be screened from the thoughts and ideas which usually hypnotize it.*

These books are profusely illustrated with mind diagrams showing the components of psychic consciousness and the inner design of the subtle body.

Explained Series

Bhagavad Gita Explained

Uddhava Gita Explained

Anu Gita Explained

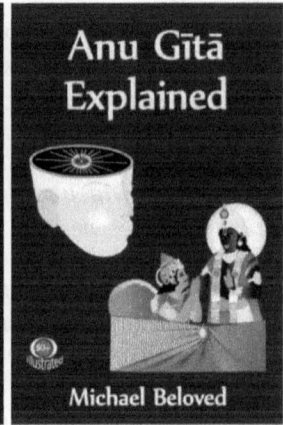

The specialty of these books is that they are free of missionary intentions, cult tactics and philosophical distortion. Instead of using these books to add credence to a philosophy, meditation process, belief or plea for followers, I spread the information out so that a reader can look through this literature and freely take or leave anything as desired.

When Krishna stressed himself as God, I stated that. When Krishna laid no claims for supremacy, I showed that. The reader is left to form an independent opinion about the validity of the information and the credibility of Krishna.

There is a difference in the discourse with Arjuna in the Bhagavad Gita and the one with Uddhava in the Uddhava Gita. In fact these two books may appear to contradict each other. In the Bhagavad Gita, Krishna pressured Arjuna to complete social duties. In the Uddhava Gita, Krishna insisted that Uddhava should abandon the same.

The Anu Gita is not as popular as the Bhagavad Gita but it is the conclusion of that text. Anu means what is to follow, what proceeds. In this discourse, an anxious Arjuna request that Krishna should repeat the Bhagavad Gita and again show His supernatural and divine forms.

However Krishna refuses to do so and chastises Arjuna for being a disappointment in forgetting what was revealed. Krishna then cited a celestial yogi, a near-perfected being, who explained the process of transmigration in vivid detail.

Commentaries

Yoga Sutras of Patanjali

Meditation Expertise

Krishna Cosmic Body

Anu Gita Explained

Bhagavad Gita Explained

Kriya Yoga Bhagavad Gita

Brahma Yoga Bhagavad Gita

Uddhava Gita Explained

Kundalini Hatha Yoga Pradipika

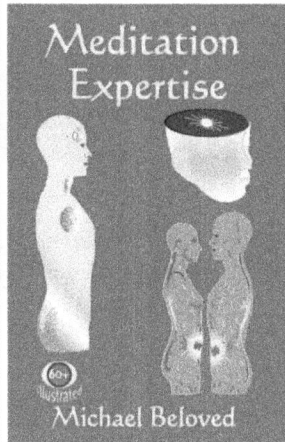

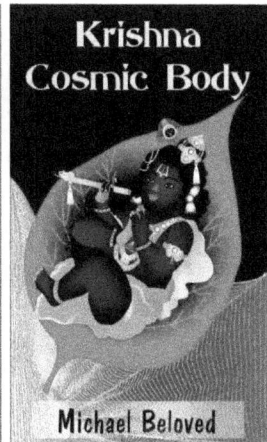

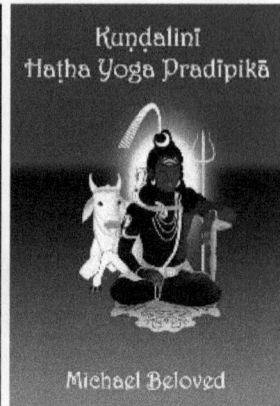

Yoga Sutras of Patanjali is the globally acclaimed text book of yoga. This has detailed expositions of yoga techniques. Many kriya techniques are vividly described in the commentary.

Meditation Expertise is an analysis and application of the Yoga Sutras. This book is loaded with illustrations and has detailed explanations of secretive advanced meditation techniques which are called kriyas in the Sanskrit language.

Krishna Cosmic Body is a narrative commentary on the Markandeya Samasya portion of the Aranyaka Parva of the Mahabharata. This is the detailed description of the dissolution of the world, as experienced by the great yogin Markandeya who transcended the cosmic deity, Brahma, and reached Brahma's source who is the divine infant, Krishna.

Anu Gita Explained is a detailed explanation of how we endure many material bodies in the course of transmigrating through various life-forms. This is a discourse between Krishna and Arjuna. Arjuna requested of Krishna a display of the Universal Form and a repeat narration of the Bhagavad Gita but Krishna declined and explained what a siddha perfected being told the Yadu family about the sequence of existences one endures and the systematic flow of those lives at the convenience of material nature.

Bhagavad Gita Explained shows what was said in the Gita without religious overtones and sectarian biases.

Kriya Yoga Bhagavad Gita shows the instructions for those who are doing kriya yoga.

Brahma Yoga Bhagavad Gita shows the instructions for those who are doing brahma yoga.

Uddhava Gita Explained shows the instructions to Uddhava which are more advanced than the ones given to Arjuna.

Bhagavad Gita is an instruction for applying the expertise of yoga in the cultural field. This is why the process taught to Arjuna is called karma yoga which means karma + yoga or cultural activities done with yogic insight.

Uddhava Gita is an instruction for apply the expertise of yoga to attaining spiritual status. This is why it is explains jnana yoga and bhakti yoga in detail. Jnana yoga is using mystic skill for knowing the spiritual part of existence. Bhakti yoga is for developing affectionate relationships with divine beings.

Karma yoga is for negotiating the social concerns in the material world. It is inferior to bhakti yoga which concerns negotiating the social concerns in the spiritual world.

This world has a social environment. The spiritual world has one too.

Currently, Uddhava Gita is the most advanced and informative spiritual book on the planet. There is nothing anywhere which is superior to it or which goes into so much detail as it. It verified that historically Krishna is the most advanced human being to ever have left literary instructions on this planet. Even Patanjali Yoga Sutras which I translated and gave an application for in my book, **Meditation Expertise**, does not go as far as the Uddhava Gita.

Some of the information of these two books is identical but while the Yoga Sutras are concerned with the personal spiritual emancipation (kaivalyam) of the individual spirits, the Uddhava Gita explains that and also explains the situations in the spiritual universes.

Bhagavad Gita is from the Mahabharata *which is the history of the Pandavas. Arjuna, the student of the Gita, is one of the Pandavas brothers. He was in a social hassle and did not know how to apply yoga expertise to solve it. On the battlefield, Krishna gave him a crash-course on yogic social interactions.*

Uddhava Gita is from the Srimad Bhagavatam (Bhagavata Purana), *which is a history of the incarnations of Krishna. Uddhava was a relative of Krishna. He was concerned about the situation of the deaths of many of his relatives but Krishna diverted Uddhava's attention to the practice of yoga for the purpose of successfully migrating to the spiritual environment.*

Kundalini Hatha Yoga Pradipika *is the commentary for the Hatha Yoga Pradipika of Swatmarama Mahayogin. This is the detailed process about asana posture, pranayama breath-infusion, complex compressions of energy, naad sound resonance intonement and advanced meditation practice.*

This is the singular book with all the techniques of how to reform and redesign the subtle body so that it does not have the tendency for physical life forms and for it to attain the status of a siddha.

These books are based on the author's experiences in meditation, yoga practice and participation in spiritual groups:

Specialty

Spiritual Master

sex you!

Sleep Paralysis

Astral Projection

Masturbation Psychic Details

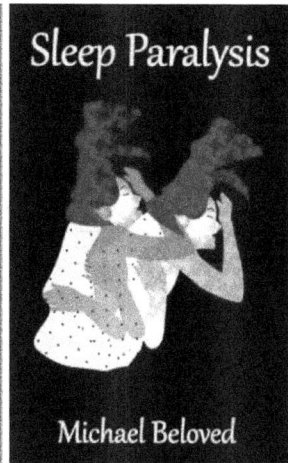

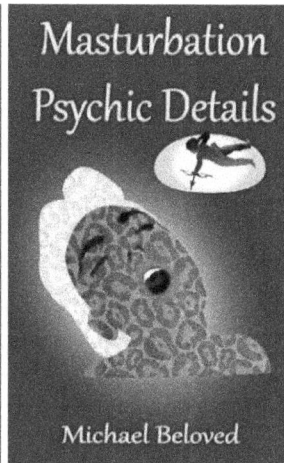

In **Spiritual Master**, *Michael draws from experience with gurus or with their senior students. His contact with astral gurus is rated. He walks you through the avenue of gurus showing what you should do and what you should not do, so as to gain proficiency in whatever area of spirituality the guru has proficiency.*

sex you! *is a masterpiece about the adventures of an individual spirit's passage through the parents' psyches. The conversion of a departed soul into a sexual urge is described. The transit from the afterlife to residency in the emotions of the parents is detailed. This is about sex and you. Learn about how much of you comprises the romantic energy of your would-be parents!*

Sleep Paralysis *clears misconceptions so that one can see what sleep paralysis is and what frightening astral experience occurs while the paralysis is being* *experienced. This disempowerment has great value in giving you confidence that you can and do exist even if you are unable to operate the physical body. The implication is that one can exist apart from and will survive the loss of the material form.*

Astral Projection *details experiences Michael had even in childhood, where he assumed incorrectly that everyone was astrally conversant. He discusses the life force psychic mechanism which operates the sleep-wake cycle of the physical form, and which budgets energy into the separated astral form which determines if the individual will have dream recall or no objective awareness during the projections. Astral travel happens on every occasion when the physical body sleeps. What is missing in awareness is the observer status while the astral body is separated.*

Masturbation Psychic Details *is a surprise presentation which relates what happens on the psychic plane during a masturbation event. This does not tackle moral issues or even addictions but shows the involvement of memory and the sure but hidden subconscious mind which operates many features of the psyche irrespective of the desire or approval of the self-conscious personality.*

inVision Series

Yoga inVision 1

Yoga inVision 2

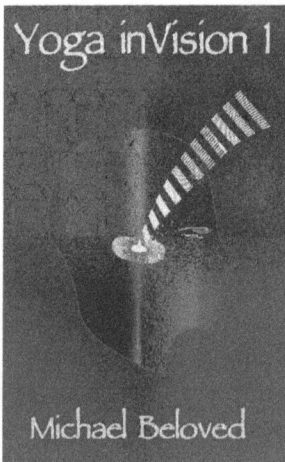

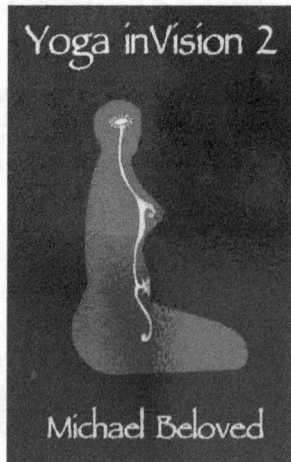

Yoga inVision 1, the first in this series, describes the breath infusion and meditation practices during the years of 1998 and 1999. There are unique, once in a lifetime as well as recurring insights which are elaborated. inFocus during breath infusion and the meditation which follows is an adventure for any yogi. This gives what happened to this particular ascetic.

Yoga inVision 2 reports on the author's experiences from 1999 to 2001. Each day the experience is unique, illustrating the vibrancy of practice. Many rare once-in-a-lifetime perceptions are described.

Online Resources

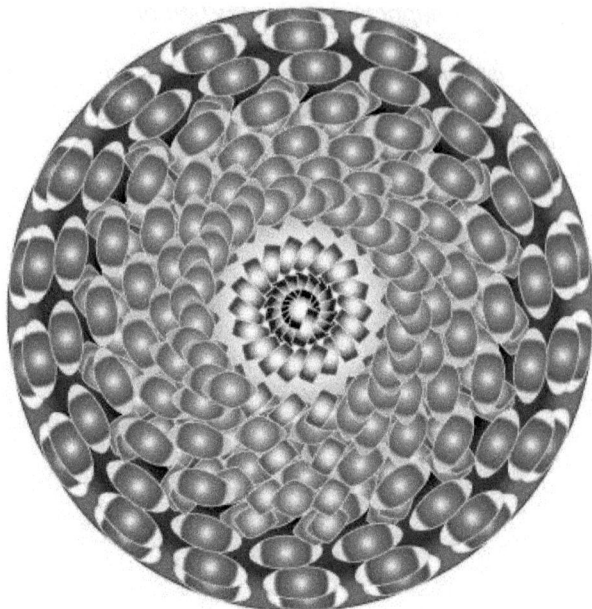

Email:	**michaelbelovedbooks@gmail.com**
	axisnexus@gmail.com
Website:	michaelbeloved.com
Forum:	inselfyoga.com
Posters:	zazzle.com/inself